Generation
Hope

Paperback: 978-1-955671-34-7
E-Book: 978-1-955671-35-4

Except where noted below, all images are courtesy of the author and publisher.

Page 9: Private Rocket: "billionaire space race" by Schot, De Volkskrant, Netherlands

Page 57: "Public Predictions for the Future of Workplace Automation: Two-thirds of Americans expect that robots and computers will do much of the work currently done by humans within 50 years…" Pew Research Center, Washington, D.C. (March 10, 2016) https://www.pewresearch.org/internet/2016/03/10/public-predictions-for-the-future-of-workforce-automation/.

Page 61: Institute for Fiscal Studies (@TheIFS), "Real household disposable income is expected to regain its pre-COVID levels by 2023–24," Twitter post, October 27, 2021, https://twitter.com/TheIFS/status/1453349318761533442/photo/1.

Page 64: Figure adapted from "Home Ownership—3. By ethnicity," Gov.uk, accessed July 2023, https://www.ethnicity-facts-figures.service.gov.uk/housing/owning-and-renting/home-ownership/latest.

Pexels: Ahmed akacha xii.

Stock.adobe.com: Jasmin Merdan 20; V.R.Murralinath 48; Niks Ads 72, 124; ruslanita 104; Southtownboy Studio 150; dr322 176; Riccardo Niels Mayer 207; saiko3p 232, 280; visoot 258; Adam Ján Figel' 308; PRASANNAPIX 334.

Freepik: 251.

otterpine.com

Generation Hope

how inclusive economics can help us all thrive

Arunjay Katakam

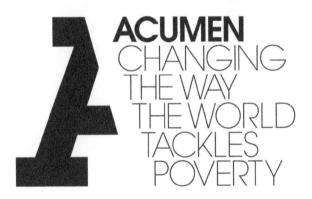

Acumen is changing the way the world tackles poverty.

For over 21 years, Acumen has been a global leader in social and economic transformation, solving problems of poverty and building a world based on dignity. Your donation will help support innovative companies, inspire new leaders, and scale impactful solutions in energy access, smallholder farming, and other critical work at the intersection of climate and poverty. Acumen has invested over $154 million in philanthropic capital and has impacted the lives of over half a billion people.

To my parents, Sabrina and Asoka; my late grandmother, Hermione; my late grandaunt, Kausalya; and Shantiben for influencing me during my formative years by teaching me valuable life lessons and helping ground me.

Preface

The desire—and the ability—to make money came to me early. At age 11, I was selling and trading snacks at my boarding school. This entrepreneurial streak continued through my teens and into my thirties, and my experiences over those years helped me understand both the impact that entrepreneurs make on society as well as the flaws in the system. That dual-track learning process would continue as I went on to work for a global accountancy firm before launching a series of startups designed to help improve financial inclusion in developing countries.

I grew up in India in a fairly affluent family, but I saw a lot of poverty. I couldn't ignore it and often wondered why that was so, since most others seemed to ignore poverty quite easily...but it would take me three decades to be able to do something about it.

My mother introduced me at age 13 to meditation. In case that sounds too otherworldly or specifically Indian, I should point out that every faith and culture has a tradition and practice of meditation. As the saying goes, to pray is to talk to God and to meditate is to listen. Over the past 30 years, I have slowly increased my consciousness—moving away from narrow-minded self-interest and wanting to be super rich, toward a desire to help humanity. I left a career in investment banking along the way to work in international development.

But my knowledge of the international development and payments industry led me to realize that our current economic system only works for some, and that we need to proactively shift our consciousness if we're going to reimagine a better world that tackles the ultimate challenge: leaving no one behind.

My desire to help humanity has grown stronger and stronger, along with a simple belief that each one of us can make a difference. But despite spending the past decade of my life trying to improve the lives of the poor through my work in financial inclusion, I must admit that the overall progress the international development sector has made is very little. I realized this most powerfully during the pandemic. Although 500 million more people have gained access to the formal financial system in the last decade by opening a bank account for the first time, most of those new accounts are dormant or empty—the economics haven't changed.

No doubt their individual circumstances varied, but the end result was that for the majority of 500 million people, their shiny new bank accounts had no real or perceived value. A bank account, in other words, turned out to be not so much a real invitation to a seat at the economic table, but something more like an element of the dress code for those already seated. Meanwhile, the same economic systems that left the better part of 500 million people with just the outer trappings of financial inclusion continue to leave more than half the world's population behind entirely. In other words, the feudal system still lives with us today. And we can still feel its effects: injustice, inequality, and extreme poverty. Yet I had to believe—and do, very strongly—that change is possible, and we can create a world where everyone thrives.

In May 2020, when I was facing this realization, I serendipitously met a life coach who challenged me to think beyond the realms of what I thought was possible at the time. Then in early 2021, I listened to Anand Giridharadas's book, *Winners Take All: The Elite Charade of*

Changing the World. It not only struck a chord, it shook me to my core, and it helped me see my own participation in our economic system. *Generation Hope*, at its heart, is my personal response to Giridharadas's clear-eyed and unsparing analysis and the challenge he proposes.

You may not agree with everything I say, but we don't need to agree on every little detail in order to take better actions. The idea that we are all alone unless we're with someone just like us is just another unconscious story that drives us to unhelpful places, leaving us all feeling polarized and powerless.

I am not an economist. Neither am I a sociologist or an historian or a politician. Over the last two decades, I've had a front-row seat in finance and development, on both sides of the rich/poor coin. This book is based on my observations as a recovering wealth-chaser and, above all, as a father.

Table of Contents

Part 3. The Scope of Impact

Introduction

"Why are you so worried about our planet's trajectory?"

As we look at each other through our screens, Erica shifts uncomfortably in her chair and ponders the question for a moment. It is August 2021, and I am interviewing students on track for their master's degree in economics. Millennials, especially those on the younger side, as well as their Gen Z counterparts, are often said to feel jaded about our future—why wouldn't they? As a millennial myself, and someone who has undergone a journey from a self-centered sense of scarcity to become a conscious consumer with an abundance mindset, I see that discontent as something more hopeful. But as I conduct the research that will become this book, I want to hear directly from the freshest minds studying economics.

My goal as I am writing is to understand where this jadedness comes from—the historical, political, economic, and cultural foundations that got us where we are today. Even more than that, I want to understand where we're actually going. At the moment, it's clear that our trajectory is aimed toward destruction, in one way or another. But is it possible to make adjustments to that path, and if so, who's going to lead us? That is exactly why I'm talking to people like Erica.

Even through the distance of a Zoom call, there is a buzz of energy about her: "Oh my god, misallocation of resources," she says. "There's just so many examples, and by putting money into the wrong streams, a lot of great solutions are being left out or overlooked and don't even have the chance to grow."

I have similar concerns: we live in a dog-eat-dog world where competition is a matter of survival. This has created an economic system with such a strong vortex that, if we don't do anything to change it, will suck us in and ultimately lead to destruction. Erica agrees.

"The other night, I woke up at 4:00 a.m., and the thought that just wouldn't leave my mind was that we don't know how much time we have here on the planet. I had these pictures of wildfires going through my head and it left me with this feeling that we must do something now."

"And yet," she continues, "it is so frustrating because people still focus too much on the wrong things—not only where money goes, but where people work." And she is right. We are in this perilous moment in our planet's history, and underlining the climate crisis is our economic system.

Our conversation varies widely as we discuss the many problems that are, of course, valid for countries or for companies, including the cost-of-living crisis. Erica gets animated and I can feel her frustration when she says, "But in the grander scheme of things, they're not as big of a problem as climate change—people losing their loved ones, people losing their homes, people losing their way of life." We agree that this is a real threat and we're already seeing it, with ever-increasing natural disasters caused by climate change displacing people. There could be 1.2 billion climate refugees by 2050, and climate migration will have significant implications for international security, instability, conflict, and geopolitics.[1]

Erica goes on: "Unfortunately, people just don't react to it. If your company has bad quarterly earnings or has bad earnings, and you're on the stock market, everyone's going to work their ass off to turn it around, and kind of show, hey, our company's not gonna go down. But for the whole planet? That kind of doesn't happen."

A lot of people care about our planet in this way, and like many in her demographic, Erica is doing something about it.

As we spoke, she pulled out book after book that informed her opinions. She told me about the startup she's part of that is working on plastic pollution in the oceans. And, as is typical for high-achieving students, she was involved in societies at her school. This combination of awareness and action sets the "conscious millennial" apart from their peers and older counterparts. And it runs counter to the narrative that we are all resigned to a doomed fate.

"So, what gives you hope?" I ask her.

She responds cautiously. "New movements like the Green Deal and all those new types of deals and incentives for the environment. I really hope that they will do what they're supposed to do, and that it's not just another way of generating revenue or generating public image for companies."

Erica represents a growing chorus emerging among our generation, with more frustration being directed toward our current economic system. Climate, racial, and gender injustices have entered our collective awareness—concerns about the people and planet we live with now, and what we're leaving behind for future generations. But so far, when this frustration has found political expression, the results have ranged from unfocused and thus ineffective movements (e.g., Occupy Wall Street) to the rise of authoritarian figures who fuse legitimate economic grievances with class warfare and often overt racism.

Movements have found more traction in artistic expression. Consider the astonishing worldwide response to the Spanish thriller *La Casa de*

Papel (distributed by Netflix as *Money Heist* to the English-speaking world). Set in Madrid, the series tells the story of a mild-mannered, mysterious genius known only as "the Professor" who recruits and rigorously trains a group of people to lay siege to the Royal Mint of Spain. Once inside, the Professor's gang takes hostages to keep the police at bay while they occupy the Mint for 11 days, running the presses nonstop and escaping with more than 980 million euros.

The Professor makes it clear that his gang's action is aimed not at "stealing" what belongs to someone else, but rather at open rebellion against late-stage capitalism. The gang captures the support of a sympathetic public, who gather outside the Mint holding signs and shouting encouragement. The show appears to have tapped into something powerful: in 2020, it became the most in-demand show in the world, beating out *Game of Thrones, The Walking Dead,* and other streaming favorites. Netflix figures indicate that the show is most popular in Spanish-speaking countries (no surprise), as well as Brazil, Italy, Turkey, the Arab world, India, and other countries with especially striking income inequality.

It has apparently not caught on in Nordic countries.[*]

Storytelling plays an important role in raising awareness—for example, documentary films like *The Game Changers, What The Health, Cowspiracy,* and *Blue Planet* call attention to their respective issues in a way that captures attention and sparks a conversation. In becoming aware, we start out ignorant to something, then we learn more about it in a way that completely changes our perception of that thing. But awareness is only part of the equation. Combining awareness with action—that's where consciousness happens, as demonstrated by Erica's climate concerns leading to her priorities in work and study. Someone

---

[*] Which, incidentally, don't have the problem with wealth and income inequality that much of the rest of the world shares.

who watches *Cowspiracy* and then becomes vegan has raised their level of consciousness. But even when a documentary tops all the charts and increases our collective awareness, without action, the change that the filmmakers hoped to inspire remains theoretical.

Consciousness is not a state of arrival; we each express different levels of consciousness for different things at different times. In my own life, I am much more conscious about our planet than I used to be, meaning my awareness is at a level that has changed my actions. For example, like Erica and many of our generation, I shun disposable plastic. Yet I am sure there are many things I haven't yet learned. For those things, my consciousness remains low. Unfortunately for us and our planet, our current economic system is being driven by low consciousness. To function, it must exploit and extract from people, animals, and planet alike; to function well, consumers are better off not thinking about that reality. If you're wondering how those who amass wealth using this model manage to not care about the effects it has, this is why. If their awareness has been raised—and that's a big if—it hasn't affected them deeply enough to turn into a conscious change in behavior. They are happy to continue exploiting people, animals, and planet in the name of growth and prosperity because growth and prosperity are where their consciousness sits.

Such mentalities are informed by previous advancements made by capitalism, and yes, the progress humanity made in the "special century" (1870–1970) was radical and transformative. But despite the rate of technological change that followed in the last 50 years, we have seen comparatively little progress relative to that era.

Buckminster Fuller, one of the intellectual godfathers of today's integrated approach to sustainable design, was born in 1895—the millennial of his era—and died in 1983. In his last book, *Grunch of Giants*, he continued his effort to put forth an original blueprint of living sustainability for humanity. He wrote:

I do know that technologically humanity now has the opportunity, for the first time in its history, to operate our planet in such a manner as to support and accommodate all humanity at a substantially more advanced standard of living than any humans have ever experienced.[2]

Turns out, Fuller was so far ahead of his time that we're only just now catching up to some of his ideas—off-grid housing, "two-way TV," and mass customization, to name a few. Sadly, in the third decade of the 21st century, we are actually further away from his vision of equitably dividing the resources of our planet to provide people all around the world with a substantially more advanced standard of living. Technologically advanced housing and transportation have been developed, but access to them has not, and what we have developed has managed to increase greenhouse gasses to a dangerous level. If not reversed soon, thriving will be off the table. Our survival is at risk.

However, I believe that the opposite can be true.

We may have continued our polluting ways uninhibited for at least another decade before awareness impacted those in power enough to inspire action—but the COVID-19 pandemic interrupted that pattern. The dramatic shift in status quo put us on the cusp of a seismic shift, which some say set the world back many years in terms of achieving our Sustainable Development Goals (SDGs). Anecdotally, many of us noticed the lack of airplanes in our skies; pollution data from 10 UK cities during lockdown showed that nitrogen dioxide levels and small particle pollution were significantly lower than usual for spring 2020;[3] and according to US space agency NASA, satellite images showed a dramatic decline in pollution levels over China, which is "at least partly" due to the economic slowdown prompted by the coronavirus.[4] And, given the unprecedented adoption of technology, the pandemic has unlocked a genie we can't put back in the bottle.

My brother is a full-time architect and couldn't work from home until March of 2020, when suddenly he found himself working from home five days a week. Before the pandemic, there were set ways of working. Now, employers who have asked people to come back to work have lost some of their employees to more flexible organizations. Similarly, before the pandemic, there had been an assumption that the government was responsible for keeping us safe. Very quickly, we saw that most governments could not enforce rules strict enough to stop the spread of COVID—it was down to each citizen to do their bit. And as we saw in the climate data above, it was once easy to think the damage couldn't be undone, but we were amazed at how quickly nature could right itself when our collective behavior changed.

We can't unsee what we've seen—pre-pandemic thinking no longer holds up. We can't waste this golden opportunity. Our planet isn't going to wait for us to sort out our issues slowly. Just as oppressed and mistreated people eventually revolt, the planet has had enough too.

Approximately 51 billion tons of greenhouse gasses are added to the atmosphere every year, and the conclusions of the UN's 2018 Intergovernmental Panel on Climate Change (IPCC)'s special report "Global Warming of 1.5° C" were startling. Just a half degree more of warming would mean substantially more poverty, extreme heat, sea level rise, habitat and coral reef loss, and drought.[5] Israeli historian and philosopher Yuval Noah Harari has said that "Homo sapiens as we know them will disappear in a century or so,"[6] and António Guterres, secretary general of the UN said, "We are on a catastrophic path. We can either save our world or condemn humanity to a hellish future." A year later he added, "We are on a highway to climate hell with our foot on the accelerator."[7] And we cannot prevent this unless we act immediately to cut emissions deeply.

Things that we have been able to disregard in the past are becoming harder and harder to ignore. On the whole, previous generations focused mostly on wealth creation without consciously considering the broader implications of those actions. As a result, even the most complex social problems of our time, from poverty to climate change to political violence, are all fundamentally economically driven. Even if you live under a rock and/or don't believe in global warming, you have to acknowledge that burning our planet and destroying each other cannot be the solution to our economic problems. And because our economic system doesn't care about negative externalities, it isn't going to fix itself. As we learned during the COVID-19 pandemic, some problems require each of us to participate in their resolution.

For those affected by increasing wealth disparity or who lack systemic access to power, participation may seem overwhelming. And by "those of us," I mean most of us. Fifty years ago, the middle class was on the up, creating stability and purchasing power even if you weren't born into wealth. Visionaries like Fuller were predicting we would continue that trend until we had accommodated all of humanity. But the advent of Reaganomics shortly after triggered a massive shift in global wealth, and everyone but the upper-income households have suffered significantly.

This hollowing-out of the middle class is a result of many factors— economic, political, and social. For decades, rich countries have been shedding semi-skilled manufacturing and other jobs by which people could earn sufficient income without a university degree. Partly because of these dimmer economic prospects, and partly in response to fast-shifting cultural norms, family formation has declined as well; single parenthood, which is highly correlated with poverty, has risen dramatically in the West. Far fewer people belong to labor unions, which themselves haven't kept pace with the demands they should make. And although the major cities have always been beacons of opportunity for ambitious people, they are increasingly the only places where decent jobs can be found—which of course pushes the cost of living in those metropolises ever farther beyond the reach of all but the most privileged. Ultra-gentrified city centers are ringed in by high-rise public housing and council flats, effectively taxpayer-subsidized servants' quarters occupied by the service workers who keep the cities humming but could never afford to live in them.

PRIVATE ROCKET

And what solutions do the ultrarich have for us? When billionaires zoom off to space with the idea of advancing humanity, many of us with our feet on earth see a demonstration of their selfishness. The 2021 movie *Don't Look Up* satirized this component of our society—one that allows us to bypass scientific fact and ignore the threat of our own self-destruction in order to bolster short-term gains for the rich.

Over the last decade, a rise in consciousness primarily among millennials has begun a subtle shift away from wealth creation at any cost to a search for more sustainable ways to progress—at least the millennials who can't rely on the bank of mom and dad. Nobel prize-winning economist and professor Joseph Stiglitz is known to tell his students who want to be wealthy that they have one crucial decision to make in life: choosing the right parent.

Today, the top 26 billionaires own $1.4 trillion—as much as half the world's population (3.8 billion people). Are those 26 individuals (almost all male) so much smarter than those fighting for their survival? All of them were born into some level of wealth, and 15 of them were born into great wealth. Being born into the right family and living in the right neighborhood have become increasingly more important ingredients for "success" in life than any others.

But are we so different from the rocket-building, trust-fund-baby billionaires? Even as we slowly move away from materialism, we find other ways to turn up our noses at "the other." You must have noticed how we still try to differentiate ourselves in some way, usually to demonstrate our superiority in one form or another. Failing to keep up with the Joneses is still perceived as evidence of socioeconomic or cultural inferiority. We unconsciously feed the need to be superior with our habitual spending and economic practices while marching in the streets to promote awareness of racism, sexism, and all forms of discrimination. But it all comes from the same need to differentiate ourselves.

As humans, we are wired to be selfish and self-centered—it is a primal instinct required for our survival, evident throughout history. Which country hasn't behaved in a barbaric manner at some point or another? Capitalist societies hold us to that level of consciousness, constantly making us feel inadequate so that we rely on productivity and products to meet those needs. As long as we stay stuck in that system, we will think only about ourselves, forgetting that everyone and everything around us is connected, and our behavior will continue to reflect that selfishness.

Meanwhile, we are just as wired to be altruistic as we are to be selfish, often helping others without expecting anything in return. When this part of us takes center stage, we thrive. As our consciousness rises, we realize that we are complete as we are. Awareness tells us there is no need to be superior and nothing to be gained from wasting our time trying to demonstrate our superiority. Actions then translate to skipping the designer handbag or Rolex watch or certain job or house or lifestyle as a means of fitting in. I can't help but think of a line in Charlie Mackesy's *The Boy, the Mole, the Fox and the Horse* that stood out to me as I read it to my children: "Always remember you matter, you're important and you are loved, and you bring to this world things no one else can."[8]

And, I'm encouraged by Fuller—whose vision isn't yet out of our reach:

> *Never forget that you are one of a kind. Never forget that if there weren't any need for you in all your uniqueness to be on this earth, you wouldn't be here in the first place. And never forget, no matter how overwhelming life's challenges and problems seem to be, that one person can make a difference in the world. In fact, it is always because of one person that all the changes that matter in the world come about. So be that one person.*[9]

When we see ourselves and each other as individuals who matter, with or without any other social signifiers, the barriers between awareness and action begin to come down. Change only requires awareness of what is going on around you in that case, because you don't have to be affected directly in order to become conscious about your actions.

I realize that consciousness can have a whiff of "woo woo" about it, but it is simply the state of being aware of, and responsive to, your surroundings. Have you ever found yourself at a place you routinely go to even though you were planning to go somewhere else? You must have responded to your surroundings in order to get there safely, but you didn't make any active choices to do so. In my research on this topic, it blew my mind to realize that we have an innate preference for functioning on autopilot, largely because conscious thought is a

"Always remember you matter, you're important and you are loved, and you bring to this world things no one else can."
—*Charlie Mackesy*

relatively scarce resource. It can typically only be used to process seven to ten pieces of information at once, and that process can be expensive in terms of calories expended. So wherever possible, we use the unconscious mind, reserving the conscious for problem-solving around anything that we don't yet know how to address unconsciously.

The moment we realize something is wrong, we have the chance to make a conscious choice about it. Awareness creates the opportunity; action determines whether we remain part of the problem (see: slavery, suffrage, the ozone layer). Without that realization, we live in blissful ignorance we are raised into. From the age of 11, without my parents explicitly conveying wealth as a value, I harbored a strong desire to become super rich. It took me three decades and the shifts in awareness that I outline in this book to realize that my dream was part of the problem, and nearly all that time to change my actions. But allow me to demonstrate the same progression of change with an easier example first.

When I was 13 years old, after a large family gathering for Christmas, my parents rented a minibus and drove 22 of us down to Goa, India. The morning after we arrived, we headed off to the beach. The weather was perfect—a beautiful sunny day without being too hot to enjoy it. As I was walking on the beach, I opened an ice cream that was wrapped in a plastic cover and immediately, unthinkingly discarded the wrapper onto the beach. My older cousin, who lives in Singapore, was outraged.

She stopped, pulled me back, and asked, "Who do you think is going to pick that up?" Then she proceeded to give me a spiel about how bad it is to litter and how I'd be fined if I did that in Singapore.

I cringe now remembering my response: "This is India. Everybody does it."

But from that day on, with her tart "So what?" in mind, I stopped littering completely. No matter where I was.

Two things happened. First, I had been made aware that my action did, in fact, merit some thought. Second, I felt an impact of that action. Concern for the earth wasn't enough for me at first—it was when I realized that persisting in such behavior would affect my standing with my cousin, whom I admired and whose good opinion I valued, that I really paid attention. Then I could understand the bigger picture. I became conscious of my actions, and I could no longer litter. Eventually, that level of consciousness turned into an almost unconscious level of good behavior.

Years later, on another beautiful sunny morning, my son was on a play-date with his friend, rolling around doing somersaults down the soft green hills. His friend's mom came up to me and asked about the beer can in my hand—a little relieved to find that I hadn't cracked one open. Without thinking much about it, I had picked up the discarded empty can and held it in my hand until I could find a rubbish bag to put it in. A couple of decades after my cousin scolded me, I had finally gone from unconscious littering, to conscious awareness of my choices, to picking up other people's litter as a matter of course. I had grown from being part of the problem to becoming part of the solution, and as my son follows my example and picks up litter on his own, I believe that solution will continue on. When I spoke with Erica and heard about everything her team was doing to clean up the oceans, it inspired me further, and I'm certain I have more growth yet to come.

At the end of my call with Erica, she added, "We can do this—change is possible."

Whole-society problems require whole-society solutions. Never has this been more the case than in today's world, where the most important challenges facing business and society are problems that no single organization, sector, nation, or global region can solve by acting alone. Low consciousness leads us to believe that only what affects us personally matters, but as long as there are billions of individual people just trying to survive, the whole of humanity will fail to thrive.

Make no mistake: a part will always find their own way, as has been the case for centuries, even if that is a way off the planet. But the beauty of our need to cooperate when competition fails is that, when we raise our consciousness, we can't help but spread it.

This book is an attempt to raise your consciousness, perhaps not to scold you as my cousin scolded me, but to leave you hopeful, energized, and excited. First through awareness, then your connection to it, and finally by empowering and encouraging you to act.

This is why I see us as Generation Hope: as jaded as millennials and younger generations have a reputation for being, it's because we are more conscious of what needs to change. Indeed, hope stems from the actions we take as our awareness grows—which opens up a potential path toward an economic and societal future that we can shape. This alternative, often referred to as the third way*, suggests that we can make transformative changes by starting with ourselves and then expanding our impact to the broader community. It involves shifting our mindset from one of scarcity to abundance, embracing inclusivity, and fostering a sense of interconnectedness.

The responsibility for making these changes rests upon our generation. By acknowledging that change begins within ourselves and that our collective efforts can shape a new narrative for our economic and social systems, and by adopting a mindset of abundance, raising our consciousness, fostering community, and advocating for inclusive economics, we have the potential to create meaningful impact and contribute to a more positive and sustainable world.

---

* The term "third way" refers to a political, social, or economic philosophy that seeks to find a middle ground or alternative approach between traditional ideologies. It often emerges as a response to perceived shortcomings or limitations of existing systems. The concept of a third way suggests that there is an alternative path that combines elements from different ideologies to create a more balanced, practical, and inclusive solution

Change is never easy; however, as we embark on this journey of trans-formation, the process itself brings about immediate benefits. As each of us takes steps to evolve, we experience personal growth, increased happiness, and a sense of thriving in the present moment. This un-derscores the idea that positive change is not solely a distant goal but a rewarding and fulfilling process that positively impacts our lives here and now.

You may not yet feel this hope, and you may not agree with everything I say in the coming pages, but we don't need to agree on every little detail in order to take better actions. The idea that we are all alone unless we're with someone just like us is just another unconscious story that drives us to unhelpful places, leaving us all feeling polarized and powerless.

Similarly, our current economic system is a story we tell ourselves about our relationships to money, abundance, and each other. It was not written from start to finish before being handed down to us—it is simply a collection of decisions made over time, which means every decision we make reinforces or reinvents it on some level.

Our generation loves the story of the underdog—the YouTube gamer who became a millionaire, the Instagram influencer who partnered with a huge brand that changed her life. But those are the dreams of a dying system. If we can influence the stories we tell ourselves first, as individuals and as societies, we have the ability to unlock a huge latent reservoir of potential. We can build a new system—a new world—from new levels of consciousness. We can create the kind of future that Fuller dreamed about, rather than the one that gives Erica and the rest of our generation nightmares.

The rest of this book is an exploration of that dream. While reading cover to cover is an option, each chapter's insights can also stand on their own. Part I, comprising chapters 1 to 3, delves into "The Scale of the Problem," addressing the macroeconomic challenges that humanity collectively faces.

Transitioning to Part II, which encompasses chapters 4 to 8, we embark on "The Shape of Change." Here, the focus shifts to our personal engagement with our current economic system. Because economic structures are shaped by bottom-up participation, chapters 5 and 6 take a deep dive into our intricate relationship with money. After we decide to take a new approach to our personal finances, we can consider an alternative to our failing system—the five-step framework of inclusive economics—introduced in chapter 7.

As we stride into Part III, spanning chapters 9 to 12, "The Scope of Impact" unfolds. These chapters illustrate the power of unity as we shift the spotlight onto community-centric values. With this as our anchor, we can finally navigate toward collective prosperity, as the last chapters demonstrate how it is not only attainable but imperative for us to learn to thrive both individually and as a whole.

Ultimately, writing this book has only reinforced my hope that we have more than dreams at our fingertips. Change is happening right now. Over the coming chapters, I'll share stories that will give you hope and inspire you to take action. But first, we need to find out how we got here. Buckle up, we're heading for a crisis.

Part I

The S
of the
Probl

scale

em

Chapter 1
Crisis a

d Crossroads

Humanity has shown amazing resilience in the past decade, from individuals withstanding personal loss to countries surviving economic shocks. Most importantly, this horrible time has shown us that it is possible to make wholesale changes to our lives—and change is not easy. They say never let a good crisis go to waste, and I believe that is true in our post-pandemic era as much as it was when the Second World War laid the foundations for a host of social and economic reforms. We now have the opportunity to change the world for the better. Will we take it?

Shakespeare said that some are born great, some achieve greatness, and some have greatness thrust upon 'em—and that turns out to be true about innovation as well. One need look no further than the innovative responses society had to the pandemic *that was thrust upon* us. Sectors from education to healthcare, and food service to filmmaking, all scrambled to innovate their operations for a world in lockdown, fueling a rapid adoption of digital technologies in which even the baby boomer generation was forced to get digitally savvy. Without the lockdowns, they may never have had an incentive to make the leap to adopt technology beyond the basics.

Interestingly enough, most if not all of the digital technology that became commonplace after the start of national lockdowns had been available for at least five years prior to 2020. However, it took the pandemic to scale adoption from a very small percentage of people to the mass market.

No one would have thought the change that took place during the pandemic would have been possible. It may have taken another 10 years or more to reach these levels of digital adoption. It's a natural human instinct to resist change, mostly due to the fear of the unknown. The pandemic gave us two choices: adapt or face the consequences—in this case, potentially death. When you have to choose between the two, survival instincts kick in, and for most people, resistance to change disappears. Our need to survive eclipses our fear of the unknown.

Pre-pandemic, who would have imagined the need for, or possibility of, restricting people's movement in democratic countries? Yet after COVID-19's rampage through northern Italy, it was clear that the burden on countries' healthcare infrastructure needed to be managed, and until a vaccine could be developed, social distancing was the only way to do that. In March and April of 2020, as country after country went into national lockdowns, by and large people accepted the restrictions placed on them for the greater good of society. Most people were confined to their homes for large parts of the year. Every one of us experienced some version of these restrictions, demonstrating to ourselves and each other the sacrifices that people will make to survive.

With lockdowns came a major economic impact. If the economy shrinks by 0.25 percent for two quarters, we're in a recession and all financial markets start teetering. During the first year of the pandemic, the bottom fell out. This is not to say that the pandemic was a good thing or that it didn't matter. Of course it did—1.6 billion people lost their jobs, with approximately 400 million of those jobs not expected to come back; 200 million people were pushed into poverty, and the poor and lower middle class were disproportionately affected. Supply

chain disruptions led to major logistical problems, which further compounded the economic woes of those less fortunate. According to the
International Monetary Fund, the pandemic was the worst economic
downturn since the Great Depression (1929).[1]

Yet because of our resilience and ability to adapt, the economy is
still working.

National lockdowns also meant remote working became the new normal, after gaining momentum for the five years prior to 2020. That
meant a certain part of the workforce already knew how to do it, but
the majority had to figure it out under challenging circumstances.

Outside of the pandemic, remote working does create opportunities
for those who cannot relocate. It also helps provide flexibility to those
who find it difficult to be at an office the whole day—including parents,
who need to do the school run or tend to appointments. During the
work-from-home period of 2020–2021, people and businesses got a
taste of new potential working arrangements and what that might look
like for both parties. Some businesses thrived in this model, giving up
their office space and permanently shifting to being "remote-first." A
few pioneering companies said their employees can work from home
indefinitely, and the majority have considered some form of a hybrid
model.

But many businesses quietly learned which of their white-collar jobs
can be done remotely—and chances are, they will ultimately offshore
many of them. One study found that 65 percent of Americans "expect
that robots and computers will do much of the work currently done
by humans within 50 years." We can forget about robots for a minute,
because many jobs are being replaced by other humans in countries
with lower cost bases. This had already been happening consistently
for the last two decades, and the pandemic has further accelerated
the pace.

Costs aren't the only concern. After initial mandates to a full return to the office were met with stiff resistance and resignations, leaders realized that it is virtually impossible to get everyone back five days a week—especially those folks they hired remotely during the pandemic. Hybrid situations aim for two to three days a week, which is still a tough ask for some people. It fascinates me, because working from home isn't all roses, yet for most (myself included), there is a preference to work from home.

What gives us the right to work from home when it was absolutely normal to work five days a week at the office? I'm not sure. Leaders who live in the past—and are paranoid about productivity—are asking the same question. But it seems like after we let the genie out of the bottle, we can't put it back.

Some of the biggest businesses in the world showed their true colors in how they dealt with their return to office policies, and they lost a lot of talent to those who were offering permanent remote roles, forming one part of the #GreatResignation and #QuietQuitting.* Businesses who understand this shift in employee preferences will continue to attract the best talent, but the change has to be more than just allowing employees to work remotely.

When it comes to culture, the expression "corridors of power" highlights the fact that location really matters—the most important decisions are made at headquarters, and only by those who have access to decision-makers. We've all had experiences where occasionally colleagues meeting in person have forgotten about those online, especially when it is just one person joining remotely. Being in the building provides access to those physically present in a way that people working remotely just don't have. Missing the side chats that happen at the water cooler or when meetings are concluded and people are

* The other part is people wanting to follow their purpose.

walking back to their desks are other dynamics that disadvantage re-mote workers. This is a culture-based dynamic that points to deeper reform that is needed—as I'm sure many have discovered after switch-ing companies to one that has "kept up with the times," only to find they are back to square one.

I started working from home in 2016 when I joined an all-remote company. It was great—but only because I was able to go out too. I could have coffee with former colleagues and meet people for work. I joined a coworking community on a pay-as-you-use plan, which al-lowed me to pop in whenever I wanted to. When lockdowns happened, I was stuck at home with my four white walls, and it wasn't so great anymore—I missed social interactions and a change of scenery. Par-ents with young kids working from home because of COVID found it incredibly hard to juggle work and family life. Even though the kids have gone back to school now, lockdown was its own trauma, with the entire family working or studying from home. My wife now works from home permanently as well, and that's another dynamic to con-tend with. Previously, when you were at work you were at work, and at home you were home. While you might have received the odd call or text asking about something, there was a separation. Working from home provides easier access for those at home—a spouse, parents, family members, or kids—to make a request. Home-related interac-tions inevitably interfere with your work, and vice versa, in ways that previously didn't happen unless you were a "workaholic."

Some sort of hybrid is certainly the way forward, which will look dif-ferent for different companies based on their needs and their culture. It will take a few years for all this to shake out and for new norms to be formed. In the meantime, we have an opportunity to shape this change, rather than be shaped by it. For example, in 2019, my family moved homes and I lost access to my coworking community. Initially, there weren't any coworking spaces in my new neighborhood at all, while community spaces sat unused. Post-pandemic, new coworking spaces have mushroomed along with new community spaces, and old ones in some areas have been refreshed. In the UK, the government has funded Barclays Bank to help to expand Eagle Labs—comprising around 30 tech hubs located all over the country. Many of them were built out of old Barclays branches that became redundant as more and more banking went online. Coworking spaces for those who cannot afford private spaces would help us all adjust to the future of work.

Instead, the pressure to perform in any circumstance is high, the support for doing so remains low, and psychological safety—the ability to work in a place where you are not condemned for expressing your opinion or ostracized for your differences—is rare. Working a dead-end job that pays just enough to keep the lights on while being constantly gaslit and undermined by a boss who simply doesn't care is no longer enough when it's become clear that companies are in fact capable of change. While such treatment may come from an individual, it is the toxic company culture that creates and tolerates their behavior, and companies that are only concerned with profits will be the worst offenders.

Reskill training is another option for those being replaced by low-cost workers and robotics, and Sweden is leading the way. They've set up a network of job security councils jointly run by industries and unions that retrain laid-off workers in skills that are still in demand but out of reach of automation. Moreover, while unemployed and learning new skills, workers are buoyed by a safety net that includes generous jobless benefits. Around the world, the average age of workers who need to be retrained goes down every year. Increasingly, workers only in their mid-thirties are finding that their skills are out of date. Yet over the past two decades, most countries in the West, particularly the US, have been slow to follow Sweden in responding to this need.[*2]

---

* The US spent just 0.03 percent of its GDP on labor training in 2015, a decline of 63 percent from 1993 levels.

In other words, it's up to us to save our jobs and our sanity. Relying on business or governments to protect your job or train you for a new one is a foolhardy strategy, and perhaps it always has been. But more advancements than we thought possible happened in the pandemic, and I believe we can trigger those advancements whenever we want to when we come together as a community.

£ € $

It's not by accident that many of the most successful entrepreneurs on our planet, from Steve Jobs and Bill Gates to Mark Zuckerberg and Jack Dorsey, as well as media moguls Oprah Winfrey and Ellen DeGeneres, all dropped out of the education system to kickstart or accelerate the information age.

With every passing decade of the last century, more and more emphasis has been placed on how broken global education is—a system that is, bizarrely, still rooted in the industrial age. While it has been a key factor in improving people's standard of living, education is more closely controlled by parents who are desperate for their children to do well and move up in society than by anyone working to increase general well-being. Every effort is made to educate kids in the "best" schools— never mind that their rankings are based on outdated scoring systems.

How much do you remember from what you were taught at school? As someone with dyslexia, I struggled to learn and suffered in exams. I'm not alone, and it's not just dyslexia that's to blame. The dominant approach to teaching—rote memorization—was designed for a time when information was not available at our fingertips. Relevant skills and knowledge can no longer be gained by learning in this way, which makes the ability to spit them out in exams to score high marks irrelevant. Yet this mode of teaching is still prevalent across the world. The educational progress of seven- and eleven-year-olds in England is assessed by standardized assessment tests (SATs) administered in primary schools. This is common practice all over the world. While there have been efforts to move away from standardized testing in the US (where SATs were invented) with the introduction of the Common Core curriculum standards, progress has been slow and painful.

So why is education still failing so many people, myself included? Sal Khan of the online learning platform Khan Academy offers a helpful analogy. Imagine if the way we are taught at school was the model for how we do other things, such as building a house:

> So we bring in the contractor and say, "We were told we have two weeks to build a foundation. Do what you can." So they do what they can. Maybe it rains. Maybe some of the supplies don't show up. And two weeks later, the inspector comes, looks around, says, "OK, the concrete is still wet right over there, that part isn't quite up to code...I'll give it an 80 percent." You say, "Great! That's a C. Let's build the first floor." Same thing. We have two weeks, do what you can, inspector shows up, it's 75 percent. Great, that's a D-plus. Second floor, third floor, and all of a sudden, while you're building the third floor, the whole structure collapses.[3]

That's the current education model. In school, we go to lessons where we are taught concepts, we go home and do homework. That model is repeated—lessons followed by homework—until there is a test. The best students might get 80 percent of the test right, others will score much lower, and we all move on from the foundation to a more complicated subject. That is repeated for months and years, building new knowledge on incomplete knowledge. If we go back to the house Khan is describing, it's no wonder the whole structure collapses.

It's obvious that the process is flawed. We can even see when it is the contractor's or inspector's fault, in cases where the school system, the teachers, or the curriculum are obviously lacking. But by artificially constraining how long we have to do something—standard measurements by grade and class period—we have prioritized time over quality, ensuring a variable outcome. Worse still, even though we've made an effort to inspect and identify the gaps, we continue to build right on top of the collapsed structure year after year, while countless kids fall through the cracks.

That is exactly what happened to me at school—disengaged, I sat at the back of the class and played chess or (when I could get away with it) stayed out of class entirely and played cricket. Each year, I scored 40–50 percent and moved to the next grade. My foundations were nonexistent. By the time I had to sit for my class 10 board exams (GCSE/grade 10 equivalent), I was going to several private tutors in a desperate attempt to catch up. It was a miracle that I managed to scrape through. After taking a gap year and doing some soul searching, I was lucky to have the opportunity to start again at university.

Looking back, I recognize and appreciate how lucky I was. Not only could my family afford the extra teaching, but I also realized that I wanted to do well in school. That was largely due to two factors: my grandmother and my grandaunt, who frequently drilled the importance into my head. As it happened, my friend circle at school included the kids who did really well. But I was also friends with the students "at the back of the class" and could easily have been influenced differently.

The rift was too big to bridge, and I struggled despite the tutors and my best efforts. During my gap year, my parents arranged for me to spend time with three family friends in their businesses as an apprentice of sorts. I learned to assemble computers, fix telephones, and begin programming. While I was keen to study computer science, I didn't have the grades in math and physics to get in. Accounting was the default option.

The subjects I chose at university—accounting and economics—were not taught at foundational school level, so everyone started together with the basic concepts. For the first time, I realized how important it was to learn the basics and build from there. I put away my chess set, sat in the first row, and absorbed as much as I could.

To help bring more kids like me to the proverbial front of the class, Sal Khan founded Khan Academy, an online learning nonprofit educational organization, in 2008. Twelve years later, Khan Academy has more than 71 million registered users from 190 countries. At the heart of its learning model is teaching for mastery, not for test scores. We see this all the time in other disciplines: in a martial art, you practice the white belt skills as long as necessary to master them before you move on to become a yellow belt. Likewise, when learning a musical instrument, you practice basic scales and movements until you've mastered them before going on to more advanced levels.

And that's before the pandemic upended our lives. Like businesses and governments, schools across the world had to instantly adjust to lockdowns. Some did better than others. Even though remote learning had been around for more than a decade, most schools failed to adapt and the level of education provided decreased. In India, where schools were closed for two years, it affected the education of nearly 290 million children. While remote education was widely offered in India, four out of ten students were unable to go online. Those who went online are still struggling with learning loss, mental health issues, trauma, and poverty. They are being called a "lost generation," and for India, whose working-age population is projected to peak at 65 percent in 2031, what was once seen as an advantage is likely to turn into a burden if many of them are undereducated and underemployed. This is just one example of a worldwide generation affected by disparate access to resources during one of the most formative stages of life.

While cost and geographic barriers continue to limit access to specialized schooling, efforts over the last decade doubled during the pandemic as Khan Academy and others—such as Outlier.org, edX, Coursera, DataCamp, Udemy, Codecademy, and Andela—attempted to fill the gaps that schools were missing and ultimately to change the status quo. Khan's mission is to help open more opportunities for people in the creative world, where almost everyone can participate as an entrepreneur, an artist, or a researcher, compared to the industrial world and its associated jobs. While the concept of remote learning is as old as correspondence courses, today it's often discussed in the context of massive open online courses, or MOOCs. Organized by companies, universities, and nonprofits, MOOCs provide education in the form of online lectures, quizzes, and projects, allowing large numbers of students to learn at a flexible pace while using different models. These platforms are gaining significant traction, but education has never been about academics alone. Kids go to school to become well-rounded citizens—and that comes with pitfalls of its own.

While schools attempt to provide physically secure environments, most don't provide emotionally secure environments. Kids are chastised for the smallest mistakes. Instead of teaching for mastery, schools are in some race to cover syllabus material, and homework is part of that race. Similarly, being late to school is an offense—in the UK, children are made to stand in a separate "late line" as some sort of repercussion for something they have little control over. This dynamic isn't necessary by any means. My kids' school asks parents to drop off their children by a certain time like all schools, but they firmly believe that it is okay if you are late. It's an alien concept to most, but the school believes that children shouldn't be stressed at home or at school.

As education moves to remote learning models, especially for older kids and college students, it will be important to create the right environment for learning, similar to coworking spaces. I expect more and more study centers to pop up—places where students come to study regardless of which school or university they are part of. If we can teach people not just skills but to have a creative approach to learning, they will be empowered by learning for mastery and able to build new skills much more easily when automation changes things.

Unfortunately, schools have struggled to keep up as the world changes —governments have been slow to react and, with the exception of the pandemic, the private sector doesn't have the impetus to change rapidly. Reimagining the way we educate our children comes at the expense of profits or larger government spending, and the incentives apparently aren't there. Meanwhile, the building is still crumbling. If we don't prioritize physiological safety or aim to develop children with active minds in a digital world, all while fostering compassion for others and confidence to be themselves, we will continue to perpetuate a dysfunctional world. I was lucky that my struggles at school taught me how to embrace, even celebrate, failure. But this didn't come from the schools I attended, and that kind of teaching needs to be baked in by design rather than be left to luck.

Governments, nonprofits, and businesses that operate schools have failed to deliver on so many levels. And a lot of this failure can be attributed to our current economic model, which is so deeply entrenched that even the people who lead nonprofit schools are unaware of what they are perpetuating: the school system was designed to teach you how to be an employee or a doctor or a lawyer, period. Never about money or innovation, skills acquisition, or equitable living.

Take the emergence of ChatGPT for example. Students who are adept enough at obtaining formal examination responses through AI are demonstrating skills that would be rewarded in the adult world: efficiency, innovation, and technological adaptability. Instead of being taught how to use those skills ethically and responsibly, they are simply punished. Experts are asking: Is it time to ditch formal examinations altogether? Even before ChatGPT, qualifications had been losing their value. The rate of change is outpacing our education system's ability to deliver the skills we need. Joshua Wöhle, serial founder in the edtech space, says:

> *The average time a skill stays relevant used to be over ten years. In 2022 it was four, down from five in 2017. Soon, it will be shorter than the time it takes to get a degree. The logical endpoint is that qualifications, as we know them, will lose their value. With it, the entire model of "learn first, apply second" will become obsolete. And as the value of any particular skill decreases, the value of your ability to adapt and learn as you go along will soar.*[4]

As we enter the exponential age,* our education system, which already couldn't switch from the industrial age to the information age, needs to make an even bigger leap to reflect the changing world we live in.

£ € $

As with most technology and science, modern medicine made great strides in the 20th century. Infant mortality has drastically decreased, life expectancy has increased, and quality of life, for the most part, has greatly improved—at least to those who have access to surgical operations and lifesaving interventions.

But only five billion people have access to that medicine,[5] which means over two billion people are completely left out. And given the way these calculations are made—estimations with a lot of assumptions—the last billion of that five billion people are likely to have very little access to medicine, if any at all. In 2017, the World Bank and WHO published a report that said, "At least half the world lacks access

* Exponential age: driven by quantum computing, artificial intelligence, and supercomputers (smartphones) in the hands of more than half the world's population.

"The entire model of 'learn first, apply second' will become obsolete."
—Joshua Wöhle

to essential health services, while 100 million people are pushed into extreme poverty because of health expenses every year."[6]

For over a decade, efforts have been underway to remotely administer basic healthcare services, but they have been met with limited uptake. Mera Doctor, which let people chat directly with a trained, licensed doctor through an Android app (like WhatsApp with a doctor) launched in 2010. It raised $2.81 million in funding and served over 700,000 patients across India, but folded before the pandemic.[7] Similarly GSMA's mHealth program failed to get traction despite the potential to reach women and children who lack access to essential healthcare and nutritional information.

Then came the pandemic. Overnight, the health sector had to figure out how to treat outpatients remotely, and healthtech and telemedicine took off. Some did better than others in the way they were able to embrace and adopt technology. From getting online consultations to ICU nurses holding iPads for folks to talk to their family members, technology enabled us to achieve outcomes that previously required in-person interactions. Slowly and over time, online processes are improving, providing better user experiences. But there is a dark side too. The medical profession is a noble one, yet scandal after scandal quietly rocks the foundations of the industry. The main culprit? Yes, you guessed it: our current economic system. Private hospitals all around the world have a conflict of interest between their duty to treat patients and the financial targets they have to meet—especially those that are listed on stock markets.

Public hospitals are not immune either. A recent independent inquiry into maternity practices at two National Health Service (NHS) hospitals in the UK uncovered hundreds of cases in which health officials failed to undertake serious incident investigations. Grieving families were denied access to reviews of their care and mothers were blamed when their babies died or suffered horrific injuries. A total of 201 babies and nine mothers could have or would have survived if the NHS trust had provided better care, the inquiry found. An obsession with "natural births" rather than caesarean sections combined with a shocking lack of staff training and oversight of maternity wards resulted in a toxic culture in which mothers and babies died needlessly for 20 years while "repeated failures" were ignored again and again.[8]

The inquiry's report makes for grim reading, and my heart goes out to all the families that have suffered so gravely. Even though the NHS hospitals are funded by the government and are not-for-profit, money played a key role in these catastrophic blunders. The evidence points to the decade of NHS underfunding since 2010, despite cash boosts in 2018 and 2019.

Post-pandemic, the UK's beloved NHS seems to be falling apart. Remote consultations continue beyond the pandemic, and the process of administering telehealth will continue to get better and better—but how will that process be utilized? Rather than remote care providing healthcare to those who previously didn't have access to medicine, the squeeze on the medical system has forced remote care to become a way to meet the current load. Recently, a friend's grandmother was treated in a hospital in the US and rather than a doctor being physically present, a different remote doctor "attended" to her every time she was checked.

No doubt, technology can play a big role in healthcare and save lives as a result. But which way is it going to go—an increase in superprofits for the wealthy (the slow privatization of the NHS) or an increase in healthcare for the poor? Or perhaps both? Superprofits will likely continue to be prioritized due to the pressures from Wall Street and the investment community, and there will always be efforts to increase healthcare for the poor, led by Good Samaritans. But even the most well-intentioned are likely to have their hands tied by those who control capital. If we can find a way to scale true impact investing, we might finally be able to unlock the potential for the greater good of humanity we saw during the pandemic, without the pressure of a crisis.

£ € $

Healthtech, edtech and remote working were all in nascent stages, and the pandemic gave them a huge shot in the arm. The health, education, and employment sectors in general have been vastly undermined through reduced funding and reduced unionization. The rise of neoliberalism (detailed in chapter 3) over the past three decades has left these sectors vulnerable while making super winners of the rest. Without controls in place, it is highly likely these factors will be used to create superprofits, rather than being used to better serve society. The precedent has been set.

The tech industry really didn't need to be put on steroids—in the 10 years before the pandemic, it created more billionaires than all other industries combined.*[9] But that's exactly what happened. Two years into the pandemic, it became apparent that COVID-19 shifted economic fortunes. Despite the rapid adoption of technology and wholesale change to the workforce, education, and health systems, to name a few, the increased need to shop from home changed the marketplace as well. Unfortunately, it enabled capital-intensive firms to take business from smaller firms while also benefiting from lower corporate taxes and lower interest rates, boosting their profits as share prices skyrocketed and wealth inequality was exacerbated overall.

---

* Although other sectors produce a fair share of billionaires, this number cannot match individuals who have minted their money by operating in the tech industry.

Amazon, one of the biggest winners from the pandemic, saw its stock price nearly double in the first part of 2020. It reported $108.5 billion in sales in the first three months of 2021, up 44 percent from a year earlier. This came with $8.1 billion in profit—an increase of 220 percent from the same period that last year,[10] while its valuation reached an all-time high of almost $2 trillion.

Apple, Microsoft, Alphabet (Google), Tesla, Nvidia, and Meta platforms (Facebook) were big winners too. Apple's stock ended 2021 close to a record—not just for the company but for any company, ever. Despite facing supply chain challenges and its stores closing worldwide, the iPhone maker was on the cusp of a $3 trillion market value, almost triple its pandemic low in March 2020. Microsoft was firing on all cylinders as well, and it already had more cylinders than most. Its cloud platform and Office 365 tools have been a mainstay, but Microsoft has a finger in many other digital pies, including the hiring market (LinkedIn), business applications (Dynamics), and gaming (Xbox). Google's parent Alphabet went into the pandemic as a powerful advertising company. It came out of it as one of the main engines of a booming digital economy. Tesla, the electric car pioneer, became the first $1 trillion automaker and made its cofounder and chief executive the richest man in the world. Nvidia graphics chips have become the main workhorse behind artificial intelligence and other data-intensive applications that are fueling the rise of giant cloud data centers. And even though it was a bruising year for Meta (Facebook), its share price has weathered the reputational hits, reaching a record $1 trillion for the first time in June 2021.

In the private markets, venture capitalists made hay as the investment industry continued to exhibit immunity to COVID-19—and the numbers we saw were truly staggering. The top two years ever of venture investment came during the pandemic. The $307 billion invested in venture-backed startups in 2021 almost doubled the previous year's record, bringing the total invested to nearly $750 billion over a span of four years.[11] Unicorn after unicorn, occasionally decacorns and even centicorns,* pop up in the news on a daily basis as startups raise hundreds of millions—war chests that disrupt (more accurately, destroy) the competition so that the winners can take all.

While some individuals, companies, and countries stand to benefit, many countries, companies, and individuals are left in a far worse position. Technology has opened the door to serve populations that were previously unprofitable, and entrepreneurs who truly believe they are delivering value—a win-win if you will—are excited about the possibility. But that's not exactly how it plays out. Building a startup to help the poor and making hundreds of millions doing it means you're either extracting too much (even if the product is free) or could provide an even better service that's more tailored to their needs. Capital isn't the scarce resource it used to be, but that should justify a more expansive use of it rather than outsized 10x–100x returns, all in the name of risk.

Economists are calling the post-pandemic era a K-shaped recovery, in which some measurements go up and others go down. From an economic standpoint, a full recovery is when a country repasses its previous high of GDP output,† and stock markets do the same. When the stock market crashed and fairly quickly rebounded in March 2020 (largely due to the stimulus packages that were passed), it was considered a V-shaped recovery. You might have also heard of W-shaped recovery, where there is a partial rebound, then a dip again before a full recovery is made. While this dip-and-rebound happened after the

---

* A unicorn is a startup company valued at $1 billion or more. Unicorns with over $10 billion in valuation have been designated as decacorn companies. For private companies valued over $100 billion, the terms centicorn or hectocorn are used.

† Gross domestic product (GDP) measures the monetary value of final goods and services—that is, those that are bought by the final user—produced in a country in a given period of time (say a quarter or a year). It counts all of the output generated within the borders of a country.

2008 global financial crisis, in reality, we did not actually recover from the crisis itself. No matter what the charts showed, GDP is a flawed metric. The governments and media told us growth and GDP recovered and repassed its previous high, but a disproportionate amount of the new GDP went to the super-rich (who were flush with cash after the bailouts and put it to work). When you remove the super-rich from the numbers it becomes clear why the impacts (lower purchasing power) are still being felt by the many who were deeply affected. I see the same thing happening again, and with the recognition of a K-shaped divergence between the haves and have-nots, I fear that this time it will be even worse.

The pandemic was a great opportunity to use public resources and create social programs to benefit the less fortunate, but instead, wealth inequality has continued to widen. Why the disparity? As soon as the pandemic hit, governments around the world announced fiscal and stimulus packages, but they all directly or indirectly benefited wealthy individuals far more than low-income people.

Instead, we need a different measure to influence policy. One such measure is Gross National Happiness (GNH), a multidimensional poverty index that Bhutan formally adopted in 2008. The GNH was trailblazing in that it provided the world with proof-of-concept for moving beyond GDP measurement and taking a holistic view of social development. It aggregates Bhutan's performance across nine domains and 33 development indicators into a single number between zero and one, addressing several shortcomings of GDP. For example, when industrial production increases, GDP will always rise even when it comes at the cost of environmental degradation. On the other hand, GNH may fall because it takes people's experience of their natural surroundings into account. In addition, while GDP values only market labor, GNH takes other uses of time into account, including sleep adequacy. Crucially, unpaid work (such as childcare, caring for the elderly, and domestic work) factors into the calculation of total time spent on work, which determines whether an individual has sufficient leisure time. Given the disproportionate burden of domestic work on women, this makes the GNH Index more gender-sensitive than GDP.[12]

Other countries have constructed their own versions of happiness indices, reflecting different visions for what socioeconomic development means and the constantly progressing scientific understanding of the determinants of happiness. In 2013 the United Nations General Assembly adopted Resolution 66/281, proclaiming March 20th to be observed annually as International Day of Happiness. Since then, more and more people have come to believe that our success as countries should be judged by the happiness of our people. Each year the World Happiness Report is published. It's no surprise that the Nordic countries have the highest well-being, though they are not richer than many other countries.

But to understand when the UK changed paths from being a welfare state to unequal individualism, let's look to Margaret Thatcher, Prime Minister of the UK from 1979 to 1990, known for her uncompromising politics and leadership style, so much so that a Soviet journalist dubbed her the "Iron Lady."

While I don't agree with her politics, you at least knew what she stood for and why, and I wish we had more leaders who are able to explain their position and policy clearly, rather than the populist blatant liars we have now (more on that later). In a career-defining comment, she said the following:

> *I think we have been through a period when too many people have been given to understand that when they have a problem it is government's job to cope with it. "I have a problem, I'll get a grant. I'm homeless, the government must house me." They are casting their problems on society. And, you know, there is no such thing as society. There are individual men and women and there are families. And*

no governments can do anything except through people, and people must look to themselves first. It is our duty to look after ourselves and then, also, to look after our neighbors. People have got their entitlements too much in mind, without the obligations. There is no such thing as an entitlement, unless someone has first met an obligation.[13]

As a millennial who grew up in India, I didn't live through or even read about her policies when they were active. Perhaps in the '70s, too many people had been given to understand that when they had a problem it was the government's job to cope with it and were simply looking for handouts. But even if that were the case, it's fair to say that politicians from all parties have over-corrected. By the time the 21st century hit, so much had changed and so much more was available to the world that there would have been nothing wrong with using the surplus to look after one's citizens—without expecting them to meet some obligation first. Instead, austerity put the squeeze on public spending and made it clear who would get the benefits.

To highlight how polarized politics has been for decades, some see Thatcher's quote as one of the worst things that she said and some regard it as one of the best.

One thing Thatcher was right about: financial support would come not from a mysterious entity known as the state but from fellow citizens, also known as the taxpayers. The very idea of individualism is flawed, and not just because of our shared tax obligation. The famous saying "it takes a village to raise a child" is evident in every aspect of life. You hear it in acceptance speeches, whether at the Oscars or from a victorious sports star thanking everyone who supported them on their journey. Further, all athletes would have used a state-funded public facility to train at some point or another.

Nothing has reflected this flawed sense of individualism more than Silicon Valley. Even though founders say things like "there is no I in team" and "we couldn't have done it without you," financial reward is so heavily weighted in favor of the individuals who started the company that it would be comical if it weren't so clearly unethical. And while becoming a founder or joining a startup has been all the rage, you have to have money to do it. Get in early, and you could make a lot. Wait too long, and you only make the cut if you've already got the dough. For the most part, the tech industry is a pyramid scheme, and instead of those coming in at the end left holding the bag, it is society that has to pay.*

While Ms. Thatcher might not have agreed with "entitlements" such as individual stimulus funds or the government support of declining industries, governments that were aligned with her thinking saw it perfectly fine to support shareholders with bailouts. One of the greatest economic policy failures has been the clear priority of protecting the rich rather than the poor. In fact, from 2008 to 2018, the UK and US protected the rich and actively took away from the poor.

Even during the pandemic, when government payments were purported to go right to the people, the money didn't go to where it was most needed—to protect the most vulnerable. For example, the PPP program for small businesses in the US made businesses apply through the banks, so the businesses with the best connections with the banks got pushed to the head of the line. You can imagine that those weren't the smallest businesses or those who needed it the most.† As a result, the cost of living has risen faster post-2020 than it has in the last 30 years. And decades after Ms. Thatcher's statement above, we are seeing just how destructive those policies have been.

Less-than-conscious millennials (and older generations) will continue to believe that their benefits are merely transactional—that their

---

* As the winners take all, more people are left with less. Benefits are hollowed out in the name of efficiency (e.g., gig workers) and the masses become poorer.

† There were exceptions: countries such as Denmark and New Zealand did design programs that were very effective.

"taxpayer money" hires their teachers and other service providers, and pays for infrastructure like roads and bridges. Some who are even more extreme believe they don't benefit from any handouts at all—perhaps after being born in private hospitals, educated in private schools, etc. But while an individual's money might be able to buy such things, it can never buy freedom without protection from the state unless you somehow have a private army at your command. If only we could attribute how much of our taxes go to protecting our country and keeping society civil compared to each of the benefits we receive—be it education, social security, basic infrastructure, or corporate bailouts. As individuals are now left to fend for themselves in the wake of the pandemic, some are going up on the K-curve while others go down, all in the name of meritocracy. We have failed to provide everyone with basic skills because we have failed to invest in all of society.

To make matters worse, the pandemic ushered in an unprecedented global rise in state surveillance. In an effort to trace the spread of the disease and to enforce lockdowns, governments in democracies and autocracies alike have set a dangerous precedent by turning to surveillance technologies such as contact tracing apps. In many countries, such surveillance is used to control the population, to guard against uprisings that in many cases wouldn't be needed if their citizens weren't given such a raw deal in the first place. For all the progress we made in the 19th and 20th centuries, we're now in danger of losing (or actively taking away) the freedom that millions of lives were lost fighting for.

Against this backdrop, countries continue to misallocate resources on a global level in a way that will undoubtedly result in our extinction. The decisions we make over the next 20 years—of which the first 10 years are the most important by far—represent our one chance of saving our planet. It's one thing for someone to enrich themselves while others starve, but quite another for that same selfishness to result in the end of humanity.

Convenience and greed have been at the forefront of the past decades. We all want more: more money, more convenience, and more stuff. The economics that rewarded Wall Street's greed and Silicon Valley's individualism have thrived while ignoring its true costs—harm to our planet, unsustainability of excesses, and deep inequality.

£ € $

The COVID-19 pandemic drew back the curtain to lay bare many of society's most pernicious inequalities, which have only increased at multiple levels in various countries around the world. As a result, global leaders have been thrown into the spotlight, allowing their citizens and the public at large to see whether compassion was ever anything more than fashion. This time our leaders must put their people first, through authenticity and compassion, rather than looking for a standing ovation for a polished performance.

As the dust from the pandemic settles, will we repay everyone who has made sacrifices with a better future? Will we translate the solidarity we found during lockdowns into inclusive long-term objectives? Governments around the world are under pressure to do something, and the cupboard is bare—they don't have any fresh ideas.

Our potential is clear. We have yet another opportunity to change our world.

For me, our priorities are staring right at us: we need holistic change that revamps our current economic system, curtails emissions of greenhouse gasses, and rethinks the way we educate our kids. And given the way economic priorities seem to take precedence even in matters as serious as our future generations, the system has to be our first area of focus.

We are now at a crossroads, where the great potential we've proven we have intersects with the great destruction we've shown we're inclined toward. After the First World War, a similar opportunity ended in the Great Depression, the rise of fascism, and the Second World War.

While history repeats itself, the one difference in our current crisis is that the urgency has escalated. The scope of the problem is no excuse for inaction. To avoid a literal extinction, we must change more than we ever have. Will we take this once-in-a-generation opportunity to design our new world, or let it all fall away?

It's time to meet the heroes and heroines of the story. Introducing: Generation Hope.

Chapter 2
Outdated a

d Outmoded

As older generations in political and high-level corporate positions continue to fight progress and deny reality, millennials and Gen Z are shouldering the burden of an uncertain future. And it is no wonder we often feel jaded about that responsibility and outlook. As millennials, we should be the adults in the room making the change, but with far less power than we expected to have by this stage of our lives, how can we be Generation Hope?

Born between the 1980s and mid-1990s, millennials are the children of baby boomers and older Gen Xers. Baby boomers were obviously named by the dramatic increase in the number of children born during the post-WWII baby boom. In 1964 the novel *Generation X: Tales for an Accelerated Culture*, which named the next generation, hit the bookstands. Its aim was clear from the first line: "To get young people talking about their hates and hopes and fears."[1]

The book was an immediate bestseller thanks to its frank, powerful quotes, and "Generation X" ended up sticking as a moniker, with the "X" referring to an unknown variable or to a desire to not be defined. The natural progression would be to call the generation that followed Generation Y. But decades define us, and during most of that time period, the world was preoccupied with the turn of the century. "Millennial" as a term reflected that focus. Like Gen X, "millennial" referred to an attitude, a lens through which people viewed the near future.

As a result, leading up to the year 2000, we were all millennials—bracing for a new century, living at a time of uncertainty.

A lesser-known name for millennials is "Echo Boomers."[2] It's not surprising that this name hasn't stuck, given how much this generation has been at odds with our parents' generation. While there is usually animosity and judgment between baby boomers and millennials, there are similarities worth acknowledging.

Like baby boomers, millennials are a significant and disruptive demographic. We millennials are now the world's largest generation, and we want to be heard and respected as much as our predecessors. Now that we are approaching our thirties and forties, we are finding that voice. An overlooked aspect of this similarity is that both generations see themselves as rebels. As Greg Zoch, managing director and partner at executive search firm Kaye-Bassman, says: "A lot of people complain that Millennials are rebellious, bohemian, rule breakers—but if you talk to Boomers who went through the 1960s, well, guess what? They were called those same things."

What's more, boomers and millennials both have a sensitivity to social injustice and causes. Zoch continues:

> They approach it differently, which is a technology thing. Millennials can reach more people on social media than we ever could before, but they're not afraid to march. Boomers marched in Mississippi for Civil Rights; Millennials rallied for the Occupy Wall Street movement. It's the values that are similar.[3]

With that said, millennials do things very differently from their parents and grandparents, and that goes for more than emergent technology use.[4]

In 1968, if you bumped into a thirty-year-old, there was a 56 percent chance that they were married, had children, had a full-time job, and owned a mortgage. Today, however, a thirty-year-old is less than 23 percent likely[5] to have those trademarks of settling down, and that percentage is dropping each year. Meanwhile, 69 percent of millennials say that they crave adventure[6]—something I totally relate to, having lived on a plane and friends' couches for much of my late twenties and early thirties, buying airplane tickets rather than paying rent. Equally, a friend who settled down early, married at 22—something considered absolutely normal for the previous generation—says she considers it a child marriage and feels she was robbed of her youth.

Take the example of Sofia and Andrew, who met in 2013 in Washington, DC, and struggled to find their way through the demands of raising a family in this era. As recent graduates of elite US universities, each were pursuing prestigious careers: Andrew teaching physics, Sofia working as a science writer for a leading magazine. Their decision to marry shifted their ambitions rather than amplifying them. It forced a familiar reckoning: How would the needs of the household be met—both immediately and when children came? What forms of paid work would be compatible with the division of responsibilities? As devout Catholics, Sofia and Andrew were also acutely aware of the spiritual nature of these questions. Is our paid work a means of self-actualization, or purely a way to put bread on the table—or both, or neither?

When they met in their late twenties, DC made sense for them both. It is one of the key US cities that draws ambitious young people from all over the world. But even after they combined incomes once married, they needed every cent of what they made to stay afloat. That feeling of the tail wagging the dog became even more pronounced when their first child was born. It was time to make a decision.

As of 2023, Sofia and Andrew live in rural Pennsylvania, now with five children. Andrew teaches physics and coaches the robotics team at a nearby high school, while Sofia occasionally writes and edits for her old magazine. Teaching is a union job with a modest but steady income and excellent benefits, including health insurance for the whole family, a retirement pension, and crucially, long breaks in summer so the children can spend meaningful time in Wisconsin every year with their mother's side of the family.

Even with the pay cuts they sustained, the seven of them live comfortably on Andrew's salary. They drive reliable used cars and seldom eat out. Sofia buys organic flour in bulk to bake the family's bread, and she and the older children tend raised garden beds that produce many of the herbs and vegetables the family consumes. Andrew's parents live nearby, as do his sister, her husband, and their five children, so there is usually family around when extra hands are needed. As Sofia puts it, they have everything they need and a lot of what they want—and the peace that only comes from knowing the difference between the two.

Striking that balance is a feat that only a minority of our generation has accomplished. In fact, most millennials in developed countries are worse off when compared to their baby boomer parents. For instance, when baby boomers were at the median age of 35 in 1990, they owned 21 percent of the national US wealth. At the writing of this book, the millennial cohort won't turn 35 for another two years, but as of now, they own just 3.2 percent of national wealth.[7] With less means and higher expenses than previous generations, millennials can't buy the same stuff (houses, cars, etc.) even if they want to. Millennials are the first generation to not have a better life than their parents, in spite of how hard they've tried. This is why things like "the bank of mom and dad" and the significance of inheritances has increased—at least for the lucky few who have inheritances coming their way.

Another differentiator for this generation—as predicted by William Strauss and Neil Howe in their book *Millennials Rising: The Next Great Generation*—is that millennials are "civic-minded," having a strong sense of community, both locally and globally.[8] In fact, almost 50 percent of millennials say they'd be more willing to make a purchase from a company if their purchase supports a cause, and 37 percent say they are willing to pay a bit more for that benefit as well.[9]

The generation that raised the baby boomers had come through incredibly difficult times, when money and resources were limited and paying as little as possible was a high priority. For two generations—boomers and Gen X—economic abundance grew while mindsets of scarcity remained. Millennials and their younger counterparts see things differently. Perhaps the knowledge that we're burning our planet has given us some perspective. A recent special report by the Intergovernmental Panel on Climate Change (IPCC), a group of scientists whose findings are endorsed by the world's governments, described this moment as "code red for humanity."

The main focus of the report was to identify the increase in global temperature and its cause. Key findings were twofold: that global surface temperature was 1.09°C higher in the decade between 2011–2020 than between 1850–1900, and that human influence is "very likely" (90 percent) the main driver of the global retreat of glaciers and the decrease in Arctic sea ice since the 1990s. It's become clear that due to the warming we've experienced to date, we can expect a significant jump in extreme weather over the next 20 or 30 years and things are unfortunately likely to get worse than they are now. The dangers of warming our planet are no longer something distant, impacting people in faraway places. According one of the report's many authors, Dr. Friederike Otto from the University of Oxford, "Climate change is not a problem of the future, it's here and now and affecting every region in the world."[10]

At the time of this writing, approximately 51 billion tons of greenhouse gasses are added to the atmosphere every year. Although this amount may fluctuate from year to year, the overall effect is an increase. You don't have to believe in global warming to accept that this isn't a good thing.

While the downsides to warming and greenhouse gas emissions are clear, scientists are hopeful that we can halt and possibly reverse the rise in temperatures *if* we can cut global emissions in half by 2030 and reach net zero by the middle of this century. To reduce greenhouse gas emissions from 51 billion tons to zero, we need new zero-carbon ways to generate electricity, to grow food, make things, move around, and heat and cool our houses. And we need ways to calculate the true costs of all that power.

To use just one example, it costs $10 of electricity to power a cell phone for 10 years. "Sounds like a pretty good deal?" says Rebecca Henderson in her book *Reimagining Capitalism in a World on Fire.* Not when it comes from coal-fired electricity. Henderson calculates that $10 worth of coal-fired electricity causes $8 of harm to human health plus another $8 worth of climate damage, adding up to at least $26 per phone—that's a 160 percent increase when we look at the true and total cost of electricity. [11]

But the current economic system not only hides these indirect costs, it rewards growth at *any* cost. And millennials and Gen Z are paying the majority of that bill.

£ € $

If it seems like everything has gotten even worse since 2020, it's because it has—but it also hasn't. Beyond the toll the pandemic has taken on human life and public health, incomes took a substantial hit from the initial COVID-19 lockdowns, intermittent restrictions on public mobility, and the disproportionate impact on smaller, more labor-intensive organizations across the globe. During the pandemic, 1.6 billion people lost their jobs. But these problems weren't introduced in 2020. The pandemic simply drew back the curtain to lay bare society's most pernicious inequalities, which had already increased over the last decade.

Gone are the days when a person could get a job for life. Over the last decade, large corporations have been steadily cutting jobs, outsourcing, offshoring, and sometimes rehiring the same people as contractors rather than employees, all to either protect or increase profits. A lot of this disruption is being made possible by advances in technology, and we're not even at the stage where our world is run by robots.

Offshoring jobs—the relocation of a business process from one country to another—has gained momentum over the last two decades for work such as call centers, computer programming, reading medical data such as X-rays and magnetic resonance imaging, medical transcription, income tax preparation, and title searching. The decreasing costs of transportation and communication, combined with substantial disparities in pay rates, have made offshoring from wealthier countries to less wealthy countries financially enticing for many companies.

In his book, *The Globotics Upheaval: Globalization, Robotics, and the Future of Work*, Richard Baldwin starts by defining the term "globotics" as a combination of globalization and robotics.[12] This is not old wine in a new bottle. Globalization is no longer simply the trade of goods and services across boundaries. It is "telemigration"—a widespread, new form of work that allows workers to sit in one country and work in offices in another. And Baldwin's book was written *before* the pandemic. Now that we're all working from home, what difference does it make if we're in London or in the tropics as long as we have high-speed internet?

Given the difference in cost base, responses from there is a huge economic pull toward telemigration. Employee benefits in the US account for approximately 30 percent of total compensation[13]—a substantial cost that companies can avoid by hiring contractors. In 2019, *The New York Times* highlighted the substantial size of Google's two-tier "shadow work force": 121,000 temps and contractors (compared to their 102,000 full-time employees) who make less money with different benefit plans.[14]

Now don't get me wrong, increasing productivity or efficiency is important. The point I'm making here is that large organizations have so much market power* that they can get away with shadow work forces—who are paid less than their full-time employee counterparts who are essentially doing the same jobs.

As technology continues its simultaneous evolution and expansion, a greater portion of traditional employment will most certainly be at risk for recategorization in this way, or complete elimination. In fact, much of this is already happening under our noses. The World Economic Forum estimates that by 2025, 85 million jobs will be displaced globally by the shift in division of labor between humans and machines.[15]

For well-defined, repetitive tasks, computers are already replacing human operatives outright. This extends beyond factory machines. Examples include the robo-advisor as an investment portfolio manager, e-discovery robot lawyers, and the digital doctor. As a result,

* Market power refers to a company's relative ability to manipulate the price of an item in the marketplace by manipulating the level of supply, demand, or both.

many traditional middle-class occupations can and will be eliminated, allowing the super-rich (who own a vast majority of these supercomputers) to capture even more value.

The paradox is that the vast majority see what's coming but don't see it coming *for them*. Recall the study I cited in the previous chapter that found 65 percent of Americans expect that robots and computers will do much of the work currently done by humans within 50 years. The catch is, an even bigger number—80 percent—of Americans believe *their own jobs or professions* will be safe and will still exist 50 years from now.[16] The math doesn't add up, but that's because we all suffer from status quo bias (more on that later).

TWO-THIRDS OF AMERICANS EXPECT THAT ROBOTS AND COMPUTERS WILL DO MUCH OF THE WORK CURRENTLY DONE BY HUMANS WITHIN 50 YEARS...

% of adults who say that in the next 50 years robots and computers will do much of the work currently done by humans

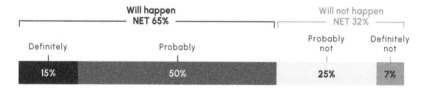

...BUT MOST WORKERS EXPECT THAT THEIR OWN JOBS WILL EXIST IN THEIR CURRENT FORMS IN FIVE DECADES

% of workers who say the jobs/professions they work in now will/will not exist in 50 years

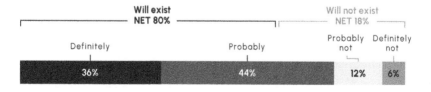

Note: Second chart based on responses from those who are currently employed on a full- or part-time basis

Source: Pew Research Center; survey conducted June 10–July 12, 2015.

Good education has considerable power to increase equality on a number of levels. Education can help tackle gender disparities in wages, poverty, reproductive autonomy, and political power. It can dramatically improve the health outcomes for women and children. And in theory, over time, education leads to skilled work that decreases income inequality. But since 2005, US offshoring of skilled work, also known as knowledge work, has dramatically increased as well.

Make no mistake: the current economic system provides absolutely no incentive for companies with large work forces to either keep or reskill their people as technology eliminates job after job. This system is solely driven by the need to protect or increase profits. And as mentioned in the previous chapter, our education system, still stuck in the industrial age, continues to fail us.

In the industrial age, society was a pyramid. At the base of the pyramid, you needed human labor. The middle of the pyramid comprised information processing and a bureaucracy class, and at the top of the pyramid sat the owners of capital, entrepreneurs, and the creative class. Unsurprisingly, education mirrored that pyramid, where those from prestigious universities found their way to the top, high school/labor training attendees were at the bottom, and everyone else made their way in the middle. That model no longer makes sense. Automation disrupts the information processing at the middle of the pyramid. At the bottom of the pyramid, those who have managed to educate themselves or who have access to smartphones are becoming gig workers—rideshare drivers, food delivery drivers—only because computers and robots can't do these jobs yet.

This outdated pyramid model is precisely why education has been built around limited access. An increase in tertiary education reduces the wages of highly educated workers because their supply goes up, and it simultaneously raises the wages of the less-educated workers because their supply goes down. Universities become prestigious based on historic achievements and current rankings, leading to high-paying jobs. To maintain this perception, professional certification structures create low pass rates for professional exams, using a bell curve in order to avoid flooding the market with professionals. This keeps doctors' and lawyers' incomes high, for example, while blocking competition from nurses and paralegals. The cycle is meant to serve the universities and those they certify, not the individuals they are training to serve. In a 2018 working paper, "Regulation of Charlatans in High-Skill Professions," the model concludes that licenses enrich the incumbent providers of a service and hurt consumers—not sometimes or in certain scenarios, but every time.[17]

Writer David Brooks highlighted another cog in the education-to-high-income wheel in a 2021 article in *The Atlantic*:

> As Elizabeth Currid-Halkett reported in her 2017 book, The Sum of Small Things, *affluent parents have increased their share of educational spending by nearly 300 percent since 1996. Partly as a result, the test-score gap between high- and low-income students has grown by 40 to 50 percent. The children of well-off, well-educated meritocrats are thus perfectly situated to predominate at the elite colleges that produced their parents' social standing in the first place. Roughly 72 percent of students at these colleges come from the richest quarter of families, whereas only 3 percent come from the poorest quarter. A 2017 study found that 38 schools—including Princeton, Yale, Penn, Dartmouth, Colgate, and Middlebury—draw more students from the top 1 percent than from the bottom 60 percent.*[18]

Affluent parents of millennials are baby boomers, and it's their limited mindsets (scarcity from their parents' war experiences) that have reinforced the prestige and exclusivity of tertiary education institutions and professional certifications. But limiting access to education has widened inequality, and a decade of austerity has made that inequality even worse.

Around the world, governments are choosing austerity, actively de-creasing public spending in an attempt to shrink the state. In the UK since 2010, public sector workers have seen an average salary decrease of 4.5 percent in real terms, while private sector wages remained flat over the same period. Government budgets for public services including transportation, defense, social housing, justice, and the environment have been significantly reduced, and health and education budgets haven't grown fast enough to keep up with the demand for their services.[19]

It has become abundantly clear that as the UK population grows older, this is a form of economy that will only become more inhumane. Most people experience the squeeze in longer waits in government-funded hospitals run by the NHS, longer commutes on public transport, tighter school budgets at state schools, and the mirage of homeownership. The decade of austerity (2010–2019) has also reduced government funding to local governments, known as councils in the UK, which provide care for many of the country's elderly and disabled.

Governments briefly paused austerity during the pandemic, but they weren't ready to reverse what they had done. After the pandemic, the cost-of-living crisis has increased financial pressure on the working class, while further austerity policies have returned. The UK chancellor's budget for government spending and taxation announced in October 2021 was meant to feel good, but a closer look shows that his pledges ring hollow. On the one hand, the chancellor declared it to be a budget for "the age of optimism," creating an economy of "higher wages, higher skills, vibrant communities and safer streets." Great. But buried deep inside the documents, the picture was much grimmer. Over the five years that follow, real household disposable income is expected to grow by just 0.8 percent per year, well below the historical average, and is expected to be 28 percent (£9,000 per capita) below the pre-2008 trend. The chart below shows the impact—the working class is projected to be almost 30 percent poorer 14 years after the start of the austerity decade.

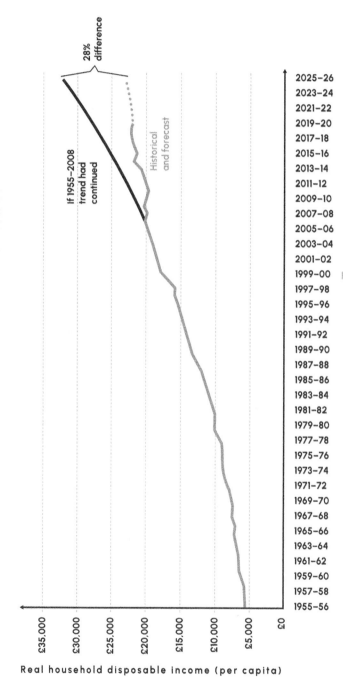

REAL HOUSEHOLD DISPOSABLE INCOME IS EXPECTED TO REGAIN ITS PRE-COVID LEVEL BY 2023–24

28% difference

If 1955–2008 trend had continued

Historical and forecast

Real household disposable income (per capita)

£35,000
£30,000
£25,000
£20,000
£15,000
£10,000
£5,000
£0

2025–26
2023–24
2021–22
2019–20
2017–18
2015–16
2013–14
2011–12
2009–10
2007–08
2005–06
2003–04
2001–02
1999–00
1997–98
1995–96
1993–94
1991–92
1989–90
1987–88
1985–86
1983–84
1981–82
1979–80
1977–78
1975–76
1973–74
1971–72
1969–70
1967–68
1965–66
1963–64
1961–62
1959–60
1957–58
1955–56

Note: Figure shows mean per capita real household disposable income.

Economic and Social Research Council

UKRI

Institute for Fiscal Studies

High inflation, rising taxes, and poor growth will keep living standards virtually stagnant for another half a decade. So bad is the picture in the UK that the head of the Institute for Fiscal Studies, Paul Johnson, tweeted (in response to the October 2021 budget): "This is actually awful. Yet more years of real incomes barely growing. High inflation, rising taxes, poor growth keeping living standards virtually stagnant for another half a decade."[20]

Sadly, the November 2022 budget was even worse. Yet more austerity measures due to rising interest rates means the British people are suffering even more, and here's Paul Johnson again: "The truth is we just got a lot poorer. We are in for a long, hard, unpleasant journey; a journey that has been made more arduous than it might have been by a series of economic own goals."[21]

True optimism seems to be owned by the wealthy. As of this writing, the richest 1 percent of the global population own 44 percent of the world's wealth, while 57 percent of the global population have a wealth range of under $10,000 and own just 2 percent of the world's wealth.[22] This gross wealth inequality is glamorized in media and social media, which continues to amplify the lives of the rich and famous. There is a growing unrest between the haves—who flash their cash, fancy cars, yachts, jets, and multiple homes—and the have-nots, who are worrying about making ends meet. Or worse.

The 2011 riots in England, more widely known as the London Riots, saw looting and arson as well as mass deployment of police and the deaths of five people as thousands of people took to the streets during a five-day period in August. While the causes, both immediate and long-term, have been the subject of media and academic debate, socioeconomic causes focusing on unemployment and spending cuts are presumed to be at least a contributing factor.

In 2020, widespread Black Lives Matter protests and calls for greater racial equality prompted former Prime Minister Boris Johnson to launch a cross-government inquiry into systemic racism—a form of racism that is embedded through laws within society or an organization, which continues to contribute to race-based inequality across many different economic indicators. The commission aimed to examine "all aspects of inequality—in employment, in health outcomes, in academics and all other walks of life." The starkest divides have been found in measures of household wealth, reflecting centuries of white privilege that have made it particularly difficult for people of color to achieve economic security.

One US study followed the same sets of families for 25 years and found vast differences in wealth across racial groups. In that period of time, the wealth gap between white and African American families nearly tripled, from $85,000 per household in 1984 to $236,500 in 2009. The study concluded that the main factors contributing to the wealth inequality included years of home ownership, household income, education, and familial financial support and/or inheritance.[23]

In the UK, white British people have home ownership rates nearly double than that of Black Caribbean people and more than triple that of Black African people. Conversely, these minorities are vastly overrepresented when it comes to private renting and social housing. Only Indian households, which make up just 2.5 percent of the population of England and Wales according to the 2011 census, have higher home ownership rates than white British households.[24]

And all of this was before COVID-19 blew wealth inequality apart. The rich more than doubled their wealth during the same period that the public sector declined—and then they doubled it again during the pandemic, as not even the black swan pundits could predict that a major pandemic would lead to a stock market bubble and record new listings. It's not just wealth inequality, either. Black and

Latinx Americans were infected with COVID-19 at disproportionately higher rates than white Americans,[25] in addition to existing
racial health disparity. Black women in the US, for example, face a
pregnancy-related death risk that's three to four times higher than
that of white women.[26]

PERCENTAGE OF HOUSEHOLDS THAT OWN THEIR HOME

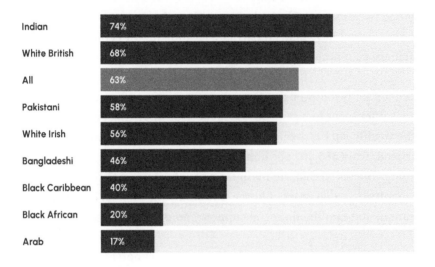

Indian	74%
White British	68%
All	63%
Pakistani	58%
White Irish	56%
Bangladeshi	46%
Black Caribbean	40%
Black African	20%
Arab	17%

The initial lockdowns across the globe and intermittent restrictions
on public mobility compounded inequality by disproportionately affecting household incomes. The majority of low-income households
took a far bigger hit than wealthier households. Smaller firms in the
unorganized sector, which tends to be more labor intensive, were also
harder hit. To rub salt into small business owners' wounds, business
from smaller companies, which were mostly physical stores, moved
online to more capital-intensive large companies, which used their
capital to scale up their online presence. At the same time, large companies benefited from lower corporate taxes and lower interest rates,
as most central banks around the world lowered interest rates and
flooded the system with liquidity to contain the impact of COVID-19.

When the money supply increases and assets remain constant, the price of assets increases—which means stock prices and asset valuations went up for the "big guys" as well. And since financial assets are owned mostly by the better-off sections of society, their wealth increased as the rest of the world struggled.

In this context, a recent report by Oxfam noted that in India 84 percent of households suffered income losses in 2021, while the wealth of the richest segment increased. Workforce flexibility was a key determinant here as well. Only 20 percent of workers with a high school degree or less could work from home, and 39 percent of workers living in households earning $40,000 or less lost work during the pandemic.[27]

Of the 1.6 billion people who lost their jobs, 400 million of those jobs are not expected to come back. Rich countries were better positioned to look after their unemployed citizens with a raft of schemes aimed at helping them, though bureaucracy limited access for some of the most needy. And there were companies, big and small, who looked after their employees and supported them in the ways they could, despite their own economic challenges. It's hard not to imagine, then, that many of these job losses came down to the need to balance the books—especially the jobs that aren't coming back. When spreadsheets make firing decisions, any crisis becomes an opportunity that's not to be wasted.

In reality, financial responses to the pandemic have largely benefited the rich and not the poor. Wealth disparity and rising temperatures threaten our survival on this planet, while persistent racial, gender, and economic inequality threatens our humanity—and underlying it all remains an economic system that rewards growth at any cost.

£ € $

"The divide between the haves and have-nots is getting worse really, really fast."
—Nick Hanauer

If current trends continue, the 2011 London riots and 2020 unrest will serve as mere movie trailers of the uprising to come. Across the pond, Nick Hanauer, an American billionaire venture capitalist, says he "sees pitchforks coming," and I do too. In a *Politico* piece that landed between the riots and the COVID-19 pandemic, he warned us (emphasis mine):

> *The divide between the haves and have-nots is getting worse really, really fast. In 1980, the top 1 percent controlled about 8 percent of U.S. national income. The bottom 50 percent shared about 18 percent. Today the top 1 percent share about 20 percent; the bottom 50 percent, just 12 percent.*
>
> *But the problem isn't that we have inequality. Some inequality is intrinsic to any high-functioning capitalist economy. The problem is that inequality is at historically high levels and getting worse every day. Our country is rapidly becoming less a capitalist society and more a feudal society.* ***Unless our policies change dramatically, the middle class will disappear, and we will be back to late 18th-century France. Before the revolution.***[28]

It's important to note that inequality isn't the monster we're trying to tackle. Inequality can exist in a world where everyone thrives. There's nothing wrong with some people being filthy rich—as long as everyone else has a decent standard of living. The problem of this generation is that only a small percentage of people are wealthy, and life is a daily struggle for the rest. History has shown us, over time, that level of disparity boils over into revolutions.

Even though it might seem like the vested interests of this outmoded system are so strong that change may not be possible at all, conscious millennials are already making a difference. As they get into positions of power, be it in large corporations, governments, etc., they are starting to ask the tough questions—and they are not taking no for an answer. From Greta Thunberg to Alexandria Ocasio-Cortez to Malala Yousafzai and thousands of other young leaders who are driving change, it is this generational change that gives me great hope.

As more and more people become conscious of climate change, there has been a wave of anti-consumerism and a move away from buying stuff for stuff's sake. One study found that more than three out of four millennials choose to spend money on an experience or event instead of a possession.[29]

A recent survey found that 72 percent of consumers buy more environmentally friendly products now than they did five years prior, and that 83% believe it is important for companies to design products that can be reused or recycled.[30]

E-commerce companies have noticed that people are willing to pay more and wait longer for sustainable products in order to reduce their carbon footprint. Many now offer the option to delay shipment of some items so that you can get them all together in one package, reducing packaging material and the carbon emissions of that extra delivery.

Even as jobs were threatened by the pandemic and economic factors, the #GreatResignation has gained momentum and morphed into quiet quitting. In November 2021 in the US, the number of people leaving their jobs reached a record high of 4.53 million.[31] People are walking away because of low pay, feeling stuck, and disrespect.[32] In the past, these kinds of discomforts might have been weathered indefinitely, or until a better option came along. Having a job used to be treated as a privilege. Now, not even social conformity and conditioning can keep people from walking out.

£ € $

To be fair, the rise of capitalism undoubtedly lifted millions of people out of poverty, improved lives, provided opportunities, and drove innovation that previous generations just couldn't imagine. For many decades, the so-called American dream thrived for some in the Western world—though for fewer around the world—but at a steep cost. The US now accounts for less than 5 percent of the world's population, yet consumes 25 percent of the world's resources. With over a quarter of the world's billionaires living in the US, the American dream is simply not a model that can be scaled.

I'm not suggesting socialism or communism as alternatives. For many who grew up behind the iron curtain, capitalism was a welcomed savior. But we do need to recognize that the slow evolution of capitalism has failed to match the pace of change in the rest of the world. In the 21st century, rather than furthering society, capitalism as we know it has concentrated wealth, enabling an ever-shrinking number of people to reap the rewards of the efforts of millions, even billions, of people.

If we want to stop burning our planet and harming each other, a middle path needs to be found—one that will give us sustainable economic growth in a way that allows participation of all people, with opportunity and stability.

We need an economic model that works for all of us.

The good news is, the ripple of change happens quickly, which means we truly do have the ability to turn the tide. We have seen it in the #MeToo movement, in #BlackLivesMatter, in Greta Thunberg standing outside Swedish parliament day after day to simply be heard, and "I can't breathe" leading to thousands of protests in over 60 countries on all seven continents[*33] within a week.

---

* Yes, even in Antarctica: a group of workers at McMurdo Station in Antarctica stood in solidarity with protesters by holding signs saying "Black Lives Matter" while stationed during winter.

Millennials like us are finding our voice, and we've paid the costs of a broken system long enough. We're ready and willing to make the changes needed, and we expect to hold our leaders accountable along the way. As long as we stick together, we have a little more hope of facing a seemingly hopeless situation.

With that in mind, let's take a closer look at our broken system and the cracks we'll have to fix. Are you ready to meet the enemy—the all-powerful, all-consuming economic system we live in?

Chapter 3
The Flaws

f the System

For as disparate and polarized as all of our massive societal problems seem to be, the underlying cause is surprisingly bipartisan. And yet, together with government-funded innovation and citizen-centric regulations, undistorted capitalism is arguably the best system humans have created.

During the industrial age, products—for example, a T-shirt or a bottle of something to drink—were made, purchased, and consumed at a rate measured by GDP. We had regulations in place to protect those producing the product, as well as to protect consumers. And we made sure competition could keep the price of the product in check.

But none of that works in the information age because products have evolved. Before the internet, a product was something physical that you made a choice to buy or not buy. But the head of product at Meta doesn't manufacture anything physical. Facebook is the flagship product, and the rest of their line is digital as well—WhatsApp, Instagram, and Horizons World, to name a few. These are clearly different in nature from a company like Nike Inc., whose product lines include footwear, clothing, and sports equipment. The biggest difference is the way users value platform products over physical ones.

The value of a T-shirt is the T-shirt itself, and while there may be more demand on a particular T-shirt if it is worn by a celebrity, the intrinsic value is still very much in the physical product itself. For social media networks, the platform becomes more valuable as more people spend time on it. This means the platform is deriving most of its value from its users—taking from many and giving to the few who own the platform.

Have you heard the line, "If a product is free, you are the product?" It's certainly true for social media platforms, who have long offered free products and reaped outsized rewards. Workers on a production line are giving their time to the company to create the T-shirt but are at least getting some kind of wage in return—a unit cost. But when it comes to these digital platforms, they simply take our time to create their value and provide no tangible exchange in return.

And as the information age has progressed, a concentrated number of people continue to reap the rewards for the efforts of millions, even billions, of people. It's the first time in history that one product can be sold to three billion people, for free.

Whether it was by luck or great foresight, The Internet Corporation for Assigned Names and Numbers (ICANN) was set up in 1998 as the nonprofit guardian of the internet—providing the world with neutrality and choices that could have easily been subverted. Imagine if the entire internet were owned by one company and email by another. We would be held for ransom by those owners. Not only that, everything built on that internet would ultimately be owned by one private company who could reserve the right to change their policies as they please. It seems obvious now, but the path to ICANN wasn't always clear. From the 1970s to the 1990s, the Protocol Wars dominated political science, as engineers, organizations, and nations became polarized over the issue of which communication protocol would result in the best and most robust computer networks. This culminated in the Internet-OSI Standards War in the late 1980s and early 1990s, which was ultimately "won" by the Internet protocol suite ("TCP/IP"), replacing most other protocols. Today, thanks to ICANN, private companies provide services (e.g., domain registrars, web hosting, email providers, etc.), but you are free to go to another provider for exactly the same service to use the internet in exactly the same way as before.

This is not true for social media networks. Unfortunately, when the next version of the internet, also known as Web 2.0*, was created—based on user-generated content, primarily social media networks—it wasn't seen as a move for the public good. Instead, it became a land grab battle for private ownership. Typically, a company requires approval from anti-competition authorities to acquire a competitor, under regulations that are designed to protect consumers. However, anti-competition authorities failed to see the power of preemptive mergers, when companies like WhatsApp and Instagram were bought before they became full-blown competitors to Facebook. As a result, Facebook and its subsequently acquired properties created the equivalent of private-ownership internet.

While you can send an email to anyone regardless of their service provider, you can't do the same with instant messaging. If you want to instant message someone on WhatsApp, you can't send it to someone on Signal. You have to use WhatsApp and agree to Facebook's terms of service. Of course, you still have a choice on whether to use the service or not, but it's not the same as the rest of the internet, where you can still achieve your objective of buying a domain name and hosting a

---

* A Web 2.0 website allows users to interact and collaborate with each other through social media dialogue as creators of user-generated content in a virtual community. This contrasts with the first generation of Web 1.0-era websites in which people were limited to viewing content in a passive manner. Examples of Web 2.0 features include social networking sites or social media sites (e.g., Facebook), blogs, wikis, folksonomies ("tagging" keywords on websites and links), video-sharing sites (e.g., YouTube), image-sharing sites (e.g., Flickr), hosted services, Web applications ("apps"), collaborative consumption platforms, and mashup applications.

website with any provider of your choice. If you opt out of WhatsApp, you lose access to everyone on WhatsApp and they lose access to you.

This came to a head in 2021, when WhatsApp's terms of service changed. You see, when Facebook bought WhatsApp in 2014, it promised to keep it independent from Facebook and ad free—a promise the founders made when they launched WhatsApp in 2009. However, Facebook had been itching to integrate WhatsApp with Facebook, just as they had done with Instagram. The poorly worded terms of service appeared to be forcing users to either agree to sharing of personal data with Facebook and its various other subsidiary companies, or stop using the messaging app. In response to a storm of criticism, WhatsApp issued a clarification specifying exactly what types of user data will be shared and said that data sharing with Facebook would be limited to communication with businesses on WhatsApp.

WhatsApp lost millions of outraged users. Over the first three weeks of January 2021, Signal gained 7.5 million users globally, and Telegram gained 25 million. In both cases, the increase appears to have come at WhatsApp's expense.[1] However, almost all those who migrated to Signal and Telegram returned to WhatsApp after they realized not everyone in their contact book moved with them because they could no longer message people they were used to messaging. I have wanted to stop using WhatsApp for a few years, but haven't, knowing that it would make me a social pariah. WhatsApp's biggest market is in India, and all my family and friends are on it. Leaving the app would cut me off from them almost entirely.

These network effects* are the key difference between physical products and the products of the information age. Private companies have

---

* In economics, network effects refer to the phenomenon when the value of a product, service, or platform increases as more people use it. Network effects play a significant role in various industries, particularly in technology, social media, communication, and platform-based businesses.

a vested interest in building products in such a way that everyone has to join their product to enjoy the benefits—and this extends to physical products as well. If you want to join a friend's iPhone photo stream, you can only do so if you have an iPhone or another Apple device. You can't join from a Microsoft or Google product. Tech giants have built wall gardens*—closed loops that are not interoperable, meaning you cannot move between one service to another like you can with emails or telephone calls.

Superprofits motivated tech giants to design their products in this way, but the network effects that resulted have given them immense power over all of us—and not just when we try to quit Instagram, as we saw with the Facebook-Cambridge Analytica data scandal that was allegedly responsible for influencing the outcome of the US 2016 presidential election and the UK Brexit referendum.[2] They gave everyone the product for free, and once they got to critical mass, they used every opportunity to extract from us—whether that's by keeping us hooked, inserting advertising, or selling our data to political consulting firms like Cambridge Analytica.

The irony of it all is that before it grew into the behemoth it is today, Facebook advocated for interoperability in order to get access to users from MySpace and Friendster.

Technically, they are doing exactly what capitalism asks of them. Capitalism is based on productivity. The more you can produce, the more you stand to gain, and it is this incentive that drives innovation and efficiency. But human nature is such that, left unchecked, incentive can lead to all sorts of bad things. Facebook is only one example, and the shift from industrial age to information age isn't the only problem.

---

* A walled garden refers to a limited set of technology or media information provided to users with the intention of creating a monopoly or secure information system, only accessible on a given network.

£ € $

The thing is, innovation has happened everywhere, not just in technology. In the 1990s, just as the internet really caught on and before we knew what Web 2.0 would become, a new form of finance that entered the scene in the 1980s—neoliberalism*—went global.

Driven by international finance, neoliberalism connected the big financial capital cities around the world—New York, London, Singapore, Dubai, Mumbai, Shanghai—to ensure that a common set of policies would be pursued by as many countries across the globe as possible. This coincided with markets opening up and satellite television becoming available in emerging markets, infecting those watching with the consumeristic need for more.

During this period, those in control of international finance capital increased their dominance, supported by governments legitimating their norms and ideas. The outcome of international finance is cyclical: the centralization of capital continues, which in turn reinforces the influence of those in control of it. More recently, journalist and activist George Monbiot tells us:

> *...it has played a major role in a remarkable variety of crises: the financial meltdown of 2007–2008; the offshoring of wealth and power, of which the Panama Papers and Pandora Papers offer us merely a glimpse; the slow collapse of public health and education; the resurgence of child poverty; the epidemic of loneliness; the collapse of wildlife ecosystems and the rise of Donald Trump.*[3]

---

* Neoliberal capitalism, also known as neoliberalism, is the term used to describe the phase of capitalism when restrictions on the global flows of commodities and capital, including capital in the form of finance, have been substantially removed.

But innovation wasn't all down to the private sector, either. In fact, so much of what we have today can be traced to government funding, primarily from Uncle Sam, spurring the development of everything from the internet to the technologies at the heart of smartphones, including microprocessors, memory, LCDs, lithium-ion batteries, GPS chips, and artificial intelligence.

Regulations played their part too. For example, to avoid having all kinds of spurious medications on the market, pharmaceutical companies in the US need approval from the Food and Drug Administration before they can sell their medicines. Financial services have similar constraints: if banks were not regulated, we'd be inundated with Ponzi schemes. In fact, regulations were created in response to those kinds of abuses in the first place, to protect citizens.

However, so much has changed in the past three decades that existing regulations have not sufficed, and new regulations haven't kept pace—all while deregulation caused further damage.

What neoliberalism forgot is that vital national services cannot be allowed to collapse—which means that competition cannot run its course and that capitalism cannot run unchecked, at least in certain industries. Some industries, such as banks, railways, and airlines, are too big to fail—the entire economy depends on these companies. Allowing them to collapse would cause economic downturns with dire effects on the working- and middle-class populations, more so than using those populations to fund subsidies and rescues. Examples of this include taxpayer-funded subsidies or bailouts, made popular during the 2007–2008 global financial crisis and revisited during the 2020–2022 pandemic.

As a result, the capitalism that shaped the course of the world—that drove innovation, created products and services for the good of society, reduced poverty, increased the standard of living, and made a modest profit along the way—is dead. Today's system is all about businesses raking in megaprofits while taxpayers are handed the risks—and losses.

£ € $

So how did we get here?

The origins of capitalism as an economic system can be placed in the 16th century, but modern capitalism was born in the 18th century with economist Adam Smith as a foundational figure. At the time, capital (money) was a scarce commodity based on finite resources of gold. Thus, there was an intrinsic value to capital that doesn't hold true today.

After the Second World War, countries around the world spent the next 30 years rebuilding their economies. Most British colonies became independent, and John Maynard Keynes's economic prescriptions* were widely applied as American and British planners became determined to avoid the errors of 1918 and 1919. Those years had been a "Carthaginian peace"—a brutal peace which has the intent of crushing the losing side. The remedies Keynes proposed in 1919 had been ignored—relief, reconstruction, renewal of trade, cancellation of debts, renouncement of reparations, and integration of the vanquished. But in 1945, they were generally accepted as guideposts for the post-war order.

Governments took the lead in feeding their populations, establishing stable currencies, and restarting commercial activity. All of this

---

* The seminal works of John Maynard Keynes are *The General Theory of Employment, Interest, and Money* (1936) and *The Economic Consequences of the Peace* (1919).

pointed toward an evolution of capitalism: new roles for the state, labor unions, and corporations were formed.

The post-war commitment to a welfare state gave rise to everything that was subsequently achieved. Full employment and the relief of poverty were common goals in the US and much of western Europe. It was a mixed economy in which governments played a decisive role. Top rates of tax were high, and governments sought social outcomes without embarrassment, developing new public services and safety nets, providing citizens with an education, free healthcare, job security, a pension, and an affordable home. The baby boomer generation was on the up, and capitalism drove the innovation that would keep it there—both in the private and public sectors. And we put a man on the moon.

But the foundations of neoliberalism were also being laid, funded quietly by the rich from the 1950s on. Supporters carefully hid their influence in order to hide their intentions: they wanted to pay less in taxes and didn't want to get caught saying so. It's important to remember that the post-war top tax rate was 97 percent. Under pressure from lobbyists, governments wanted to reduce the tax rate, but due to the optics it would create, they chose to allow loopholes instead. What a mistake that turned out to be. As Robert Reich, former US Secretary of Labor under President Clinton, tells us: "The rich used to pay taxes. Now they loan money to the US government—at a profit that everyone else pays for."[4]

In the 1970s, Keynesian policies began to fall apart when many advanced economies suffered both inflation and slow growth, a condition dubbed "stagflation"—something we experienced again in 2022 as inflation hit 40-year highs in the Western world. At the time, Keynesian theory's popularity waned because it had no appropriate policy response for stagflation. As economic crises struck on both sides of the Atlantic, the door was opened for neoliberal ideas to enter the mainstream.

"The rich used to pay taxes. Now they loan money to the US government— at a profit that everyone else pays for."
—Robert Reich

The policies of neoliberalism typically support fiscal austerity (including attempts to cut government spending on social programs), deregulation, free trade, privatization, and a reduction in government spending on general welfare. Neoliberalism is often associated with the economic policies of Margaret Thatcher in the UK and Ronald Reagan in the US—both of whom were in power during the 1980s—with strong bipartisan support.

We've all heard the claims that cutting tax rates for the rich will improve the standard of living for the working class. Supposedly, top-bracket tax breaks free companies to create more jobs, pay higher wages for the average worker, and create an overall upturn in our economy—which results in increased tax revenue for the government. This is the heart of the infamous trickle-down theory.

But as George Monbiot so eloquently explains in a 2016 article for *The Guardian*, instead of trickle-down economics, citizens were tricked by economics:

> *The privatisation or marketisation of public services such as energy, water, trains, health, education, roads and prisons has enabled corporations to set up tollbooths in front of essential assets and charge rent, either to citizens or to government, for their use. Rent is another term for unearned income. When you pay an inflated price for a train ticket, only part of the fare compensates the operators for the money they spend on fuel, wages, rolling stock and other outlays. The rest reflects the fact that they have you over a barrel.*[5]

To rub salt into our wounds, those who invest in rent-seeking* companies, who seek to gain wealth without any reciprocal contribution of

---

* Rent-seeking is the practice of manipulating public policy or economic conditions as a strategy for increasing profits without any reciprocal contribution of productivity.

productivity, insist that taxes should be low to encourage "investment" (read: more private profit and shareholder value).

As Reagan and Thatcher restricted resources, they told their citizens, "Don't worry, this will benefit everyone." The promise of trickle-down economics was that a reduction of taxes on businesses and the wealthy in society would stimulate business investment in the short term and benefit society at large, at least in the long term. But that promise hasn't been kept. Economic growth has been markedly slower in the neoliberal era than it was in the preceding decades, except for the very rich. After 60 years of declining inequality in the distribution of both income and wealth, the gap increased rapidly in this era, thanks to the smashing of trade unions, reduced taxation, rising rents, privatization, and deregulation.

Tax cuts gave the wealthy more money to invest, and they did, but not necessarily in increasing the productivity that was supposed to lead to wage growth. When productivity did increase, they didn't always return it in higher wages. Instead, they used their money to organize, creating powerful lobbying forces to block breakthroughs in policy, then exploited their political influence to seize shares of national income that they neither earned nor produced. When that wasn't enough, they set up elaborate offshore corporate structures to decrease their taxes even more.

Over the last four decades of neoliberalist policies (primarily, tax cuts)—income tax, corporate tax, and capital gains tax have all declined. By 2018, the overall tax rate on the richest 400 households was only 23 percent, meaning their combined tax payments equaled less than one quarter of their total income. This overall rate was 70 percent in 1950 and 47 percent in 1980.[6]

America's wealthy switched from paying taxes to the government to lending the government money by parking their savings in government treasury bonds for which the government pays them interest. Ironically, the interest comes from an increasing portion of everyone else's taxes rather than those taxes paying for government services that everyone needs.

As a result, governments and the general public got poorer as the rich got richer. It's no wonder wealth inequality has become so utterly and completely crazy.

£ € $

To be fair, neoliberal capitalism (the trickle-down theory) wasn't conceived as a self-serving racket. Milton Friedman, a Nobel prize-winning US economist, theorized that monetary policy should be subject to rules designed to achieve price stability, and monopolized power could be seen as a reward for efficiency. Friedman instinctively took the view that government intervention was more likely to do harm than good. The most the government could do was set an appropriate structure for rules—especially the rule of law—and leave the rest to competition and the freedom of the individual to choose within a system of free markets. But Friedman's theories became polluted when they came to the attention of some very wealthy people who saw in the philosophy an opportunity to free themselves from regulation and tax.

Thus, the markets were never free. Instead, corporations were granted freedom from trade unions and collective bargaining, which gave them the freedom to suppress wages, as we're seeing now with zero-hour contracts and gig workers. Freedom from regulation meant the freedom to poison rivers, endanger workers, charge grossly unfair interest rates and design exotic financial instruments like collateral debt obligations—those bogus triple-A rated assets that caused the global financial crisis—without any consequence to the perpetrators or the rating agencies involved. Freedom from tax meant freedom from the provision of food, medicine, and basics that lift people out of poverty.

All of this is possible, maybe surprisingly so, because economics is not a science in the way we think of chemistry or physics. By using terms such as "velocity of money" and "price elasticity," we are made to believe economics is a natural science. The truth is, if one side goes up, the other side doesn't always go down. Economics falls short of the definition of a science for a number of reasons, including a lack of testable hypotheses, lack of consensus, and inherent political overtones.[7]

Economics is a social science, and its so-called theories are really social and moral constructs. As a result, economists have a surprisingly shallow (i.e., close to zero) understanding of what triggers or slows down economic growth. What policies cause entrepreneurship to increase or decrease? What incentivizes risk-taking? When should governments rely on regulation and risk regulatory capture[*] versus when should they rely on market forces and risk industry capture[†] resulting in monopolistic outcomes?

Worryingly, even today, economics continues to be portrayed as a science. "The market" sounds like a natural system that might bear upon us equally, like gravity or atmospheric pressure. But it is fraught with power relations. "What the market wants" tends to mean what corporations and their bosses want. As professor and social scientist Andrew Sayer notes:

---

* Regulatory capture is an economic theory that regulatory agencies may come to be dominated by the interests they regulate and not by the public interest.

† Industry capture or monopoly is when a few companies exist in a market with little to no competition and can therefore set their own terms and prices when facing consumers, making them highly profitable.

Investment means two quite different things. One is the funding of productive and socially useful activities, the other is the purchase of existing assets to milk them for rent, interest, dividends and capital gains. Using the same word for different activities "camouflages the sources of wealth," leading us to confuse wealth extraction with wealth creation.[8]

Treating economics as a science implies a "just the way it is" dynamic around our financial crises—that they are not man-made and certainly not the government's fault. It allows politicians to wash their hands of responsibility for their policies.

The confusion compounds as some economists, including high-profile professors at prestigious universities, are allowed to consult for the private sector, earning vast sums of money by lending their name and credibility to nothing but speculation. The documentary *Inside Job*[9] shows how some economics professors played a key role in the global financial crisis by lauding financial industry practices that weren't working, as they took home millions from Wall Street firms. As a result, those economics professors should share the blame for the global financial crisis, but instead pocketed their millions and got off scot-free—as did all the financial bigwigs—while the public was left with the losses.

£ € $

In 2018, the US Treasury released a list of 96 people that it called "oligarchs," classifying them as people with assets of a billion dollars or more.[10] The term dates back to the time of Aristotle, but in modern times is almost always used to describe powerful and wealthy Russian men with ties to the Kremlin. It's hard to say how many oligarchs there are in Russia. Some of them live large, travel widely, and are seen often in the media. Others are a lot more discreet.

Oligarchs became wealthy when the Soviet Union fell apart in the 1990s. The Soviet Union was a state-dominated planned economy, where everything belonged to the state—all factories, shops, everything. After the Soviet Union collapsed and Russia tried to build a market economy, they had to privatize all those state assets. The oligarchs had to buy them, but they bought them very cheap. As a result, football club–owning billionaires like Abramovich have pools and pools of money.

One of the most basic themes in ethics is fairness, stated by Aristotle: "Equals should be treated equally and unequals unequally." Favoritism, cronyism, and nepotism all interfere with fairness because they give undue advantage to someone who does not necessarily merit this treatment. The idea of giving individuals lucrative state contracts, allowing them to grow ultrawealthy in exchange for kickbacks—the way a recipient of illegal gain "kicks back" a portion of it to another person for that person's assistance in obtaining it—is not new or restricted to Russia. Crony capitalism* is everywhere.

The word "oligarch" is synonymous with wealthy Russian buisinesspeople, but collusion between the business class and the political class is prevalent all throughout the world—in democratic, communist, and authoritarian regimes alike. In Mexico, Carlos Slim Helú was granted control of almost all landline and mobile phone services and soon became the world's richest man from 2010 to 2013. He remains the seventh richest today.[11] In India, Reliance Industries run by Mukesh Ambani, and the Adani Group run by Gautam Adani (the 13th[12] and 24th[13] richest men in the world respectively) both benefit from friendly government policies. With 1.42 billion people,[14] India is now the most populous country in the world, overtaking China in April 2023, but the country's

---

* Crony capitalism, sometimes called cronyism is an economic system in which businesses thrive not as a result of free enterprise, but rather as a return on money amassed through collusion between a business class and the political class.

100 richest people own assets equivalent to one-fourth of India's GDP.[15] In 2015, China officially became home to the world's highest number of billionaires. Of the 1,133 billionaires they had in 2022, over 100 of them had seats in China's parliament.*[16]

Crony capitalism isn't only reserved for corporations, either. Nonprofit organizations with noble missions fall into the trap too, becoming piggy banks for their directors. The most notorious example is FIFA, the world football governing body, a nonprofit whose mission is to make football truly global, diverse, and inclusive for the benefit of the entire world. In 2015, FIFA was hit with a series of scandals, when more than two dozen FIFA officials and their associates were implicated in a 24-year self-enrichment scheme that reached the highest levels of FIFA management. In December 2022, after years of investigations and indictments, the United States Department of Justice said for the first time that representatives working for Russia and Qatar had bribed FIFA officials to secure hosting rights for the World Cup in men's soccer. Sadly, it's not just FIFA; scores of nonprofit organizations have flouted the law, muddying the waters for the ones who genuinely follow their mission and make a difference to the world.

And it all started in the US with the likes of Vanderbilt (railroads), Rockefeller (oil), and Carnegie (steel). Three of the greatest businessmen America has ever known each built their vast empires by exploiting workers and consumers, often using predatory and unfair practices. They were the most notorious robber barons† until the Roosevelt administration sued successfully to break up such monopolies.

In more recent years, the US government bailed out many of the nation's largest businesses during and in the aftermath of the Great

---

* Compared to 716 residing in the US.

† The term "robber baron" began to be used in the early 1870s to describe a class of extremely wealthy businessmen who used ruthless and unethical business tactics to dominate vital industries.

Recession of 2008. Afterward, lawmakers passed the 2010 Dodd–Frank Act in hopes of avoiding future bailouts to banks. Then, the bailouts went to the investment banks and automakers. At the start of the pandemic, the same tact was taken for the airline industry and big businesses in the wider economy. Why? Because instead of saying "never again," the law created a new orderly liquidation authority, which granted immense discretionary governmental power to bail out and regulate Wall Street firms and the wider economy. Of course, the government already had plenty of power. Indeed, it was the very power that led to the favoritism, rule-bending, and reckless risk-taking that created the Great Recession in the first place.

Aristotle considered oligarchy a deviant form of rule that tended to arise when elites became corrupt and were no longer interested in the common good but only in enriching themselves; throughout history, power structures considered to be oligarchies have often been viewed as tyrannical, relying on public obedience or oppression to exist. Aristotle pioneered the use of the term as meaning rule by the rich, for which another term commonly used today is plutocracy.

For the oligarchy or plutocracy, financial engineering, privatized profits, and socialized losses all connect to the mindset that a company's profits are the rightful property of shareholders, while its losses are a responsibility that society must shoulder.

When losses occur, large corporations, their executives, and their shareholders benefit from government subsidies and rescues, in large part because of their ability to cultivate or buy influence through lobbyists. A few people in government choose which existing regulations to enforce and which ones to bend, who gets bailed out and who doesn't—this is textbook crony capitalism: using the power of government and the rule of people to decide who will benefit and who will not, rather than the power of the market and the rule of law.

Case in point: after the fall of Lehman Brothers, the next domino was Goldman Sachs. However, at the time, the US Secretary of the Treasury was Hank Paulson. Prior to his role in the Department of the Treasury, Paulson was the Chairman and Chief Executive Officer of Goldman Sachs.

Paulson let Lehman fail, but bailed out Goldman.

£ € $

The central bank of a given country is responsible for monetary policy and is independent of the government in power. Sort of...or supposedly, anyway.

However, once an economy has been sucked into neoliberalism's whirlpool of globalized financial flows, its government has to bow to the whim and fancy of international finance capital and its policies. And poof, there goes the independence of the central bank.

Let's look closer at some other implications of globalism, which happens to constitute the salient features of neoliberal capitalism as well, given that globalization is primarily driven by neoliberal doctrine and enabled by the rise of the internet—allowing us to communicate in real time. Remember: the goal of neoliberalism is a wholly deregulated global market society, and we were well on our way until the post-pandemic supply chain issues and the Russian-Ukraine War.

First, unlike the capitalism of the past, globalization has relocated production from the developed to the developing world in order to take advantage of the comparably low wages. In developing countries, it's easy to be sold on the increase in employment and standard of living this can bring, but in reality, it is almost always exploitative. Think sweatshops—lower labor standards compared to what would be allowed in developed nations while the major benefits go to those who control international finance capital.

Second, globalized neoliberalism influences governments in developing countries to become more openly and directly linked to the interests of the "corporate-financial oligarchy" who vote on policies with their capital. In his book, *Saving Capitalism: For the Many, Not the Few*, Robert Reich highlights this phenomenon and reveals the cycles of power and influence that have perpetuated a new American oligarchy. And because neoliberalism went global, governments around the world are fearful of foreign direct investment being pulled out of their countries.

Third, neoliberalism influences fiscal responsibility.[*] Legislation was passed in country after country, and these new policies ensure that efforts to increase employment and economic activity are outsourced to the private sector instead of the government by providing so-called incentives to capital—primarily tax breaks, cheap debt, and provision of state land—in the hope of increasing employment and wage growth.

Sound familiar? It's what paved the way for quantitative easing or QE[†] in 2008, and at present, it continues to compound inequality by propping up stock markets and house prices at the expense of the real economy. Growth comes to depend essentially upon the formation of asset bubbles[‡] apart from credit-financed consumer spending, which

---

[*] Fiscal responsibility is the ability to balance between government spending and tax. It is the obligation of a state to maximize incomes by using their spending powers while also ensuring that inflation does not spiral up.

[†] Quantitative easing (QE) is a monetary policy tool invented by the US Fed during the global financial crisis (December 2008) whereby a central bank purchases at scale existing government bonds or other financial assets in order to inject money into the economy to expand economic activity. The newly created money therefore goes directly into the financial markets, boosting bonds and stock markets to the highest levels in history.

[‡] An asset bubble occurs when the price of an asset, such as stocks, bonds, real estate, or commodities, rises at a rapid pace without underlying fundamentals.

has very strict limits (remember subprime mortgages in 2008?). When COVID struck, quantitative easing was on the menu and governments around the world said, "We'll have more of the same."

By February 2021, the G20 countries collectively pumped $12 trillion into stimulus packages.[17] Worryingly, less than 1 percent went to developing countries, as the rich countries kept everything for themselves. In most cases, that money ultimately found its way to extremely wealthy people, exacerbating income and wealth inequality. The excess money supply drove up asset prices, particularly stock markets and house prices, forming asset bubbles—a phenomenon which has been responsible for some of the most devastating recessions* in history, including the worst faced by the US during the Great Depression.

This means that the growth of the economy can no longer be stimulated by the government, since neoliberal capitalists simply pocket all subsidies and government transfers as so-called incentives, with very little if any additional investment on the other side.

These three features of neoliberalism—relocation of production activities, influence on governments to become more openly and directly linked to the interests of the corporate-financial oligarchy, and a reduction of government fiscal responsibility—have important consequences.

On the one hand, when an economy grows, it is accompanied by extreme widening of income and wealth inequalities—think China, India, Brazil, Mexico, etc. Workers in developed countries are unable to increase their wages because in a global world they compete with the massive developing country labor reserves. At the same time, workers

---

* The stock market bubble of the 1920s, the dot-com bubble of the 1990s, and the real estate bubble of the 2000s were asset bubbles followed by sharp economic downturns.

in developing countries, to whom knowledge and production activities are outsourced, are unable to raise their wages due to job attractiveness,[*18] and the power lies with employers as the supply of labor is high. Labor reserves in these developing countries actually increase in relative size as additional workers in the same country decide to enter the workforce or switch jobs because of these opportunities. As a result, real wages across developed and developing countries do not increase over time, despite the increase in labor productivity and the increased profitability of companies using large workforces. Amazon is a key example, having produced an average annual return of 17.99 percent over the past five years compared to measly increases in hourly wages that sparked huge protests and workers' rights campaigns.

On the other hand, even when neoliberalism is tied to growth, it cannot be sustained. Growth grinds to a halt when there is a surplus of anything produced in the world economy. Neoliberal capitalism can offset this tendency with booms caused by asset bubbles, but even those become inoperative when the bubbles collapse, as they inevitably must. Still, the fear of an economic collapse is great, and governments pumped in so much liquidity to stop it that we've moved into unknown territory.[†19]

£ € $

As software scaled at a rate previously not seen, quickly embedding itself into every industry, our shift into the information age allowed neoliberal capitalism to take off. In the 1990s, under President Clinton, the amount of leverage investment banks were allowed increased from

---

* Job attractiveness is defined as the benefits potential employees see in an employment in a specific organization.

† To address the economic shock triggered by COVID-19, the world's four major central banks expanded their QE programs by a total $7.8 trillion to support their economies as well as the functioning of global financial markets.

5x to 30x[20] This means $1 of capital could become $30 by borrowing $29—that's a 3 percent deposit and 97 percent mortgage—causing the loan-to-value ratio of mortgages to drop to the floor in the early 2000s.

At that time, I was on a path to a career in investment banking when a friend told me that in order to succeed, I had to be so greedy that I would be willing to knock out my granny's teeth and melt the gold. Seeing what dog-eat-dog looked like in a society so far removed from thriving had a profound impact on me, and I was lucky to leave the industry in 2008, before the global financial crisis took hold.

But as we saw at the beginning of this chapter, the information age doesn't lend itself well to a capitalist model, as it creates a small number of extreme winners (for example, Elon Musk and Jeff Bezos) and a lot of losers. Technology drives increased profits and without any reason to share it, the cycle of greed continues—barring a few morally conscious individuals, like Patagonia founder Yvon Chouinard, who gave away his company to a trust and a nonprofit in September 2022. More often, when those winners can't take all, they defend controversial subsidies and bailouts that are many times greater than the measly checks US citizens received in 2020.

Corporate bailouts are requested and defended by making all sorts of claims, as United Airlines CEO Scott Kirby said in 2021 when he lobbied for further funding from the US government: "This is certainly good news for our economy, our industry, and our airline, but it's especially good news for those who have been without a paycheck, and we can't wait to welcome them back."[21]

But what actually happened was not quite as rosy for airline employees or their paychecks.

Reeling from travel bans due to the pandemic, the US airline industry accepted $50 billion in financial assistance from the government in

April 2020—more than three times the size of the industry's bailout following the 9/11 attacks. Of course, that money didn't last forever, and a second bailout of $15 billion came in December 2020.

Airlines said they needed payroll support to keep their employees connected to the airline and fully trained, so they'd be prepared to fly when the economy recovered—and so they could transport vaccines. Anyone who tried to travel in the second half of 2021 and all of 2022 knows all too well what a mess airlines and airports were, all caused by massive shortages of staff.

Here's the kicker: despite being the most expensive employment program in history (paying 40,000 people for four months at an annualized cost of over $1 million per job), American Airlines was not satisfied with keeping roughly four out of every five dollars for themselves out of government "payroll support" and were trying to avoid paying workers the remaining dollar.[22]

From 9/11 on, American Airlines has been through some rocky times. After it finally emerged from bankruptcy at the end of 2013, it had finally hit six straight years of positive net income and had banked about $17.5 billion. The airline industry became so lucrative that people wrote papers arguing that airlines collude to keep prices high. Flush with so much money, there were plenty of options for how American Airlines could spend what was in its coffers. Knowing that airlines cycle through booms and busts, it could have stored up cash reserves to buffer future crises; it could have invested in service quality or managed contract disputes and personnel issues with pilots, flight attendants, and mechanics. But it didn't do any of these things. In his investigation of what American Airlines actually did, law professor and author Tim Wu instead found that:

> ...American blew most of its cash on a stock buyback spree. From 2014 to 2020, in an attempt to increase its earnings per share,

American spent more than $15 billion buying back its own stock. It managed, despite the risk of the proverbial rainy day, to shrink its cash reserves. At the same time it was blowing cash on buybacks, American also began to borrow heavily to finance the purchase of new planes and the retrofitting of old planes to pack in more seats. As early as 2017, analysts warned of a risk of default should the economy deteriorate, but American kept borrowing. It has now accumulated a debt of nearly $30 billion, nearly five times the company's current market value.[23]

The above example is not unique to American Airlines. In fact, the biggest U.S. airlines spent 96 percent of free cash flow last decade on buying back their own shares[24]—$45 billion in total.[25] The current economic structure is optimized to extract money for shareholders when things go right and minimize the amount of shareholder money at risk when things go very wrong. That's the nature of the limited-liability corporation and the modern focus on shareholder value and capital-structure optimization, all driven by greed.

By mid-2021, the price of airline stocks were back at pre-pandemic levels. You could rationally conclude from the rise in stock prices that any government support of the airlines should involve taking a lot of equity or zeroing the shareholders. But economic practice is not rational. As Bloomberg columnist Matt Levine explains:

It's not that the CEOs of the airlines, in 2014, with perfect foresight, said "we are going to extract as much money as we can for shareholders for as long as we can, and then leave the government holding the bag." It is...a lot like that...but that was not their conscious choice; that was, like, capitalism's choice.[26]

This is common practice across other sectors too. Stock buybacks have boomed—from 2010–2019, companies in the S&P 500 Index spent a whopping $5.3 trillion on buybacks, representing 54 percent of net income,[27] as the buyback system turned out to be a tax-efficient dividend. It's important to note that there is nothing wrong with stock buybacks or paying dividends to shareholders—though it only works when markets are going up, as they did from March 2009 until the pandemic. For example, Bank of America bought back $18 billion in stock in the two years leading up to 2007, before its stock fell 60 percent in 2008. Similarly, AIG repurchased over $6 billion in stock in 2007 before seeing its price plunge 96 percent in 2008.

What I really want to highlight here is the fact that funds were not saved for a rainy day—there is little incentive to do so, and when a crisis hit, the taxpayer footed the bill. And if the government isn't left holding the bag, the workers are—in some cases terminated even after two decades of service.

As Michael Douglas's *Wall Street* villain Gordon Gekko famously said, "Greed is good"—and capitalism thrives on greed at all costs. In the good times, dividends are paid out, and in the bad times—especially with the demise of labor unions and dilution of labor laws—employees are either laid off or asked to take a salary cut. The profits are privatized but the losses are socialized.

£ € $

Every time someone criticizes the current economic system, they are called a socialist and disregarded. Once again, I am not endorsing socialism in any way, and I am happy to defend capitalism very strongly. Capitalism has one distinct advantage: incentive. But at the other end of the spectrum, while socialism has lots of issues, it does put people first. Neoliberal capitalism took the prioritization of capital, which had been vital in previous eras, to a new extreme, and even though human capital drives value, people are hardly prioritized.

You and I don't have to agree on why the system is broken—we just need to agree that the system is broken. Without being able to name the flaws of our current economic system, in which the few benefit at the expense of the many, we'll never be able to repair it. Especially because none of our leaders are even thinking about the underlying economic system.

The global financial crisis in 2008 resulted in discontent as well as a long period of austerity, where governments cut spending on social programs and general welfare to reduce debt. In response to desperation and fear of more adversity, populists and nationalists came to power across the world. People voted for Brexit in the UK and Trump in the US—politician after politician who promised the moon knowing full well that the rocket can't get off the ground. Sadly, but not surprisingly, none of these new leaders increased general welfare.

Donald Trump's campaign promise to "drain the swamp" became a rallying cry for many Americans fed up with politics as usual. He vowed that he would take on the "power structure" in Washington and drain the swamp of all the lobbyists who had hurt the country's working class. But the swamp not only survived Donald Trump, it thrived as at least seven former industry lobbyists were in Trump's cabinet—and dozens more held political appointments.[28] Far from draining the swamp, Trump and his political appointees filled it to the brim.[29]

Even Barack Obama, elected in 2008 as the conscious millennials' president of choice, couldn't grasp the negative impact the policies of the Great Recession would have. In 2009, the Obama administration appointed Timothy Geithner and Larry Summers, two men who played a critical role in deregulation of financial services during the Clinton administration. It was a clear signal to Wall Street that they could carry on with business as usual. It is no wonder that, in the wake of the financial crisis, no bonuses were clawed back, no charges were brought, and not one person went to jail.

Neoliberalism's triumph reflects the failure of the left as well as the right. When laissez-faire economics led to catastrophe in 1929, Keynes devised a comprehensive economic theory to replace it, and when Keynesian demand management hit the buffers in the '70s, there was an alternative ready. But when neoliberalism fell apart in 2008, there was...nothing. The left and center have produced no new general framework of economic thought for the past 80 years.

The powers that be knew with the fall of Lehman Brothers that the entire financial system was poised to collapse like a house of cards. And in hindsight, perhaps that wouldn't have been as bad as what happened next. With the wholesale collapse of faith in the 21st century, money became our God. And because "the money that money makes, makes even more money," a cycle of greed, panic, and spending has begun that our current economic system will not and cannot stop, no matter how fast the planet burns around us.

This wasn't the change Obama had hoped for or the fresh start that voters go to the polls to secure—because no political policy can make us more conscious citizens.

Neoliberalism got us here; something else has to get us out. The solution starts with belief.

Part II

The Shap Char

e of
ge

Chapter 4
Who's Rea

y in Control?

Collective consciousness is a set of shared beliefs, ideas, and moral attitudes that operate as a unifying force within society. In general, it does not refer to the specific moral conscience but to a shared understanding of social norms. As generations change, so do the accepted norms—and as millennials and Gen Z continue asking questions that were previously taboo, the consciousness shifts further. For example, in the 1970s, a company would never expect to be asked about their carbon footprint or environmental strategy while interviewing someone for a job. Each new generation is brought up with different values, and this generation is not accepting the status quo and its impact on people and our planet.

This shift in consciousness has shifted the dynamics around consumerism. Many more shoppers are conscious of their actions—and the actions of the businesses they purchase from. More people have become aware of their own carbon footprint. It's commonplace to try to eat healthy, prioritize physical fitness, and practice mindfulness. People are realizing they have enough stuff. Even the practice of asking for no gifts has caught on.

Not everyone believes the movement will last. Jeff Bezos has said that Amazon focuses on two convictions: 1) people want to pay the least for a product, and 2) they want it as fast as they can get it. He went on to say that in 10 years (from a 2011 quote) this would still be true. Amazon has obviously done extremely well, yet reality is shifting, if only slightly. For the first time, these two convictions are no longer universal truths. People are willing to pay more for environmentally friendly products, products that support a cause, and sustainable products—and they are willing to wait longer to get things in order to reduce their footprint. The effect is strong enough that Amazon now offers the option of delaying shipment of some items in your shopping cart so that you can get them all together in one package, reducing packaging materials and carbon emissions caused by having to make extra deliveries.

This isn't to say a rapid change is underway, but questions raise consciousness. After a friend asked my wife why she hadn't stopped using Amazon Prime, we discussed it and decided to stop our subscription. In July 2021, I took the added step of selling my Amazon shares. We then slowly weaned ourselves off buying from them almost entirely, though it's not been easy. While collective consciousness has enabled some of the biggest movements in recent times—#MeToo, #BlackLivesMatter and #ClimateChange—movements such as #DeleteFacebook, #DeleteUber, and the boycott of businesses that don't pay taxes (e.g., Starbucks, Amazon, etc.) haven't gathered momentum as readily. Consumerism will be difficult to fully release. My personal Amazon account can attest to this with its "member since 2005" designation.

As conscious consumerism builds its momentum slowly, conscienceless capitalism is still ruling politics. Take Donald Trump's "Make America Great Again" 2016 campaign. Apart from borrowing it from Reagan's 1980 campaign, Trump used it as a tool to demonstrate that the lower middle class—most of his voter base—would economically benefit from his policies. During his 2016 run for the presidency, he came up with a simple but powerful message: I'm going to take *their* pie and give it to you. Other politicians often talk about increasing the pie so everyone gets more, but that takes time. Changing how you divide an existing pie—EU's freedom of movement rules, claiming "the other" is taking your job, build the wall, etc.—feels closer to instant gratification for those who want to believe others are taking their share. In reality, Trump only helped widen wealth inequality with major tax cuts for the rich in 2017. If Trump was serious about tackling wealth inequality, he would have rewritten the rules in a way that serves all of society, not just people like him.

Not that the Democrats really care either. Both the Clinton and Obama administrations continued the Republican Party's push for extreme globalization and worked against policy frameworks that would have mitigated the trauma associated with it.

As a result, every four or eight years, disenchanted voters change the political party in power—that is, until a dictator comes along and changes the constitution, removing term limits and holding office for life. To name a few: Putin in Russia, Orbán in Hungary, Erdoğan in Turkey, and in 2022, Xi Jinping in China.

Politicians have always had a bad reputation when it comes to honesty, but there was a time when they at least attempted to cover for their sleights. Over the past decade, blatant lies have actually driven popularity and generated votes. And virtually every issue collapses into an economic debate, no matter how loose the connections may be.

How can these patterns continually play out around the world, and who's pulling the strings?

My theory is that money is treated as a universal language all people understand. And politicians are not wrong. People want to be better off. Equally, and more influentially, the ultrarich align themselves with all the major political parties to ensure that, regardless of who comes to power, they can continue their worship of money unhindered. Legal scholar and activist Lawrence Lessig had it exactly right when he said,

"The Left and Right share a common enemy: Capitalists who corrupt capitalism."[1]

£ € $

Born the son of a Scottish chairmaker in 1823, William Macy Tweed lived the American dream. He became the ultimate powerbroker, rising from the ranks of the Odd Fellows and Mason organizations to becoming an alderman controlling the New York City government, and eventually winning a seat in the US House of Representatives. But his rags to riches ascent was fueled by corruption, and in the wake of the Orange Riots of 1870–1871, "Boss" Tweed ended up in prison. It was ultimately reporting by *The New York Times* about Tweed Ring corruption that took him down. One exposé read:

> *All the Tweed Ring were subsequently tried and sentenced to prison. Boss Tweed served time for forgery and larceny and other charges, but in 1875 escaped from prison and traveled to Cuba and Spain. In 1876, he was arrested by Spanish police, who reportedly recognized him from a famous Nash cartoon depiction. After Tweed's extradition to the United States, he was returned to prison, where he died in 1878, age 55.[2]*

Tweed is long gone, but his toxic legacy lives on in what is now called Tweedism. For example, he famously said, "I don't care who does the electing, as long as I get to do the nominating."

Lawrence Lessig, who coined the term Tweedism, goes on to call it a "genius theory" for destroying democracy. Lessig argues that if you control the nomination, then every candidate is going to worry about what you the nominator thinks, so you practically control the candidate whether or not you control the ultimate election. We saw this play out in the 2022 Republican primaries, when candidates endorsed

"The Left and Right share a common enemy: Capitalists who corrupt capitalism."
—*Lawrence Lessig*

by Trump were blindly supported by his base, though many went on to lose the midterm elections when they needed more support than just Trump's following.[3]

Let me give you another example: candidates in the US need to fund their campaigns, making funding itself its own contest. Known as the "money primary," this stage of the election process determines which candidates are allowed to run. But a money primary takes time, typically one to two years prior to the nominations. In that time, members of Congress spend 30–70 percent of their time dialing for dollars—calling people all across the country to get the money they need to run their campaigns. Lessig explains that each candidate develops "a 'sixth sense,' a constant awareness of how what they do might affect their ability to raise money."[3]

In 2011, Lessig founded Rootstrikers, an organization dedicated to changing the influence of money in Congress, and in 2016 he founded Equal Citizens, a nonprofit, nonpartisan group that is "dedicated to reforms that will achieve citizen equality." About these moves, *The New York Times* wrote: "Mr. Lessig's vision is at once profoundly pessimistic—the integrity of the nation is collapsing under the best of intentions—and deeply optimistic. Simple legislative surgery, he says, can put the nation back on the path to greatness."[4]

But reform seems more complicated than that. David Brooks, a political and cultural commentator, described the political elite as "bobos in paradise."* The bobos, he says, "have united into an insular, intermarrying elite that dominates culture, media, education, and technology."[5]

If it's not bad enough that this elite exists, those in that situation have a hard time admitting their power, much less using it responsibly.

---

* The term bobo is a portmanteau of "bohemian" and "bourgeois;" i.e., people who support bohemian or progressive values while leading privileged or bourgeois lives.

Brooks admits he himself is a bobo and that his kin have come to dominate left-wing parties around the world that were formerly vehicles for the working class. He describes how creative-class people like him pull policies further left on cultural issues, such as cosmopolitanism and identity. This creates a situation where traditional policies on labor, trade, and unions are watered down, forcing working people to leave the party. He backs this up by saying:

> *Around 1990, nearly a third of Labour members of the British Parliament were from working-class backgrounds; from 2010 to 2015, the proportion wasn't even one in 10. In 2016, Hillary Clinton won the 50 most-educated counties in America by an average of 26 points—while losing the 50 least-educated counties by an average of 31 points.*[6]

This is not just true for the US and the UK. The classic Boss Tweed political machine used to be about regional bread-and-butter politics, but it's much more sinister now—more diffused nationwide, even global. The new elite class has consolidated globally over the past two decades. I find this situation deeply depressing. Tweedism is thriving, having gone from strength to strength for over a hundred years.

Money buys political influence, and when so many people's power and livelihood depends on the supply side of the war machine, they are going to create the demand as well, regardless of who's sitting in the Oval Office. The right wing and left wing have shifted so that both are now for the rich and no one's for the poor.

£ € $

Many people believe we are in *The Matrix*. Drawing a parallel with our world, how much of the movie franchise's systematized control of reality could be true? Is it in "their" benefit—"they" being the algorithm, the politicians, the super-rich—for us to think in fear and scarcity? Is democracy itself the biggest lie of all? If so, then those of us who aren't involved in selecting the candidates are, in fact, in the Matrix. With the advent of social media, we're certainly living in a post-truth[*7] world— one where we rarely know what the truth really is. Our societies are polarized on almost every topic. If there are studies that show something, there are studies that disprove that something too, especially given special-interest-funded studies to fabricate findings that meet their needs. An example of this is when Volkswagen famously commissioned a study to hide their diesel emission levels. Now that Volkswagen has been caught cheating (and fined heavily), it is clear what was right and what was wrong, or so we think. Conspiracy theorists say the regulation to cut diesel emissions was motivated by geopolitics, in particular reducing the demand for diesel, which is extremely cheap to produce in Arab nations. But in most cases, the issues aren't so black and white—yet we still become married to our individual viewpoint, regardless of whether it is right or wrong, and cling on to it for dear life. Often, at least one if not both of the sides clinging to their opposite view has bought into some level of propaganda.

It's no secret that disinformation and fake news have dominated our media over the last decade. On Twitter (now X), fake news stories are 70 percent more likely to be retweeted than true stories, which take about six times as long to reach 1,500 people as it does for false stories to achieve the same reach. And it isn't just sharing—social media users are more likely to believe fake news as well.[8]

Social networks ceased to be free speech platforms a decade ago when they moved from reverse chronological display (newest post at the top) to one showing content driven by proprietary algorithms.

---

* Post-truth was added to the *Oxford English Dictionary* in 2016 and is defined as "relating to or denoting circumstances in which objective facts are less influential in shaping public opinion than appeals to emotion and personal belief."

Twitter, Facebook, and other social media platforms take what people say online and sort it via artificial intelligence and machine learning algorithms, then selectively show content to you based on what you have clicked on in the past and what people in your network are engaging with.

In our desire to help others in our network, we spread misinformation—and in most cases, it is false information that is not meant to hurt anyone. When you receive a forwarded message and send it on without knowing that a piece of information is untrue, you are not spreading false information deliberately. On the other hand, *disinformation* is false information deliberately spread to deceive people. There are armies of political cyber hackers and their minions who have been hired to use bots to fabricate and spread content that is completely false with an aim to destabilize foreign governments or influence elections.

Disinformation is big business for everyone involved—both the perpetrators and the social networks—as we saw with Cambridge Analytica in the previous chapter. And it's not just cyber hackers; governments across the spectrum are involved too, as was exposed by the Snowden revelations. Expect the commercialization of social media manipulation to continue to grow by both state and private actors.

There are massive dangers to both individuals and society associated with this technology. The algorithms are optimized to serve up more and more of what you and your network click on—be that meditation, outdoor adventures, soccer club Real Madrid, or Baby Shark. It's naive to think that it's better for you if they show you content you like rather than you having to sift through all the content yourself. When you lose control of choosing what you read, you have to trust those choosing for you. This is why some traditional media agencies work so hard to maintain trust and, in some cases, neutrality. Think Associated Press, Reuters, the BBC in the UK, and *The Wall Street Journal* in the US. But a large share of experts say that among the leading concerns about today's technology platforms are the ways in which they are exploited by bad actors who spread disinformation as well as the privacy issues arising out of the business model behind those systems.

Bad actors or not, politicians have embraced technological amplification. Many have learned to write the kind of provocative posts that get amplified by the algorithms. By writing explosive things about their perceived enemies, they generate attention, and attention helps them to raise funds—the new "dialing for dollars" Lessig warned about. Unfortunately, there is no algorithmic reward for compromise.

A group of researchers from Brazil's Federal University of Minas Gerais and the Qatar Computing Research Institute analyzed 70,000 articles from four major news organizations (BBC News, *Daily Mail*, Reuters, and *The New York Times*) to measure the correlation between headline sentiment and popularity. Although results varied from publication to publication, the general finding was that the more extreme the emotion is in a headline, the more likely it is to be clicked on. This runs both ways, the group said: "A headline has more chance to be successful if the sentiment expressed in its text is extreme, towards the positive or the negative side. Results suggest that neutral headlines are usually less attractive."[9]

You're more likely to click on a story that says, "This is the best" or "This is the worst" than "This is quite okay." These headlines are known as clickbait. If you momentarily lapse and click on a sensational social post once because your curiosity got the better of you, the algorithm learns a little bit from that interaction and serves up similar stories in the future. If you or your network also engage with this subsequent content, then the algorithm serves up more and more of the same content. This is also the way advertising is shown to you—as depicted in the movie *Social Dilemma.** Those who are susceptible to what the technology serves up to them end up trapped on social media.

This cycle is why social networks like Facebook amplify false information and polarizing content—it's what the algorithms have been designed to do. The global social problems posed by Facebook's algorithm in particular have led tens of millions of its 2.9 billion users around the world into a black hole of misinformation, a quagmire of lies, and a quicksand of conspiracy theories.

The sad reality is that social media has changed our values. It has made us value things that are more inane, vacuous, or even damaging. In 2018, computer science philosopher Jaron Lanier delivered a sobering prognosis on the spiraling corruption of our social networks: "I can't call them social networks anymore. I call them behavior modification empires."[10]

This is perhaps the biggest danger facing democracy today.

Louisa Heinrich, human-centered technology leader and advocate, articulates this warning well when she says, "There is a gap between the rate at which technology develops and the rate at which society develops. We need to take care not to fall into that gap."[11]

In the past, politicians and their backers controlled information quite easily. But the internet has made the flow of information more and more difficult to control (though of course some countries do it anyway, at any cost). The new strategy is to flood us with lots and lots of information, most of it bogus or fake, simply to stay in front of their potential donors and voters.

---

* The movie *Social Dilemma* describes the dangerous impact of social networking, which Big Tech uses in an attempt to manipulate and influence. I would recommend you watch it, if you haven't already.

"There is a gap between the rate at which technology develops and the rate at which society develops. We need to take care not to fall into that gap."
—*Louisa Heinrich*

Disinformation, misinformation, and fake news are such serious issues that there is concern over how users will sort through fact and fiction in the coming decade—all while the term "fake news" is being used to discredit the truth. Make no mistake: our ignorance is being weaponized against us, and the war of information has and continues to influence democracy by swaying public opinion before it's time to vote.

And it is not just public opinion and voting that's at stake. In May 2022, Food and Drug Administration (FDA) Commissioner Robert Califf, said, "I believe that misinformation is now our leading cause of death," naming ongoing COVID-19 vaccine hesitancy, the number of people taking Ivermectin, and the prevalence of vaping as examples of the problem. Asked what keeps him up at night, he went on to say, "the proliferation of false and misleading health information, particularly online—and the distrust in institutions, data, and expertise that it has wrought."[12]

Why do we fall for fake news? In a 2019 study, researchers Pennycook and Rand concluded that people are more likely to fall prey to fake news because of lazy thinking than due to any conscious or subconscious desire to protect their political identities. Rand goes on to say: "People [who] believed false headlines tended to be the people [who] didn't think carefully, regardless of whether those headlines aligned with their ideology."[13]

So how can we know what's true and what's not? In short, we must make an effort, learn to control our own flow of information, and do our own fact checking. Over time, I've stopped reading any social media feeds—this has a twofold effect of helping me avoid content rabbit holes, known as doomscrolling, and allowing me to trust the authenticity of the news articles I seek out. I also stay away from clickbait headlines and stick to two or three trusted media outlets that I visit from time to time.

Algorithmic "news" is just one facet of one of the biggest problems our generation faces: people aren't as free to choose as we'd like to believe. We talk about being in a free market or a free society, but nearly 70 percent of digital ad spending goes though just three companies—Google, Amazon, and Facebook. These artificial monopolies get to decide for everyone—what you can watch, what you can listen to, who you talk to, who you're influenced by, and who you vote for. Our interests themselves are manipulated such that even our choices are difficult to claim as entirely our own.

£ € $

The illusion does not end with choice, how much a vote counts, or what comes through your newsfeed of choice. Wealth itself is a sham.

Bezos may be one of the richest people on the planet, but like most billionaires, his actual net worth is based on shares. If he were to liquidate a significant portion of those shares in order to access their actual cash value, that value would tank—killing a lot of his net worth even as he attempted to access it. In fact, that's what happened to Elon Musk. Musk's fortune once sat as high as $340 billion in late 2021. As he attempted to access his wealth to buy Twitter, Musk saw his wealth plummet to $137 billion by the end of 2022. He became the only person in history to erase $200 billion from their net worth and is now the holder of a Guinness World Record, demolishing the previous record: a $58.6 billion loss by Japanese investor Masayoshi Son in 2000.[14]

What is wealth actually? Extreme wealth is buying power and political power. Notice how several billionaires acquired media outlets (e.g., Bezos with *The Washington Post*, and Musk with Twitter). They own their banks too, in a different sort of way. There is a saying that goes something like this: if you owe the bank $100,000, the bank owns you;

if you owe the bank $100 million, you own the bank. All billionaires owe billions in debt though their companies—it's how they became billionaires in the first place. Ultimately, wealth equals power.

Billionaire Chamath Palihapitiya, an early senior executive at Facebook, SPAC* sponsor, and the founder and CEO of Social Capital, says there are 150 people who control the world. If we are in the Matrix, these would be the entities feeding off our energy, even in our most well-intended moments.

I wanted to make millions as a pathway toward helping the poor. In 2014–15, I applied for and won a Grand Challenge grant from the Bill and Melinda Gates Foundation to simplify mobile money—my idea was to create a calculator-like device that you could use to make payments where there was no network coverage. However, assumptions from the Gates Foundation became obstacles soon after. They were sure it would only be a matter of time before everyone had a mobile phone, though as of this writing eight years later, that future has still not come into view. I ultimately chose to stay in the startup game, driven by a belief that making a "big enough" impact must start with having enough success (read: money).

From a young age, I was led to believe that money was the most important indicator of success—not by my parents, but by society at large. Story after story showed me that those who made millions would then turn their attention to philanthropy, making them not only successful but "good" as well.

---

* A SPAC, or Special Purpose Acquisition Company, is a type of investment vehicle that is created for the sole purpose of raising capital through an initial public offering (IPO), with the intention of using that capital to acquire an existing operating company. SPACs are sometimes referred to as "blank-check companies" because they don't have any specific business operations or assets at the time of their IPO.

What I later learned is that our brain is divided into three parts. The oldest part of the brain, known as the reptilian brain, was developed about 400 million years ago and consists of the main structures found in a reptile's brain. It is located deep within our head, fitting just on top of our spinal cord. It controls our most basic functions—heart rate, body temperature, blood pressure, breathing, and balance. It also helps coordinate with the other two "brains" within our head. The reptilian brain is reliable in that regard, but it tends to be somewhat rigid and compulsive. It is in control of our innate and automatic self-preserving behavior patterns, which ensure our survival and that of our species.

Whenever you hear something bad—news, danger, gossip—your first instinct is to check if that might affect you or those around you. If it doesn't, your reptile brain dismisses it. This is why we are less sympathetic to macro events than those in our immediate circle. When something does affect you, the reptilian brain sends a signal to your body: *full alert*. Our fears are heightened, and our attention is diverted.

To recall a concept from chapter 2: after feeling the effects of the long period of austerity after the 2008 global financial crisis, slim but effective majorities of people in full alert mode voted for Brexit in the UK and Trump in the US. Around the world, more and more populists and nationalists were brought into power. People listened as politician after politician promised the moon—knowing full well that the rocket couldn't get off the ground.

People believed that these new leaders would increase general welfare. It is clear now that none of them had the people's interest at heart. A slim but effective margin of people still fail to see that the leaders they voted for merely represent the interests of those with money, not the people who elect them. In this way, Tweedism is alive and well. Those who control nominations control the elections, and

"The greatest trick the Devil ever pulled was convincing the world he didn't exist."
—*Charles Baudelaire*

nominations are controlled by money. This has been the biggest illusion of all: that people in power can or will help us—not only Johnson and Trump, but Obama and Merkel or Gates and Musk as well.

Ultimately, if that kind of power is an illusion, waiting for the elected or the rich to save us isn't outsourcing our own power. It's merely outsourcing our responsibility—to ourselves, to each other, and to the planet.

My idealistic view is that awareness can be enough. But while explaining what happens during election campaigns should enable people to make better choices about who represents them, in reality, many people vote for the same political party for life, following in the footsteps of their parents and grandparents.

Fortunately, I've also come to realize that not everyone has to change— a small number of people can make an outsized difference. In this way, the growing movement toward collective consciousness already is in direct opposition to the apparently powerful few. If money is made where our attention goes, and power is concentrated around the way money is made, the solution is to turn our attention away from the reptilian brain and into our higher aspirations. After all, as Baudelaire so famously said, "The greatest trick the Devil ever pulled was convincing the world he didn't exist."

The growing movement toward collective consciousness is a direct opposition to the powerful few. Their power being an illusion means our powerlessness is an illusion as well. To outsource the change— to wait for the apparently powerful to create the change we hope to see—is to relinquish our own power.

Next, with the myth of centralized power debunked, we can now explore an even more powerful illusion of recent times: money itself.

Chapter 5
The

loney Illusion

In my twenties, I was really fascinated with the idea of passive income, from property portfolios to lifestyle businesses. I had read various books on the topic and met people who had managed to pull it off, so I had fingers in many pies. These days, there is a nicer name for that: a portfolio career. In practice, I was always starting something new, never quite finishing or staying focused on anything I had started.

Focus seems to be the exception rather than the norm, and it's easier to see the pitfalls of distraction in others rather than ourselves. Someone I know comes to mind immediately: she is absolutely brilliant in her micro niche, and even though she recognizes that, the temptation to offer her clients other ancillary services is too great to ignore.

Somewhere along the line, both she and I were taught or told to maximize revenue from existing clients. For her, that meant offering them ancillary services that she was perhaps not best suited to offer. So many business owners/freelance professionals end up falling into this trap, spending valuable time and money building suboptimal solutions and then wondering why it isn't working as we had envisioned. I've experienced the same temptation and the consequences of indulging. Over time, you get bogged down with the ancillary services rather than thriving on what you're really good at. Yet when you stay focused on those strengths, you get even better, you can become well-known for them, and you stay in flow along the way. In the long run, you really enjoy what you're doing and end up making more money anyway—and when that last part happens, it's just a bonus, not the motivation behind your decisions.

There is something ironic about setting out to earn money passively but getting so distracted that even more effort is expended. The problem begins with the motivation to earn more (and more) money. Where older millennials like me wanted the passive revenue of the dot-com boom, social media influencing is now the rage. Why? For people who grew up online and already spend most of their time sharing carefully edited videos and swapping product recommendations, the opportunity to make a living off their content can be alluring. And I get it. Doing something you love without a boss telling you what to do seems like a dream job and the ultimate way of expressing yourself. It's their version of digital products and passive revenue—so it's no wonder that 54 percent of Gen Zers said they'd become influencers if they could.[1]

The appeal of creative freedom and flexibility is stronger than ever, and tons of options have emerged since the pandemic radically altered how people work and live. It's not just influencing anymore—it's whatever we can build. Younger people especially don't want to live a corporate life. They want to have fun while being part of something relevant and embedded in the culture.

That all sounds great, but at what cost? For starters, that specific version of fun, freedom, and meaning is limited to a relatively small group of people. To be an influencer, you need at least 500,000 followers, and only 1% get there. After all, if everyone was an influencer, who would be their audience? Social media influencers are highly paid because they have built an audience that can be monetized. And that brings up another problem for those who have built large audiences and increased their consciousness: for the most part, influencers persuade you to buy stuff, and mostly stuff you don't need.

The problem comes when you realize that you're fueling the fire that's getting more people to buy more stuff. For me personally, I might not have been caught up in the social media version of influencing, but the allure of passive income was not much different. Somewhere along the way, "making millions to do good" convinced me to consider all kinds of money-making avenues that didn't do any good along the way.

Fast forward several years: in April 2016, I stopped buying stuff. Completely. Influenced by the minimalist movement and the environmental impact that buying stuff was causing, I was serious about it. My wife and I had just had our first child, and for the first few months, a package arrived every day. Each new delivery felt sickening, and I had to do something to stop.

So I didn't buy a single item for the whole year. After that, I adopted a replacement only policy, including my iPhone. Instead of getting the latest model every year, I decided to only upgrade once every three years—planned obsolescence had grown annoying, and I had grown out of the need to derive status from FOMO.[*]

However, at the exact same time, I made a deposit to join the waiting list for a Tesla Model 3.

This felt reasonable. I liked the idea of going electric, and at the time I thought I was planning for the future. My turn would come along in 2019–2020, just about the time I needed to buy a new car. I had rationalized that the Model S was too big and flashy, but the Model 3 was reasonable—including its then $35,000 price tag. But I also have to admit that it was cool to say "I'm in the queue."

I didn't realize it at the time, but I hadn't yet rid myself of deriving status from external objects. In fact, my desire to make (and spend)

---

[*] Fear of Missing Out.

millions was still burning strong, in part because it's an unquenchable desire. After a certain point—once needs are met and bills are no longer a driving concern—money doesn't buy happiness. The super-rich know this all too well, and we see it in them. Whatever they have is never enough. Yet somehow, we've all bought into the mindset that having millions is the path to satisfaction and success. And among conscious millennials, this mindset extends to the belief that being wealthy is the only way to make "real" change.

And so, in that same period of time, I launched yet another startup, and *this* one was going to make it big.

£ € $

For centuries, the vulnerable have been taken advantage of while the apparently powerful attain more power. This is how the animal kingdom works—survival of the fittest. We ought to be beyond that by now, yet there are entire industries built for the sole purpose of ripping people off. In the financial world, payday lending and for-profit colleges come to mind, especially in the US. Perhaps they started with good intentions, but greed took over—and sadly, greed knows no limit.

To name one unfortunate example, former British prime minister David Cameron was also a part-time advisor to Greensill Capital, and from those positions, he wooed investors and lobbied the UK government to bend the rules so that Greensill could receive COVID Corporate Financing Facility loans.[*] In two and a half years, Cameron made over $10 million from the very firm that lost investors billions[2] and put $435 million of taxpayer money at risk.[3] All this despite the

---

[*] The fact that he was cleared of any wrongdoing by two government inquiries only goes to show that the rules meant to regulate lobbying are outdated and completely unfit for their purpose.

fact that Cameron is expected to inherit million-pound legacies from both sides of his family.

In the UK parliamentary committee's inquiry, Cameron said that he "was not motivated by money,"[4] but how could one possibly give him the benefit of doubt? Perhaps if he'd donated even 10 percent ($1 million) to the charities that he selected for donations in memory of his son, he could have lent some credibility to that statement.

Without political affiliation, I had admired Cameron throughout that time in his life. My heart went out to him and his wife Samantha when their first son, Ivan, died in 2009. He was six years old, having been born with a rare combination of cerebral palsy and a form of severe epilepsy called Ohtahara syndrome, requiring around-the-clock care. No one deserves that kind of heartache and loss. Today, his reputation is in tatters, like so many other politicians and businessmen (who got caught).

In 2020, Netflix published an investigative docuseries called *Dirty Money*, which exposes brazen acts of corporate greed and corruption and underscores the fact that what might be good for business is often bad for consumers.

If you think what Cameron did was bad, watch the episode on Trump, or his son-in-law Jared Kushner who stars in my favorite episode, "Slumlord Millionaire," with this tagline: "As Jared Kushner rose from real estate heir to White House advisor, reporters and housing advocates uncovered disturbing patterns at his properties."

If you haven't watched it, I encourage you to. Reactions have been extremely positive, with Rotten Tomatoes calling *Dirty Money* informative and appalling. Brian Lowry of CNN explains that "for pro-business advocates of deregulation, *Dirty Money* offers a simple yet powerful rejoinder: Look at the terrible, unethical behavior that corporate entities try getting away with when they think nobody's looking."[5]

The commonality for all these companies featured on the show? One individual sits at the helm, setting the tone for the whole organization—and for that person, money is so clearly the motivator that they don't care about the consequences of their actions. Especially those that ruin people's lives. To the viewer, it appears that their hearts must be made of stone. Or perhaps this is what it truly means to be made of money.

£ € $

When you realize that money is a means to an end and not an end in itself, your focus can move from chasing money to something else, something higher. No longer optimizing your earnings requires an increase in consciousness so that meaningful work, creating impact, and contributing to society become on par with items necessary for survival—not luxuries we can only access once we're rich.

With a few exceptions, almost everyone I meet wants to earn a lot of money. Society has ingrained in us the idea that money is equivalent to success. Even though I grew up in a fairly affluent family, the desire and ability to make money came easily to me, so I got sucked into the vortex and developed a strong desire to be super rich from a young age. At age 11, I hoarded snacks in boarding school, then offered them to others days before we got our next quota—sometimes at 100 percent interest (I'll give you one packet of biscuits and you give me two back in a few days).

This entrepreneurial streak continued through my teens and into my thirties, though at age 13 I was also introduced to meditation by my mother. In case that sounds too otherworldly or specifically Indian, I should point out that every faith and culture has a tradition and practice of meditation. As the saying goes, to pray is to talk to God and to meditate is to listen. Over the past 30 years, I have slowly increased my consciousness—moving away from narrow-minded self-interest and wanting to be super rich—toward a desire to help humanity. I left a career in investment banking along the way to work in international development.

I'm not the only one who has experienced this shift. Most notably, more people than ever are getting off the 9-to-5 hamster wheel and searching for their purpose in life. Burnout and mental health are no longer taboo topics; and the #BigShift, #GreatResignation, and #QuietQuitting have seen people leave their exploitative jobs in droves. We are willing to earn less money to do more meaningful work, and we have reduced our consumption levels (though not often to a no-spend level). Altruism is also on the rise, highlighted once again by inspiring responses to the pandemic. From running food kitchens to assisting the elderly with their food shopping, this challenging time highlighted our desire to be in community and has, in that way, been an amazing triumph for humanity.

Many people who leave their soul-sucking jobs for more fulfilling work make the leap to entrepreneurship and never look back. They become the entrepreneurs running calls from Starbucks, joining coworking spaces, and becoming digital nomads.

New research conducted by the *Harvard Business Review* on the meaning of work shows that more than nine out of ten employees are willing to earn less money to do more meaningful work. Across age and salary groups, workers want meaningful work badly enough that they're willing to pay for it. Perhaps the trillion-dollar question, then, is this: Just how much is meaning worth to the individual employee?

HBR asked, "If you could find a job that offered you consistent meaning, how much of your current salary would you be willing to forego?" On average, the research pool of American workers said they'd be willing to give up 23 percent of their entire future lifetime earnings in order to have a job that was always meaningful. To put this figure in perspective, consider that Americans spend about 21 percent of their income on housing. Given that people are willing to spend more on meaningful work than on putting a roof over their heads, the 21st century list of essentials might be due for an update: "food, clothing, shelter, and meaningful work."[6]

Between 2016 and 2020, I worked with inclusive fintech startups, mentoring over 20 of them during that time. I also spent a year venture building, working deeply with startups to help them scale. Each of these companies aimed to help the poor and also wanted to be unicorns. Startup after startup launched with great visions, only to end up with mission drift* as investor priorities took over.

One day after interviewing a gig worker, detailed later in chapter 8, I was so affected by his story—working six days a week away from his family and still struggling to make ends meet—that it took me half an hour to recover from the call. The suspicion that had been getting bigger in my mind for a few months became clear: those two objectives—helping the poor and becoming a unicorn—don't go together. If you want to be a unicorn, go be one. But purporting to help the poor at the same time will either land you in no-man's land or shift you upstream to more profitable customers. Those who have succeeded, and there are a few, simply fleece the poorest: making millions (or billions) from a startup meant to help the poor means you're either charging them too much (yes, even if it is free) or that you could actually provide them with a better service. I realized that the most genuine way to create impact is to do so while making a living rather than going for a big payoff. As an entrepreneur, it took me a while to change my mindset from the former to the latter. Once I finally did, I felt liberated and ready to actually facilitate change, knowing that I had no financial conflict of interest and only a desire to help.

---

* Mission drift in startups refers to a situation where a company gradually shifts its focus, goals, or core values away from its original mission or purpose.

Just 20 years ago, my story would have been odd. If someone who was doing fairly well in life said they wanted to change careers to follow their "purpose," people would have thought that person was crazy. Even today, the concept is alien to those who are stuck with traditional ideas.

Take author and hit podcaster Jay Shetty. His parents, like most Indian parents, believed you are either a lawyer, a doctor, or a failure. All through his teenage years, they pushed him to choose between medicine and law. But even though he grew up in the UK and started off in the corporate world, the pressure of it all sent him to India, where he became a Hindu monk for three years. Wanting to bring some of that ancient wisdom into the modern world, Jay started making videos in 2016. Viewed first by a million people, then 5 million, 10 million, 20 million people—today his videos have been viewed over a billion times. What's incredible is that his parents, who pushed him to do either medicine or law, would have actually pushed him into a career that is likely going to be automated, de-commoditized, and de-professionalized in the near future. Instead, he effortlessly earns tens of thousands of dollars per appearance, rubbing shoulders with all sorts of interesting people. There was no career path in that, and his parents didn't even know this job existed.*

There's also Simon Sinek who, in 2009, started a movement to help people become more inspired at work and in turn inspire their colleagues and customers. Since then, millions have been touched by the power of his ideas, including more than 28 million who've watched his TED Talk based on *Start with Why*—the third most popular TED video of all time.

Another notable Simon—Simon Squibb, an investor, serial entrepreneur, and chief executive—founded The Purposeful Project. Simon

---

* I recommend listening to Jay Shetty's podcast, *On Purpose*.

started his first company at 15 years old when he was homeless, and now his goal is to help 10 million people become entrepreneurs. This is an exciting goal, and I believe there are at least a thousand people like him. That means, collectively, we can help billions of people become entrepreneurs or better entrepreneurs.

Now, if you are reading this and feeling frustrated that you haven't found your current purpose, I feel you. Not everyone can or wants to be an entrepreneur, and that doesn't mean they should be left out *or* taken advantage of in these movements. The truth is, entrepreneur or not, your purpose is something that intrinsically motivates you. It's something that constantly nags at you and urges you to do something about what you're seeing around you.

For some, their purpose is so clear it's like they were born with it. But for most of us, it's much harder, and we may spend 10, 20, 30 years, or our whole lives, searching for our life's purpose. The key point here is that trying to "figure out" your life's purpose is futile. Instead, do what's right in front of you. What makes sense for you to pursue *now*, given your current skill set, passion, and opportunities? Over time, you evolve and so does your purpose. My purpose has changed several times over the course of my life, and it will change again. Each time, I pivot and move forward. Sometimes your purpose is staring you in the face, but you miss it because it doesn't look sexy enough to pay attention to or because you're so focused on some abstract idea of the future that you can't see what's right here, right now.

Movie star Jonah Hill was so moved by the work of his therapist, psychiatrist Dr. Phil Stutz, that he decided to use his skills and make a documentary film called *Stutz*—both as a heartfelt tribute to the man who helped him, and to help others. The film chronicles the life and career of Hill's therapist while also exploring some of the tools Dr. Stutz uses with his clients and explaining them so simply that anyone can use them. You can either watch the movie or read

Dr. Stutz's book, *The Tools: 5 Tools to Help You Find Courage, Creativity, and Willpower—and Inspire You to Live Life in Forward Motion.*[7] If you want to go further, read his second book *Coming Alive: 4 Tools to Defeat Your Inner Enemy, Ignite Creative Expression and Unleash Your Soul's Potential.*[8]

Once you identify your current purpose, it will help you begin to thrive. Make your purpose and values very clear, and people will self-select to join your mission. For instance, my purpose is to help others thrive—just a few people like you, whose paths cross mine. It has helped me attract like-minded people whom I enjoy working closely with. There are several resources that can help you move toward your purpose. One is On Purpose (www.onpurpose.org)—a community that helps you find your work in the world, work that matters, and work you care about. You learn on the job, doing real work in purpose-driven organizations while at the same time going through an intensive learning and development program. The other resource is ThriveNow (www.thrive-now.org)—a collection of tools, articles, and videos that have helped me find and recalibrate my compass along my journey.

Fundamentally, there are two types of businesses you can work for. Vishen Lakhiani, founder of Mindvalley, calls them Humanity-minus or Humanity-plus.

Companies and businesses that are solely driven by profit motive are Humanity-minus. Nothing is intrinsically wrong with them, but I'd struggle to get excited about their mission and support them when they are not contributing to society, or worse, if the company is engaged in dubious marketing, selling products that are harmful like junk food, while making you feel like it's a healthy choice. Other examples of Humanity-minus companies are ones that are engaged in unsustainable practices, either directly like the oil and gas giants or indirectly by funding or providing services to those engaged in unsustainable practices.

In contrast, Humanity-plus companies are interested in our general welfare. They push boundaries and find ways to deliver holistic outcomes for all stakeholders. These could be startups focused on cleantech (renewable energy and alternative fuels) or companies that I call conscious companies, ones that are making a positive difference in people's lives and for our planet (I go into detailed examples in chapter 9). In an ideal world, these are the companies we should be starting, supporting, or working for.

Powerful missions are not only for new industries. Companies in traditional industries like banking, airlines, retail, and more all have an opportunity to upgrade their purpose. While I have never had the opportunity to fly on Southwest Airlines, many cite it as a great example of a company positively contributing to society. They focus on being customer-centric, uplifting customers' experiences by going above and beyond to care for their passengers. Companies don't have to repurpose themselves, they just need to care about their people (employees, suppliers, and customers) and our planet.

Author Paul Skinner beautifully explains how any company can do this in his book, *The Purpose Upgrade: Change Your Business to Save the World. Change the World to Save Your Business.*

In Skinner's book, you will meet the social entrepreneur who repurposed a previously "boring" office supply business to fund microfinance initiatives that reach millions of the people most exposed to poverty, so that "even a bad day at the office saves lives." Skinner also highlights how the leaders of a coal-mining business repurposed their enterprise first as an industrial chemicals company and then more spectacularly as a sustainable living business, generating unprecedented shareholder returns by aligning their objectives with the United Nations' Sustainable Development Goals. They are now changing the lives of smallholder farmers, redirecting the food system to a more sustainable model, and harnessing the power of the world's biggest brands to provide more nutritious food on a healthier planet.[9]

Whatever you decide to pursue—be it starting a business, joining a business, pursuing a side hustle or a cause outside of work, finding your creative spark and sharing it with the world, or devoting 110% of your time and energy to raising amazing children, Vishen Lakhiani says there's really only one thing you need to remember: "You don't have to save the world. Just don't make it a worse place for the next generation."[10]

Create anything—new companies, new products, new services. What matters is leaving the world in a better place for the next generation.

But in the process, it's important to be careful to not get caught up in a different hamster wheel—chasing fame, followers, and dollars. Following your purpose without also shedding the need to chase money is just moving from a corporate hamster wheel to an entrepreneur hamster wheel.

£ € $

Measuring success by your bank account balance and keeping up with the Joneses are not how you find collaborators, friends, or happiness. Money is not an innate human need, even though the need to signal that we are "better" is part of our genetic sense of survival. In recent years, we have taken that impulse to its extremes, inadvertently participating in the very system that keeps us frustrated and struggling.

Joshua Fields Millburn, best known as one half of The Minimalists, was living the American dream—doing "better" than that, by most standards—becoming the youngest director in his company's 140-year history, earning a remarkable six-figure income and an accumulation of the trinkets of success. But when his mom died and his marriage

"You don't have to save the world. Just don't make it a worse place for the next generation."
—Vishen Lakhiani

ended in the same month, he realized he had been so focused on success and achievement, especially on accumulating stuff, that he wasn't living *his* dream. He said, "It sort of took getting everything I thought I wanted to realize that everything I ever wanted wasn't actually what I wanted at all."[11] As a result, Millburn and longtime friend Ryan Nicodemus built a movement out of minimalism, helping over 20 million people live meaningful lives with less.

What I take from his example is that you can let society decide when you have made it, or *you* can make that decision. The latter requires you to raise your consciousness by extracting yourself from all the noise that is created to keep you buying more stuff—for which, of course, you always need more money.

We all know that guy who thinks he hasn't "made it" yet, but maybe one day he will if he keeps pushing. From the outside, it looks like he already has; after all, he has a beautiful family, two healthy kids, and lives in the tropics with a house on a hill with a beautiful view of the sea and a swimming pool. But still, it is not enough for him. The truth is, it never will be—not if he and his wife maintain the same consumerist mindset. Consumerism and materialism have infiltrated our culture by design to get us to spend money. In the same way that Valentine's Day, Mother's Day, Father's Day, and other random "days" require purchases in order to prove our love for each other, our current economic system perpetuates consumerism by ensuring that you want more—not because you actually do want more, but to drive "growth."

Growth is the foundation of capitalism, as a corporation's primary obligation is to their shareholders for whom they have to keep delivering increased revenue. Late-stage capitalism[*] has driven the need

---

[*] Late-stage capitalism, in its current usage, is a catchall phrase for the indignities and absurdities of our contemporary economy, with its yawning inequality and super-powered corporations and shrinking middle class.

for ever-expanding corporate profits, and it fuels our global addiction to stuff—companies are structured with a need to keep growing, so we are conditioned with a need to keep buying. How do they get people to part with their money for stuff that they don't need? Advertising, in part. A successful advertising campaign is driven by a good story, so we're told story after story of why we need this or that, when in reality our lives (for the most part) were just fine as they were.

The truest story is that "they" depend on us to keep spending. Just like the human energy source in *The Matrix*, our mindless, desperate, or even well-intended spending makes the wealthiest even wealthier—all while doing nothing for our own lives and certainly not for the betterment of the planet. Case in point: if we were to collectively reduce our consumerism by 10 percent, each of us would increase our personal savings by enough to feel more comfortable—and we would likely trigger a global recession.

In fact, this is exactly what happened in Japan when their economy stagnated in the 1990s after its stock market and property bubbles burst. Companies focused on cutting debt and shifting manufacturing overseas, so wages stagnated and consumers reined in spending. This triggered a period of economic stagnation and price deflation known as Japan's "Lost Decade." Equity values plunged 60 percent from late 1989 to August 1992, while land values dropped throughout the 1990s, falling an incredible 70 percent by 2001.[12] The Japanese economy eventually outgrew this period, but it did so at a much slower pace than other industrialized nations.

Money is central to almost everything required in every society on earth, and those societies require us to spend, not save it. But how often do we confuse money itself with what we'd like to do with that money, in turn missing the forest for the trees? And do we conflate money with happiness because of the story we're told about it?

There is more to money than meets the eye, and more money to be had than the advertisers and neoliberalists would have us believe.

£ € $

What is money in the first place? How do those pieces of paper or plastic, coins in our pockets, or digits on a screen hold so much power over our lives? What are they, really?

The best description I have ever heard is this from a dear friend of mine, Anne Folan: "Money is stored energy. Think about it. Every note or coin in your pocket, all those digits on your smartphone, are nothing more—but also nothing less—than the vessel containing the symbolic stored value of the sweat and brain power that you or someone else put out into this world."

If money is energy, the banking system is the grid where energy is collected, stored, and then distributed at the system's discretion. But like our utilities, the financial grid is not cooperative. For those with generational wealth, the energy of money feels like living right next to a power station—easy access, probably taken for granted. Every so often, when there isn't enough energy on the grid, commercial and central banks create more out of thin air, and as we saw during the pandemic, there seems to be no limit to how much they can create. For example, central banks around the world created $12 trillion for COVID-19 relief, and you can guess where almost all of it went: to the wealthy.

So much of our culture is propped up on the idea that money will make or break our happiness and well-being that there must be some connection between money and happiness, right? If there weren't, you'd be less likely to stay late at work (or even go in at all), or struggle to save money and invest it profitably. But because of this belief, we crave money. We chase money, idolize money, and expend tremendous amounts of energy trying to get the money we want—just so we can save money, spend money, and give money to those we care about.

Money doesn't buy happiness, but it sure can make you miserable. There's a reason why your lucrative promotion, five-bedroom house, and fat 401(k) isn't cheering you up, though that reason might be more complicated than we can possibly imagine. Fortunately, we don't have to untangle the relationship between money and happiness ourselves. In the last 25 years, economists and psychologists have banded together to sort out the hows, whys, and why-nots of money and happiness—especially the why-nots. Why is it that the more money you have, the more you want? Why doesn't buying the car, condo, or cell phone of your dreams bring you more than momentary joy?

One idea that many have held is that happiness peaks once your salary hits $75,000. It's a conclusion drawn from a 2010 study by Nobel laureates Daniel Kahneman and Angus Deaton. The study found that the correlation between emotional well-being and income plateaus once a person earns $75,000. In a nutshell, earnings above $75,000 won't make you much happier than you are at that moment.[13]

These days, you can find studies that support both sides of almost any argument, so it is no surprise that new research from the University of Pennsylvania is challenging that frequently cited finding. The study, published a decade later in 2021, looked at data on 33,391 employed adults in the US, found that people's experiences of well-being and life satisfaction does continue to rise with income—even above that $75,000 mark.[14]

To settle this, we can go to a third study by Michael Norton, a Harvard Business School professor who has studied the connections between happiness and wealth. In a paper published in 2018, Norton and his collaborators asked more than 2,000 people who have a net worth of at least $1 million (including many whose wealth far exceeds that threshold) how happy they were on a scale of 1 to 10, then how much more money they would need to get to 10. "All the way up the income-wealth spectrum," Norton noted, "basically everyone says [they'd need] two or three times as much" to be perfectly happy.[15]

Norton's study corroborates the 2010 study by Kahneman and Deaton, where the latter also found that the percentage change of wealth—not its absolute amount—was what made a difference in happiness. In the context of income, a $100 raise does not have the same significance for a financial services executive as for an individual earning the minimum wage, but a doubling of their respective incomes might have a similar impact on both.[16]

What if you're struggling to make ends meet or under huge financial pressure for one reason or another? Wouldn't everything I'm saying about purpose go out the window? No, it doesn't. In fact, it becomes even more important for those who are struggling to find contentment and hope than it is for those with excesses.

Contentment can come with relatively little wealth, but more often than not, we put ourselves under financial pressure by the decisions we make to chase what we *think* will bring contentment. Simply taking a step back to think about why we want what we want gives us a chance to make changes—from going on a spending fast like I did by buying nothing for a year to becoming more intentional with our choices. For example, many people believe owning their home will give them happiness. I'm not necessarily disagreeing. However, if you extend yourself too far to achieve home ownership, instead of making you happy, it can make you feel trapped and miserable.

In my early twenties, my uncle, who I look up to for guidance, gave me a black-and-white photo of a woman sitting outside her hut in a small village in rural India. She had a smile on her face, and she looked happy. He said to me, "Look at her, she has almost nothing, yet she is smiling." Of course, her life is hard, a struggle for survival. But we must not forget how fortunate we are and get caught up with what are in comparison minor problems.

I keep the photo on my desk, and it always reminds me to be grateful. In comparison, Wall Street traders with millions of dollars to their names are never happy with their bonus. In that world, bonuses are all relative—if you're not earning more than your colleagues, you're never content.

So then, what's the point of spending your whole life chasing money if it's not going to bring you that fulfilling happiness you crave? For many people pursuing money over the last decade, work and life balance has begun to blur. Longer hours, a feeling of overwhelm, and a never-ending need to achieve more have combined to send more than a minority of the workforce into burnout. The workplace today has found a way to extract every ounce of efficiency out of people and shows no signs of backing off. Instead of putting people first, it puts dollars first. But the pandemic showed us another pathway and many people who lost their jobs found ways to get by with less, rightfully leading to the Great Resignation and Quiet Quitting movements. As Tony Robbins famously says, "The ultimate failure is success without fulfillment."

£ € $

One thing is clear: chasing and amassing huge amounts of money won't bring you happiness.* In the process, we may not openly share how we feel; we may hide our stress behind a fake smile or justify overworking as looking after our family. But we have collectively over-indexed our careers or businesses to the point of neglect—of our health or our most important relationships. If you are living this life, I have a simple but important message for you: you deserve better. You really do.

---

* If you want to learn more about finding happiness, read *Solve for Happy: Engineer Your Path to Joy*, by Mo Gawat.

"The ultimate failure is success without fulfillment."
—Tony Robbins

There are three ways to get a sense of self-worth and validation for who we are: 1) from our own self-belief, 2) from what people say about us, and 3) from the stuff we own. The second and third require us to keep up a charade of people-pleasing or consumerism—both requiring factors that are out of our control. Of course, almost everyone wants to be thought of in a good light, and it can be upsetting when your intentions are misconstrued, but over time, if your intentions are good, they will hold firm.

But the first source of worth is internal and fully in our control. Those of us who don't care what others say about us, don't worry about our external appearances, and don't have attachments to the stuff we own have far more control of our self-worth than those dependent on external factors.

Warren Buffet, the "Oracle of Omaha," and fourth-wealthiest person on earth says it best:

> Basically, when you get to my age, you'll really measure your success in life by how many of the people you want to have love you actually do love you. I know many people who have a lot of money, and they get testimonial dinners and they get hospital wings named after them. But the truth is that nobody in the world loves them. That's the ultimate test of how you have lived your life. The trouble with love is that you can't buy it. You can buy sex. You can buy testimonial dinners. But the only way to get love is to be lovable. It's very irritating if you have a lot of money. You'd like to think you could write a check: I'll buy a million dollars' worth of love. But it doesn't work that way. The more you give love away, the more you get.[17]

The pandemic highlighted our altruistic nature as humans. For years, millions of people helped millions more, expecting nothing in return. Our interconnectivity during this era of separation has been an amazing triumph for humanity. People volunteered for everything from running food kitchens to assisting the elderly with their grocery shopping. The medical staff alone, who selflessly put their lives in danger to help society, were incredible. Cynics will say they are being paid to do their job, but those folks are completely missing the point: altruism is on the rise—and not from the sort of philanthropists who made their millions or billions of dollars and then turned their attention to doing good. People from all walks of life are making positive contributions to society by volunteering, donating blood to the Red Cross/UNHCR, supporting local businesses (even if their prices are a bit higher), and participating in fundraising events as needs arise. The concept of asking someone to make a donation on your behalf, when you've done something for them and they still feel the need to reciprocate, has also gained popularity as people realize they don't have to be remunerated for every effort they make.

Such altruism—a pursuit of happiness beyond the pursuit of money—reflects a rise in consciousness that gives me hope. But we can't stop here. As more and more of the global population joins, we raise our collective consciousness. Eventually, this will translate to better leaders and better governments. After all, the government is for the people, by the people, and of the people. If the people experience a rise in consciousness that brings more to life than money—and then act on that realization—our awakening can become a movement that strikes at the heart of our dying system.

To explain how to do that, we're going to have to go back to our ancestors. That's right: some monkeys are going to show us how money works.

Chapter 6
Normali

ed Gambling

Have you ever wondered what drives your decisions? Specifically relating to money, why do you make the decisions you make?

As consciousness rises, we shift from self-centeredness to self-awareness first—then ultimately to an awareness of our impact on other people and our planet. That level of awareness naturally increases our desire to live life in a different way. We might change some of our lifestyle habits. We might start to change financial habits by spending a little less or shifting toward minimalism. But changing our money blueprint or making bigger changes around money, like how we work or invest, is a different story.

It's not for lack of awareness—we know the impact money can have. Money is the number one issue married couples fight about,[1] and at 22 percent, it's the third leading cause of divorce, behind basic incompatibility and infidelity.[2] According to a 2018 Northwestern Mutual study on personal money matters, one in five Americans said they have financial disagreements with their significant other at least monthly. Among those surveyed, 41 percent said financial anxieties have an impact on relationships with their spouses/partners at least some of the time.[3]

But even understanding money is a challenge. We are not taught money management skills in school and have little incentive or ability to learn more as adults—even finance professionals often confess to being poor money managers. As a result, whether or not we realize it, almost all of us have an unhealthy relationship with money that affects all areas of our lives. And make no mistake: our poor money management skills come from and benefit our current economic system, which thrives in an uninformed environment. If you don't know what you are missing—in this case, how the super-rich are taking advantage of the system—you are none the wiser. Each time you're gambling, hoping for a magic outcome, they are the house, getting a small but assured outcome.

There is absolutely nothing wrong with wanting to be super rich or make millions. The problem is that only a very small percentage of people can get there. It's particularly hard to opt out of wanting to make millions when people around you and your peers are doing it. It's even harder when you believe you have the ability to do it, or if you feel that your chances are high (whether or not that's actually true). The irony is that both those who make millions and those who don't (but are still chasing it) rarely find contentment anyway.

While *capitalism* thrives on fear of losing what you've got (scarcity) and extracting everything you can (superprofits), *individuals* do not. On the other hand, individuals are more likely to thrive with boring financial strategies, like compounding interest and community care. To beat the house, we have to relearn what money is, how it works, and where the odds are skewed against us.

£ € $

Adversity is a powerful teacher. The World Wars, Great Depression, and the decades that followed programmed people to think about money in terms of fear and scarcity. Money bought food and shelter in dangerous times. But even as the baby boomers (whose parents experienced much of that adversity) "made it" in life, the scarcity mindsets they earned have lingered in the ways we think about money.

But a scarcity mindset extends far beyond how we think about money. It is an attitude that limits creativity and confines people to thinking small about themselves and all of their resources, in addition to their personal finances. We fear we aren't good enough. We fear others won't value our ideas or join us. We fear spending money, and we fear we will never make enough of it.

A fixed scarcity mindset will make you believe that you are not enough, you do not have enough, you will never have enough, and that there is very little you can do about it.

On the other hand, an abundance mindset doesn't mean having or doing it all. It is certainly important to train your mind to recognize the vast and endless possibilities life has to offer, but it is also important to learn when it is wise to say no. It is equally important to make the most of your current skills and opportunities rather than get distracted by endless possibilities. After all, there is little point in digging 10 shallow wells when you simply need to dig deeply in one spot to find water.

Stephen Covey initially coined these terms in his bestselling book, *The 7 Habits of Highly Effective People*:

> *Scarcity mentality refers to people seeing life as a finite pie, so that if one person takes a big piece, that leaves less for everyone else. Most people, particularly in the corporate world, have been conditioned to have a scarcity mentality. It's no wonder when promotions and raises are scarce, resources are limited, managers hoard information, micromanagement abounds, and generally, short-term thinking is the norm. A scarcity mentality is what keeps many of us from achieving our goals. An abundance mindset refers to the paradigm that there is plenty out there for everybody.*[4]

Yet decades after Covey wrote about the scarcity mindset of the corporate world, abundance thinking still hasn't caught on. Consumerism hasn't slowed since it hit its stride in the 1920s, despite significant global and societal changes, and despite a significant rise in consciousness in all other areas of life. For over a century, we've been conditioned to buy stuff, go on holidays, and live like the rich and famous, even if we're neither rich nor famous. Meanwhile, many of our social and cultural norms around money formed during the post-war period—times of fear and scarcity—even though that era is long gone.

A simple example: retailers give deep discounts to trigger FOMO. What is FOMO tied to? Greed that makes us want to buy or grab everything we can before we miss out. In other words, scarcity. Recently, I went into a Lidl supermarket where they have a concept called, "when it's gone it's gone." Basically, they don't restock the same stuff—so here's your one chance to buy this thing you don't really need at this great price, because it's not going to be sitting here waiting for you when you may someday need it. Similarly, I'm sure you can remember a time when you picked up free merch you didn't need, simply because it was free. I know I can.

After 70 years of prosperity alongside the growth of technology, we live in an extremely different world than our grand- and great-grandparents did—a less equal but more abundant world. Money isn't floating around and accessible to everyone, but since we're off the gold standard, there is a lot more money available per person than our forebears could have ever accessed. Yet our behaviors and happiness are shackled by the way we think about the money we do or don't have, as though the global supply could somehow run out.

This is evidence of a money blueprint—which few of us are aware we even have. Also called a money mindset, your blueprint consists of a combination of your thoughts, feelings, and actions in the arena of money. Your money blueprint consists primarily of the information or "programming" you received in the past, especially as a child. While it is possible, it is very difficult to change your money blueprint, mindset, or relationship with money as an adult. For something like that to catch on widely, it needs to be mainstreamed. Covey's writing about it decades ago was a start, but because our money blueprint is developed at a young age, unless we get it into schools, it's almost too late for most people.

I can't be the only one who was told that if I worked hard and got good grades I'd end up with a high-paying job, only to realize I was sold a broken promise of a secure future. The plan was to go get a job, then stay with the company for 40 years while they paid me a salary (with benefits) that increased every year, including a generous "final salary" in the form of a pension and other workplace perks.

For most of us, that story is a myth. It might have been true at one point, but times have changed. Over the past 50 years, pension systems, tax systems, and legal systems have drastically evolved, and we are now responsible for our own retirement savings. Some might argue that it's a good thing the government has decided to give us a bit more space and independence, but it feels like we have been abandoned to fend for ourselves with no idea how. Meanwhile, schools continue to peddle the "get good grades and a high-paying job" narrative, when the truth is far different. Job-hopping is the norm, the gig economy continues to grow, what jobs remain are threatened by robots, and the economy keeps on crashing. If you want benefits, a secure retirement, and stability, a job isn't the answer.

The government might not be responsible for personal finance, but it has a duty of care to its citizens—starting with financial education. Yet on an exam that measures students around the world in mathematics, science, and financial literacy, almost 22 percent of 15-year-olds from the US scored below a passing grade.[5] Why? The teachers don't know any better, and neither do those who set the curriculum. They were taught by an education system that's even more outdated, with little understanding about personal finance for themselves. Without their own capability to teach and no curriculum updates to back them up, the vicious cycle continues.

Equally, it should be in the interest of financial entities to have financially solvent and educated customers. Both public and private entities have the ability to change the story for teachers and parents before they pass old myths along to the upcoming generations. What happens at home may hold the greatest influence of all.

Parents who take time to teach their children the important aspects of money and some good financial habits can impart the essentials of financial education no matter what the schools teach. But if the parents don't know much about finance—surprise, surprise—neither will their kids. This is especially true if the parents have bad financial habits: constantly in debt, making bad financial decisions, or complaining about their lack of money. Parental influences, often through observations, are a big part of a child's money blueprint and stay with a child long into adulthood, often for the rest of their life, and can lead to future financial success or ignorance, as well as shaping their money habits and sense of abundance or insecurity.

Even though I grew up in India, my parents were open-minded and easygoing. They had a major influence on who I became as a person, and my siblings and I were never told to become doctors, lawyers, or engineers. They taught me how to cook, clean, dress, behave, and (what I value the most) believe in myself. They also taught me about money. When I was 12 years old, I started earning pocket money. My mother offered me 50 rupees ($0.60) a week or 200 rupees ($2.40) a month. I distinctly remember working out that some months had five weeks, so if I chose weekly, then in those months I'd get 250 rupees ($3)—weekly, please! While my parents taught me the basics, they couldn't go further than that, as they themselves were poor money managers. To this day, my parents believe they have been unlucky when it comes to investing, and that messaging has been difficult for me to overcome. It took me a few decades to discover luck has very little to do with investing.

Most parents are doing the best they can, but their limitations might actually be hurting their kids' knowledge in the long run while also keeping them locked in that tension between a scarcity mindset and a consumeristic one. And it starts early. Think about taking kids to shopping malls—such a consumerist environment—or the influence from friends who have had many similar exposures. It also extends to "alternative" approaches to parenting and talking about money—even books like *Rich Dad, Poor Dad: What the Rich Teach Their Kids About Money That the Poor and Middle Class Do Not!* mostly serve to stoke the desire to make millions. I remember reading the book 20 years ago, heavily subscribing to the Rich Dad mindset. What a deep rabbit hole that turned out to be for me.

So much has changed in the last hundred years, but the unhealthy dynamic of get rich quick schemes—from YouTubers telling you how to retire early to investing in crypto, AI, or the latest craze—is still going strong. But as Renee Christoff, the Head of Corporate Responsibility at T. Rowe Price, tells us, the real solution to scarcity is far less sexy than all that: "Improved financial capability—especially early in life—can result in improved standards of living and more stable communities."

£ € $

In an ideal world, our decisions would be the result of a careful weighing of costs and benefits and informed by existing preferences. We would always make optimal decisions, unaffected by defaults,* price

---

* Defaults refer to the preset choices or options that individuals encounter when making decisions. These defaults often have a significant influence on people's decisions and behavior, even though they might not actively think about or analyze the choices presented to them.

"Improved financial capability—especially early in life—can result in improved standards of living and more stable communities."
—Renee Christoff

framing,* and price anchors.† The work of behavioral economics—a field pretty much created by Daniel Kahneman—intends to step outside of the ideal world and instead studies the effects of psychological, cognitive, emotional, cultural, and social factors on the decisions of individual and institutions and how those decisions vary from those implied by classical economic theory. In his 1976 book, *The Economic Approach to Human Behavior,* economist Gary S. Becker famously outlines a number of ideas known as the pillars of so-called "rational choice" theory. The theory assumes that human actors have stable preferences and engage in maximizing behavior. But in reality, we all suffer from several biases. Chief among them is the status quo bias, which locks us into a prison of indecision.

The status quo bias says that we prefer things to stay as they are, or for the current state of affairs to remain the same. For example, we tend to stick with established brands even though blind tests have shown that preferences for strong brands like Coca-Cola are much lower when people are choosing based on taste alone. Another example of the status quo bias is when we fail to take advantage of investment and savings opportunities.[6] Rather than place our money in investments that have a degree of risk, we often leave our money in low-yield savings accounts. The status quo bias leads us to maintain our financial situation as it currently is, rather than taking a moderate risk to improve our financial outlook. Loss aversion, being "penny wise and

---

* Price framing is a psychological concept in behavioral economics that involves presenting prices or numerical values in a way that influences people's perceptions and decisions. The way prices are framed can significantly impact how individuals perceive the value of a product or service and whether they are more likely to make a purchase.

† Price anchors is a concept often used in marketing and sales, derived from behavioral economics. It involves strategically introducing a reference point, or "anchor," to influence how people perceive and evaluate subsequent prices. The anchor serves as a point of comparison that can bias individuals' judgments and decisions, leading them to perceive prices as either more or less favorable based on the initial anchor.

pound foolish," and the way we relate to small sums of money versus larger sums of money are all factors at play. But the larger influence is the status quo bias, built on a foundation of the fear of change, as it causes us to make the seemingly irrational decision to stay within suboptimal situations.

As we consider our choices, we focus more on what we stand to lose rather than how we might benefit. According to "prospect theory," an economic theory developed by researchers Daniel Kahneman and Amos Tversky in 1979, "losses loom larger than gains."[7] The graph below demonstrates the effects of prospect theory, which describes how individuals choose between options and how they estimate the perceived likelihood of different options.

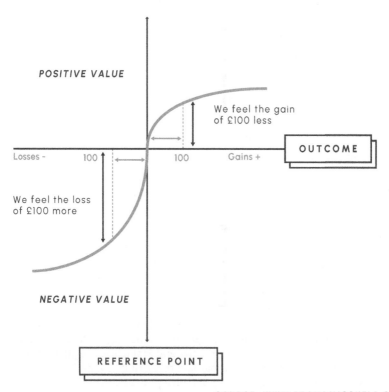

SOURCE: WWW.ECONOMICSHELP.ORG

This concept really blew my mind when I watched a TED Talk by cognitive psychologist Dr. Laurie Santos, titled "A Monkey Economy as Irrational as Ours," about how she had looked for the roots of human irrationality by watching the way our primate relatives make decisions. After studying the actions of a simple economy using monkeys, Dr. Santos discovered that we are far less sophisticated than we think we are.

She began by teaching the monkeys how to use a currency to trade for food, then created a monkey marketplace where they could exchange coins for food. She found that the monkeys don't like to save. They display greedy tendencies, often stealing from one another and from the market salesman. In another experiment, when certain foods became cheaper, monkeys would overbuy. Sound familiar?

During her TED Talk, Dr. Santos performed a simple experiment with the audience to prove just how irrational humans can be:

Pretend you have $1,000. You have two options. In option 1, you can flip a coin: heads, you win $1,000 more; tails, you win $0. In option 2, you are given a risk-free $500—a 50 percent risk-free return. According to Dr. Santos, most people will choose option 2. Sounds rational, and probably something you would do too.

In the second experiment, she gives you $2,000 and offers you two ways to *lose* that money. In option 1, you again flip a coin: heads, you risk losing $1,000; tails, you lose $0. In option 2, you can play it safe and simply lose $500 with no opportunity to gain. Interestingly, most people choose to flip the coin, taking more risk and hoping not to lose anything, rather than accepting a capped loss.

In the first experiment, you max out your gains at $2,000 if you flip the coin, but risk gaining nothing. In the second experiment, you also max out your gains at $2,000 if you flip the coin, but take the risk of potentially losing 50 percent of your capital (versus definitely losing 25% if you take the second option).

Importantly, the risk-free result (option 2 in both experiments) is the same no matter what—you get a guaranteed $1,500. However, in the second experiment, when it comes to potentially losing money versus definitely losing money, most people decide to take excessive risk by flipping the coin as per Kahneman and Tversky's prospect theory. Dr. Santos went a step further and found that the monkeys do the exact same thing! Their survival instinct is to avoid losing something they already have, but in doing so they're irrationally willing to take excessive risk.[8]

You can see how our natural instincts can drive us to make irrational decisions, especially when confronted with a complex situation that impacts survival. No wonder it's hard to change our economic behaviors—they go back 35 million years! No matter how much we have, we all suffer from loss aversion, just like our monkey ancestors.

The status quo and loss aversion biases have perpetuated our current economic system in two ways: 1) most people prefer to continue with a system they know and take excessive risks to avoid losing what they've got, and 2) companies employ experts to manipulate those biases and extract the most value they can. For example, how often have you stayed with a provider by default (status quo) even when they no longer offer the best value compared to competitors?

In politics, the status quo bias is also often used to explain the conservative mindset.[9] People who identify as conservative tend to focus on maintaining traditions and keeping things the way they are. This avoids the risks associated with change but also misses out on the possible benefits that change might bring.

You must have heard the saying "better the devil you know than the angel you don't know." We dislike uncertainty and are risk-averse when making a choice that takes us into the unknown. Even when people want change and vote against incumbents or even the establishment—as was the case with Donald Trump—they don't know which change will give them a better life. Various leaders around the world have advocated for nationalism as a solution to a country's woes and have won office as a result. But the reality is different from the campaign trail, and when in office, most of these leaders tend to favor the rich—none more so than Donald Trump, who has taken the majority of his base for an absolute ride.

Without a foundation of financial literacy or a society structured to counter our primitive survival instincts, we tend to gamble our way through life like Dr. Santos's monkeys, searching for a windfall or wishing we had one. We share in the gambler's fallacy that an event that has happened repeatedly must indicate that a different event is imminent. You'll be the one to break the streak of unhappy consumerism—it's not called retail therapy by accident. Sure, you'll fail a few more times, but eventually your startup will win big! Of course, you'll be miserable in your job a few months longer, but then it will get better. All you know is you can't stop flipping that coin, or what would be left of life?

If you don't have the financial literacy and money management skills to match, not even winning the actual lottery is a solution. Believe it or not, statistics show that 70 percent of lottery winners end up broke, while a third go on to declare bankruptcy in the three- to five-year period following their windfall.[10] How can this be? Runaway spending, toxic investments, and poor accounting can burn up even the biggest windfalls in next to no time. (Isn't it ironic that anyone can buy a lottery ticket but not everyone has access to investments? Investing the same amount that one might spend on lottery tickets would easily yield a decent return over a 40- to 50-year period).

There is a reason we like to gamble. Various studies—including Dr. Santos's monkeynomics experiments—have shown that the dopamine hit we get just as we're about to find out the result of our gamble is extremely addictive. Unsurprisingly, companies prey on these chemicals to keep us hooked.

Shows like CNBC's *Mad Money*—hosted by the energetic Jim Cramer— and updates about markets in newspapers, magazines, and online blogs have huge followings. You would think that a person who has spent a lot of hours in those spaces would be at least somewhat knowledgeable about investments. Well, no. The thing is, many retail investors are always looking to maximize their entry and exit, meaning buy when the market is low and sell when the market is high. Following financial outlooks allows them to attempt timing the market, but listening to people like Cramer is just foolhardy. In February 2023, Cramer said Silicon Valley Bank was a buy at $320. A month later it was shuttered. It's not the first time his advice was disastrous. For almost two decades, Cramer has been paid to host a show where he essentially misleads the public.

History has shown that the only way to build wealth is via long-term discipline. So why do people try to time the markets? Because we apparently have an primal urge to make quick money. Instead of investing for the long term, we try to time the markets to get that dopamine hit that comes before the win. Unfortunately, 80 percent of us lose money, on average, when the results come out[11]—all while thinking we are smarter than others for watching those market shows or that it will somehow magically work for us next time (the gambler's fallacy).

Your average Robinhood* user is like an amateur boxer going in against heavyweight champions—high frequency traders, hedge funds, etc. Even if the underdog is winning against all odds, the heavyweight champions know how to recover. Their arsenal is full of strategic

---

* Robinhood is an online financial technology broker that introduced a new trading model to allow individuals to start investing easily and efficiently with little money.

timeouts and other unsporting tactics ready to help them bounce back from inevitable blows. This is exactly what happened in January 2021 when a group of Reddit traders called r/WallStreetBets went up against hedge funds who had short positions* on GameStop, a brick-and-mortar video game retailer. Investors take short positions when they believe the value of a stock will go down. In the case of GameStop, the hedge funds theorized that given the shift to online gaming platforms, a brick-and-mortar store chain would decrease in value (think brick-and-mortar video rental chain Blockbuster versus Netflix). The Reddit traders had noticed the short positions on GameStop (how much any given stock is short is public data) and rallied their group to buy a lot of GameStop. As more and more Reddit traders bought GameStop, the price started to increase rapidly, which put a short squeeze† on hedge funds to buy the stock as their losses were increasing (therefore further increasing the demand and share price) to cover their short positions. In late January 2021, GameStop's stock price experienced an unprecedented and dramatic surge, going from around $20 per share to over $300 per share within a matter of days, largely driven by the collective buying efforts of retail investors.

However, at the height of the frenzy, Robinhood was asked to post additional collateral of $1 billion.‡ As a result, Robinhood had to restrict

---

* Short selling is a trading strategy where investors borrow shares of a stock and immediately sell them, hoping to buy them back at a lower price later and pocket the difference. This is essentially a bet that the stock's price will decrease.

† A short squeeze occurs when the price of a heavily shorted stock starts to rise significantly, forcing short sellers to buy back shares to cover their positions. This increased demand for the stock can lead to a feedback loop where the price continues to rise rapidly.

‡ Trading platforms like Robinhood have financial relationships with clearinghouses that handle the settlement of trades. Clearinghouses require collateral from brokerage firms to manage the risk associated with these trades. In late January 2021, during the height of the GameStop saga, Robinhood reportedly had to secure a large amount of capital, potentially around $1 billion, as collateral to meet regulatory requirements imposed by the clearinghouses.

their users' activity—temporarily halting them from buying or selling GameStop for a few hours while Robinhood arranged the collateral. That's all the time the hedge funds needed to regroup and sort themselves out.

The professional heavyweight champions managed to recover, even when the armatures had them on the ropes. While the connections between the hedge fund traders, brokerage firms, market makers, and clearinghouses raised questions and led to various investigations, concrete evidence of collusion or manipulation was hard to prove.

No doubt, the GameStop/Robinhood story was a thrilling ride for those participating and entertaining for the public at large, but what transpired was not very different than going to a casino. Retail trading, and buying and selling shares, is a mugs game.* Any financial guru worth their salt will tell you to auto-invest† passively for the long term.

Economist Benjamin Graham famously said: "In the short run, the market is a voting machine, but in the long run, it is a weighing machine," meaning that speculation may be rife in the short term, but it all comes down to the company's performance over time. And for media-driven businesses, feeding a voting machine makes for higher click rates and better engagement—the "voting" becomes their performance. It's good for their business and easy for us, as investors, to go down these rabbit holes of normalized gambling. While a simple monthly investment into an index fund could save us a lot of time and

---

* Mugs game is a colloquial expression that is commonly used in British English to describe an activity or endeavor that is considered foolish, futile, or likely to result in loss or disappointment

† Auto-investing refers to the practice of setting up automatic investments at regular intervals, such as monthly or quarterly. This is usually done through investment accounts or platforms where a fixed amount of money is automatically directed toward specific investment vehicles without requiring manual intervention each time.

Any financial guru worth their salt will tell you to auto-invest passively for the long term.

make us money over the long term, that would be boring and not at all fun to watch on TV.

£ € $

In the '70s, '80s, and '90s, becoming an entrepreneur wasn't an attractive career choice for young people. No one went to college to study entrepreneurship, and no one started a business in their dorm room (unless you were Bill Gates). Entrepreneurship for the young meant delivering newspapers at dawn and pizzas at night, or mowing lawns on Saturday mornings. Baby boomers did entrepreneurial work out of financial necessity, not with intentions of becoming a unicorn.

Over the last decade, we stopped regarding entrepreneurs as "those people" who went to work very early and returned home very late for little to no reward. Now, entrepreneurs are modern-day rock stars—as seen on *Shark Tank* or BBC's *Dragons' Den*. Somewhere along the way, entrepreneurship has been made to look very sexy. I know—I was part of it. One of my startups even sold to Twitter, though it was well after I had left and been washed out.

The reality is that entrepreneurs and founders are gamblers like the rest of us—only they're playing Russian roulette in a casino where venture capitalists (VCs) are the house. Sure, founders may occasionally win, and some win really big, but the VCs *always* win. Though they would have you believe otherwise, VCs take very little risk, passing the majority of it to the founders who work tirelessly to de-risk their VC's investments. And that is why most VC money is deployed to late-stage startups, when they have been through the hardest parts of building a startup and the risk is even lower (though the upside is lower too).

Once I realized the fallacies in the financial education I was taught at school—that getting an education was no guarantee of a good job and stable finances—I turned to that rock star entrepreneurial path. As I was building my first startup, I learned how hard it was to raise capital, and that access to capital is a privilege that's not easy to secure.

There are, broadly, three ways to raise capital:

1. Get an education and a "good job," and build your savings.
2. Borrow money (from friends and family, or a financial institution).
3. Benefit from generational wealth.

The richest have usually benefited from a combination of all three, as those with generational wealth almost always get an education and have access to borrowing money. And ironically, when it comes to borrowing money—the more money you have, the more people (especially at financial institutions) are willing to lend you.

In chapter 4, I said that if you owe the bank $100,000, the bank owns you, but if you owe the bank $100 million, you own the bank. Here's what that means: if you owe the bank a large sum of money, it is in the bank's interest for you to be able to continue in your business—à la Trump, who went bankrupt so many times it's hard to keep track—so that you will be able to pay them off eventually. For example, if you are having trouble meeting loan payments on a substantial amount, the bank might be willing to restructure your payment schedule, hoping to get some of their money back rather than foreclosing on your business, which might return only a small fraction of the principal. On the other hand, if you owe only a small amount the bank won't care much about your livelihood since you probably have assets they can attach to the loan that are worth that amount.

The same is true if you want to start a business with grants or funding rather than loans—having money almost always puts you at an advantage. So, if you're not *born* into a wealthy family, your chances of borrowing money are slim, fairly finite, and extremely expensive.

We tend to think of low-wage workers and gig workers as cogs in the machine, but even startup founders are taken advantage of, and they don't even know it. It's people—meaning the founders and workers who build a company—and not capital that create the value, but when you are the one chasing money, it's not possible to step outside that reality to see the bigger picture—even if that means giving your life and soul to your startup before you get washed out in a down round* or are forced to shut down your company because it's not growing at the rate your VC investors require it to.

Yet no matter how rigged the game might be toward the already rich, the fear of exiting the game runs as deeply as our monkey ancestors' dopamine-based reward centers. The mistaken belief we can exert skill over an outcome that is defined by chance causes us to overestimate our chances of winning. Thus, we create a societal preoccupation with winners against the mathematical reality of our collective long-term losses.

How do we change behaviors that go back 35 million years? Quite simply, we must evolve.

We must begin with this truth: superprofits are not synonymous with survival, and we can change our money blueprint or mindset without losing our access to community and care. If each of us increases our consciousness a little more at a time, we can become our own certainty of safety.

---

* A down round is when a round of new financing usurps control of previous equity holders because the new round of funding is lower than the previous valuation.

This is because VCs have something called a liquidation preference. This means that if a VC invests $1 million at a valuation of $2 million, the VC gets 50% and the founder gets 50%. However, in the next round, if the company raises $2 million at a $3 million valuation, then the new investor gets 66%, the original investor gets 33%, and the founder gets 0%. This is because the $1 million the first investor put in ranks higher than the founder's equity. (Cash equity ranks higher than sweat equity.)

£ € $

Two decades into the 21st century, banks are slowly beginning to realize the need to educate their customers and help them better manage their finances. This has largely happened due to the heavy fines issued to banks for mis-selling products. In 2020, US banks made $198 billion from their credit card portfolios. The vast majority of it came from the poorest consumers—those who revolve credit on their cards rather than paying it off in full. In 2018, British banks made £160 million from account fees, and 80 percent of that came from the poorest 20 percent of people living in the UK. After 10 years of activism by Martin Lewis, founder of MoneySavingExpert.com, The Financial Conduct Authority finally cracked down on unfair bank charges in 2019 to some extent—banning fixed daily and monthly overdraft fees and replacing them with a single interest rate. But it highlights the conflict of interest at play: As a bank, why would you want to educate your customers and thereby reduce your income gained by their mistakes?

If there was ever any doubt whose side the banks are on...but truthfully, they aren't even on the rich people's side. Despite all the perks offered to the rich, bankers' greed to make more and more money often see them ripping off their rich and wealthy customers too—so long as the rich are unaware of what's going on. Michael Lewis masterfully unpacks how they do this in his book *Flash Boys: A Wall Street Revolt*. They have introduced so much complexity that even the majority of people working at the bank have no clue what's actually going on.

Ignorance is not so blissful when your money is slowly disappearing into someone else's pockets. Banks, companies, media corporations, governments—they all make more money when you don't know what to do with your finances. The more debt you accumulate on a credit card, the more you'll have to pay back to the credit card company. The more advertisements are out there convincing you to buy a new car, the more money you'll spend on something you could buy secondhand—if you really even needed to replace the car you already had in the first place.

When I was 23 years old, a financial advisor conducted a workshop at the company I was working with. I lost focus as he illustrated on a PowerPoint slide the power of compounding. I thought to myself, "I'm going to be an entrepreneur. I'm going to make millions. I don't need to do any of this."

Five years later, when I was working on my first startup, a friend tried to tell me the same things about compound interest. Not only did my same old beliefs kick in, but they were further validated, as I was now on my entrepreneurial journey—any day now, I would hit my proverbial jackpot. Another eight years later, after multiple startups (and some exits, but no millions), I paid for an expensive financial course, and—guess what—I was told exactly the same thing! The only difference was that I had lost 13 years of compounding by that point.

To illustrate the power of compounding: if I had simply saved $100 a month for 13 years (an amount I could have afforded), I would have saved $15,600. Had I invested it each month with a 10 percent return, that money would have more than doubled to $32,160. In another 13 years, without any further investment, it would become $117,370. So, at just $100 a month, I lost $85,210 over 13 years ($117,370 minus $32,160).

It gets worse: add another 10 years without any further investments, and I would have had $317,725—compared to the $87,058 I had by starting 13 years later.

In April 2022, I gave a guest lecture at a top-tier business school in the UK, and I asked the students—who on average were in their thirties—how many of them had auto-savings set up. 50 percent said they did, while the other 50 percent chose the YOLO budgeting method: You Only Live Once!

Eager to make up for lost (compounding) time, I decided to start trading in the stock market. I hadn't bought and sold stocks for 15 years—I stopped when I realized that buying and selling stocks was just gambling—but the bull market rally pulled me in. And to goose up my returns, I decided to trade on margin, where you only have to put in 1–5 percent capital, but all gains or losses are yours.*

I started with $800, and it was going really well: in five months I had put in a total of $30,000 and had made roughly $90,000. I kept rolling over all my profits so at that point I had a leveraged portfolio of $1.6 million loaded up with the FAANG† stocks and the S&P 500 index. By earnings season at the end of January 2018, I was anticipating the market to go up. An increase of a few percent was all I needed to double my profits, after which I planned to scale back...or so I thought. It was also at this point that the Fed started hiking interest rates and Trump was raising tariffs against China. The markets were jittery, and despite companies posting results that beat expectations, everything went down. I was all in and got completely wiped out.

When you margin trade, you can lose more than the money you put in. Luckily for me, that wasn't the case—I lost all that I put in, but not any more. No doubt it was a difficult few days and weeks for me, but spare a thought for Alex Kearns and his family. Kearns, a 20-year-old

---

* Margin trading is when you buy and sell stocks or other types of investments with borrowed money. That means you are going into debt to invest. Margin trading is built on leverage, which is the idea that you can use borrowed money to buy more stocks and potentially make more money on your investment.

† FAANG is an acronym that refers to the stocks of five prominent American technology companies: Meta (META) (formerly known as Facebook), Amazon (AMZN), Apple (AAPL), Netflix (NFLX), and Alphabet (GOOG) (formerly known as Google).

college sophomore who was trading with Robinhood, died by suicide in June 2020 after thinking he had a negative $730,165 cash balance on Robinhood. Before he took his life, Kearns made three attempts to contact Robinhood customer service regarding the massive underwater balance, but his messages were met with automated replies.

Turns out, it was an error. The day after Alex took his life, Robinhood sent another automated email suggesting the trade had been resolved and he didn't owe any money. The email read: "Great news! We're reaching out to confirm that you've met your margin call and we've lifted your trade restrictions. If you have any questions about your margin call, please feel free to reach out. We're happy to help!"[12]

In a lawsuit settled a year later, the family claimed that "Robinhood employed aggressive tactics and strategy to lure inexperienced and unsophisticated investors, including Alex, to take big risks with the lure of tantalizing profits."[13]

In the end, the Financial Industrial Regulatory Authority (FINRA) ordered Robinhood to pay about $70 million in fines and restitution to harmed customers, the largest penalty ever handed down by the regulator. But surprise, surprise: Robinhood neither admitted nor denied the charges.

As a parent with young kids, my goal is to teach my kids what I've learned from decades of financial misadventures. But it is not easy. I'm up against our economic system, the rest of society, and our literally millions of years of monkeynomics. This is undoubtedly why people are scared of money and some even believe that it's "evil." All the financial jargon makes it hard to understand what is really going on, so we are simply taught that we need money for food and a roof over our heads. To do that, we cling onto something we think is secure and stable: a job, and perhaps a story about how that job will make everything work out in the end. And many times, it's a job we dislike.

A large part of our society relies on this "rat race" and has normalized it as though there are no other options. The sad truth is that we've been conditioned to focus so hard on survival that we don't even see the option to thrive. The good news is, once we see it, we realize we can set our own selves free.

Now this is all a bit heavy, so let's lighten things up with a joke from Greece...

Chapter 7

Inclus

⁄e Economics

Economists got it wrong (and some of them are even owning up to it): trickle-down economics don't trickle down. In fact, wealth has trickled up instead.* By the time economists began to realize this, wealthy beneficiaries had already become all too powerful, as market power got translated into political power.

Turns out, unfettered free markets, without interferences like higher taxes and regulation, are not the solution to every economic problem. Globalization and advances in technology do not, on their own, bring prosperity to all. It's beyond time to shift toward an inclusive economy in which opportunity expands for everyone, not just the rich, and prosperity is more broadly shared instead of concentrated, especially for those facing the greatest barriers to advancing their well-being.

The good news is, this economy has already been imagined, down to five specific elements: growth, participation, opportunity, stability, and sustainability—that is, inclusive economics.

£ € $

---

* And more recently it has been gushing up.

About a decade ago, when Greece was struggling to service its debt, a joke about the power of liquidity—an essential component to growth—made the rounds. It begins on a slow day in a small Greek village. The streets are deserted, and it is raining. Times are tough, everybody is in debt, and everybody lives on credit.

On this particular day, a rich German tourist is driving through the village. She stops at the local hotel and lays a 100 Euro note on the desk, telling the hotel owner she wants to inspect the room upstairs in order to spend the night. The owner gives her the keys and, as soon as the visitor has walked upstairs, the hotelier grabs the 100 Euro note and runs next door to pay his debt to the butcher.

The butcher takes the 100 Euro note and runs down the street to repay his debt to the pig farmer. The pig farmer takes the 100 Euro note and heads off to pay her bill at the supplier of feed and fuel.

The guy at the farmers' co-op takes the 100 Euro note and runs to pay his drinks bill at the tavern. The bartender slips the money along to the local prostitute drinking at the bar, who has also been facing hard times and has had to offer him "services" on credit. The prostitute then rushes to the hotel and pays off her room bill to the hotel owner—with that same 100 Euro note.

The hotel proprietor then places the 100 Euro note back on the counter so the rich traveler won't suspect a thing. At that moment, the traveler comes down the stairs and picks up the 100 Euro note. As she pockets the money, she says that the rooms are not satisfactory and leaves town.

For a village reliant on external cash, it may seem like a bad result for the money to not enter their economy. Or within the economy, that no one produced anything and no one earned anything. Yet the whole village is now out of debt and looking to the future with a lot more optimism. How? Because 600 Euros' worth of goods and services were actually produced, and each of those six people earned 100 Euros each.

Before the tourist arrived, the village folk didn't have the liquidity—aka cash—of their own, and thus borrowed goods or services on credit. When the tourist arrived, her 100 Euro note became the liquidity needed to repay what each of the six people borrowed.

This worked because people were able to produce and were willing to lend their goods and services on credit. If they hadn't been willing to provide credit, then 600 Euros' worth of goods and services wouldn't have been produced. This is the reality all around the world, in poor communities where almost everyone in the community has the ability to produce but lacks the ability to purchase.

While framed as a joke or silly story, this is actually an excellent demonstration of inclusive economics. Also known as inclusive growth or inclusive capitalism, it refers to an economic approach that emphasizes creating equitable opportunities, reducing disparities, and ensuring that the benefits of economic growth are shared broadly among every section of society. Inclusive growth also means responsible growth. It's not growth at any cost or growth for the sake of growth (i.e., to improve shareholder value). It has a longer-term perspective, with a focus on productive employment as a means of increasing the incomes of poor and excluded groups. The goal of inclusive economics is to achieve economic development alongside increased living standards in a way that not only leads to overall prosperity but also improves the well-being of all individuals, particularly those who have historically been marginalized or disadvantaged. Everyone benefits in inclusive economics, not just the richest in society.

The concept of inclusive economics has its origins in the broader fields of economics and social policy, where scholars, policymakers, and advocates have long recognized the importance of addressing social inequalities and promoting shared prosperity. While there isn't a single specific origin point for the term "inclusive economics," the principles and ideas that underlie the concept have evolved over time through various economic theories, social movements, and policy discussions.

Economists love to talk about the pie that represents the economy—how to grow it, how to slice it, who's getting the biggest share of it, whether the pie is being split fairly, etc. Over the last 40 years, the size of the pie has grown tremendously, but as inequality widened, the pie became more and more disproportionately split. This resulted in the illusion of a "zero sum" system in which people think the size of the pie is fixed. If one slice increases, another slice must get smaller—and that perception reflects reality. There are winners and losers. There are those enjoying a nine-course meal with dessert, and those going hungry. Inclusive economics seeks to increase the overall pie not just for the rich, but for everyone.

Before you get discouraged by the challenge ahead of us to achieve this goal, take heart: thinkers, strategists, activists, and many others around the world—the dreamers and the doers—are working on it. Scholars, policymakers, and advocates have long recognized the importance of addressing social inequalities and promoting shared prosperity. Key moments in the evolution of inclusive economics include:

- In the 1990s, the United Nations Development Programme (UNDP) introduced the Human Development Index (HDI), shifting the focus of development from purely economic indicators to a broader view that includes education, health, and other dimensions of well-being.
- The 2008 financial crisis, along with growing concerns about income inequality, led to renewed discussions about the need for more equitable economic systems.
- In 2015, the United Nations' Sustainable Development Goals (SDGs) encompassed a holistic approach to development that

included goals related to poverty reduction, gender equality, environmental sustainability, and social inclusion. Specifically, note Goal 8: "Promote sustained, inclusive and sustainable economic growth, full and productive employment and decent work for all."

Growing awareness of global inequalities and poverty has spurred discussions about ways to address these issues through policies that prioritize inclusive growth and social justice. Governments and policymakers in various countries continue to introduce policies and initiatives aimed at promoting inclusive growth, reducing poverty, and addressing social disparities.

Acknowledging that we can't leave these goals to enlightened self-interest* is a first step in rising consciousness. While it is true that making decisions that benefit oneself can also lead to positive outcomes for others and the greater community, if it were that easy, we would be living in an inclusive world, not one dominated by neoliberal economic woes.

Ultimately, creating a more harmonious and sustainable society requires a shift in the way we approach economics from both the bottom up and top down. This begins with growth, the first of what I see as five characteristics of an inclusive economy.[1]

---

* Enlightened self-interest is a concept that refers to the idea that individuals or entities can act in their own best interest while also considering the broader interests of others and the well-being of society as a whole. It suggests that making decisions that benefit oneself can also lead to positive outcomes for others and the greater community, ultimately contributing to a more harmonious and sustainable society.

Five Characteristics of an Inclusive Economy

1. Growth

In traditional economic theory, growth is measured by output, such as GDP. But much more is at play than simple metrics, as we saw in chapter 1. Economic growth and the transformation it brings is not just captured by aggregate economic output but includes other outcomes that measure overall well-being. For example, enough goods and services should be produced to enable broad gains in well-being and greater opportunity for all. Good job and work opportunities should be growing and incomes increasing, especially for the poorest. Economic systems should be transforming for the betterment of all, including poor and excluded communities.

Some argue that we should move away from the concept of growth being central to economic development. But with eight billion people on our planet—more than half of which lacking basic necessities—we need growth to ensure that everyone's needs are met. Just like in a jungle—where growth occurs constantly within a balanced ecosystem—responsible, renewable, and sustainable growth is what we need to focus on.

While our story about the Greek village is just a story, there are real-world organizations creating exchange of goods and services within similar communities. Grassroots Economics, a nonprofit foundation, works to empower marginalized communities to take charge of their own livelihoods and economic future. It issues its own community currency—money that is not legal tender but is honored by the community—to provide people a way to exchange goods and services and incubate projects and businesses without relying on national currency that is scarce in their community.

This concept might feel alien to many of us, but the reality is that many people have the capacity to produce goods and services and the desire to buy them from each other, independently of a national currency. Grassroots Economics has proven at the lowest levels that if you provide liquidity, productivity increases. It is a powerful and sustainable way of increasing growth—and just one way to rethink our standards of measurement.

2. Participation

People need to be able to participate fully in economic life and have greater say over their future in it. They should be able to access and participate in markets as workers, consumers, and business owners. And everyone should be rewarded for this participation—not just those who control the capital. In today's reality, you have to start with quite a lot in order to "make it," and most are not so fortunate.

Inclusive economics is based on the simple principle that people are not commodities and shouldn't be treated as such. When labor is viewed as a commodity, businesses want to pay as little as possible for it. But because people are not commodities, wages should reflect livable standards rather than the cheapest way out.

Transparency around, and common knowledge of, business rules and norms would allow people to start a business, find a job, or engage in markets. Technology could be more widely distributed and used to promote greater individual and community well-being. Workers' rights need to be modernized and social safety nets need to be built for those in need. The state will have to look after some people, but everybody else can contribute, whether that is by producing goods or providing a service. Anything that serves humanity especially—driving someone from one place to another, fixing a leak, cutting people's hair—should be compensated in a way that allows people to thrive rather than struggle to make ends meet.

3. Opportunity

Supply and demand works extremely well for nonessential products and services—when each of us has a choice, we can choose to demand

and a producer can choose to supply. But when applied to people, not so much. This is proven by the need for a minimum wage and labor unions: productive people are assets, and while they get paid for their time, very often they are underpaid. This is primarily because the world population in the last century has quadrupled, therefore the "supply" of people far exceeds the opportunities available to them.

But it wasn't just a population explosion that led to people being paid lower wages. During the industrial revolution, industrialists realized that if they got more people to work in their factories they could pay less. Soon after, the education system was bolstered to become a production line for workers.

A lot has been said about hard work and a singular focus being the key to making it in life. But like most of what we've been taught about finances and economics, it's all a myth. Billions of people work extremely hard every day, toiling for hours on end in jobs that are going nowhere while their efforts continue to be exploited. Without upward mobility, the work force stagnates and hope for a better future diminishes.

Inclusive economics ensures more upward mobility opportunities are available for more people, and that all segments of society, especially poor or socially disadvantaged groups, are able to take advantage of these opportunities. Inequality declines. People gain equal access to a more solid economic foundation, including access to adequate public goods, services, and infrastructure, such as public transport, education, clean air, and water.

When we stop treating people like commodities and instead like valued assets in our economy, the pie—meaning, available opportunities within the economy—grows manyfold.

4. Stability

So much of the prejudice and "-isms" that we're still dealing with today come from a fear that "if you have, then I won't have." But economics does not have to be a zero-sum game—my piece of the pie doesn't take away from your piece. Everyone deserves access to healthcare and education and other necessities and there are plenty of resources to make that happen. In order to do that, we need a stable economic system.

Stability means individuals, communities, businesses, and governments have a sufficient degree of confidence in their future and an increased ability to predict the outcome of their economic decisions. Systems are increasingly resilient to shocks and stresses, especially to disruptions with a disproportionate impact on poor or vulnerable communities. Individuals, households, communities, and enterprises feel secure enough to invest in their future.

Ultimately, human well-being should be the central goal of economic performance and social progress, not how someone is faring economically. Stability gives us a foundation from which we can all thrive.

5. Sustainability

Instead of growth at any cost, sustainable growth is the future, and this is only possible due to a mindset shift and rise in consciousness across the planet. Unlike our grandparents who lived through the World Wars, younger generations grew up not having to worry about survival. We are not driven purely by money, and as a result of searching for our passion, wanting to make a difference, and hoping to protect our planet, we are coming together to redefine growth to focus on positive society-wide benefits.

The make-use-dispose or take-make-waste model that the current extractive industrial complex has created is being replaced, albeit slowly, by the more sustainable "circular economy." This involves keeping resources in use for as long as possible and extracting the maximum value from them while in use, then recovering and regenerating products and materials at the end of each service life. This is moving from niche to a larger scale, with increased interest in product design for durability and repairability, which involves designing products to be durable and easy to repair in order to extend their lifespan. For example, modular smartphones with replaceable components allow users to replace only the faulty parts instead of buy a completely new phone. We are also seeing a movement toward remanufacturing and refurbishing, where companies take back used products, such as electronics or appliances, and refurbish them to like-new condition. These products are then resold, reducing the demand for new manufacturing and decreasing waste. In the clothing industry especially (traditionally one of the worst polluters), we are seeing huge growth in textile recycling (where used clothing is collected, sorted, and processed to create new textiles or products) and clothing upcycling (where discarded materials are transformed into higher-value products, such as turning old denim jeans into stylish bags).

In a circular economy, wealth is the social worth of the entire set of assets that contribute to human well-being. These assets are five kinds of capital: financial, natural, produced, human, and social—all of which have the capacity to produce flows of economically desirable outputs. The maintenance of all five kinds of capital is essential for the sustainability of economic development. Particularly in the case of natural capital, which our current economic system rarely considers an asset, human use must preserve or restore nature's ability to maintain its ecology. Therefore, decision-making must thus consider the long-term costs and benefits, and not merely the short-term gains, of human use of our full asset base.

Of course, there are many obstacles to inclusive growth. Take the example of Zambia: in 2009, an analysis by the World Bank suggested that the country's income growth was constrained by poor access to domestic and international markets and information. High indirect costs—mostly attributable to infrastructure service-related inputs in production including energy, transport, telecom, and water, but also insurance, marketing, and professional services—undermined Zambia's competitiveness, limited job creation, and acted as a major constraint to inclusive growth. The report concluded that improving quality and access to secondary and tertiary education is essential if those living in poverty are to benefit from future growth of the economy.

Weak governance and, in particular, poor government effectiveness are factors behind the market coordination failures* that create barriers to inclusive growth.[2] In the case of Zambia, weak governance and poor government effectiveness were the primary causes why the economy was performing worse than it potentially could have been.

Sadly, this is not unique to Zambia. Lack of access to quality education is prevalent across much of the developing world to varying degrees. What's more, the developed world is not immune: access is a major issue driving further income inequality around the world.

Although economists may not be known for their sense of humor, the joke about the 100 Euro note in Greece does more than lighten what is otherwise called the "dismal science." The joke also provides a more optimistic theory of inclusive growth. Along with participation, opportunity, stability, and sustainability, growth itself is a key component of an inclusive economy and one of the characteristics that can provide new economic strategies for countries around the world, from the case study of Zambia above, to the US where inclusive economics is measured in the largest 192 metropolitan cities every year.[3] The 2023

---

* Market coordination failure occurs when a group of stakeholders (typically government and private sector) could achieve a more desirable equilibrium (outcome) but fail because they do not coordinate their decision-making. The effect is often a self-fulfilling prophecy.

Brookings Institute report, which examines pandemic-era patterns of inclusive growth across the US, makes for fascinating reading.[4]

To achieve a circular economy, we must gradually decouple economic activity from the consumption of finite resources and begin to design waste out of the system. This evolution is underpinned by the shift to renewable energy sources—a transition that is already underway, but one that needs to be urgently sped up.

With the shift to a circular economy, we will be able to implement a new economic system that benefits everyone on our planet, and our planet as well. That is the goal of inclusive economics: economic and social wealth sustained over time while helping to maintain intergenerational well-being. The remaining chapters in this book will help you think differently about your participation in the current system, from wherever you fall on that spectrum of influence. But the real shift in thinking is not just about how you spend and make money within the current system. It's about how you think about the nature of money itself.

The next step beyond enlightened self-interest is to move from a scarcity-based mindset to a mindset of abundance—a necessary step for governments to appreciate their role in orchestrating a resilient transition, for business owners to relinquish the need for superprofits and harness their capacity for innovation, and for individuals to shift from being consumers to "collaborative, caring, creative citizens who can shape our communities, organisations, and nations for the better."[*5]

£ € $

---

* As Jon Alexander and Ariane Conrad eloquently put it in their book, *Citizens: Why the Key to Fixing Everything Is All of Us.*

After the 2008 global financial crisis, it became clear that the current economic system is failing. While there was no obvious alternative at that time, the notion that market power and rent-seeking are major sources of today's inequality has become mainstream over the last decade, with growing literature on what can be done about it. Many economies around the world have come to a crossroads: What is the way forward?

Nobel prize-winning economist Joseph Stiglitz and others have long argued that a central determinant of the success of an economy is its rules, and these rules are set by politics. As a result, most books on the global economy go beyond economics and into politics, and many have prescribed ways to fix democracy.

I don't disagree with the need to fix democracy to restore the balance of power. Remember the conclusion we came to in chapter 4: our democracy is a sham. But ultimately, we can't fix anything just because someone says it's a problem.

This is where consciousness and transparency come in. We can only drive change if a large enough segment of the population has that realization *and* wants to take action. In 2016, slim but effective majorities from people who wanted change voted for Brexit in the UK and Trump in the US. They had a realization of sorts, but unfortunately (though not unsurprisingly) the actions they took didn't bear fruit.

Scandal after scandal has continued to rock businesses and politicians, creating the kind of awareness that leads to discontent and hopefully action, but we need more action than just at the ballot box. Remember former British prime minister David Cameron and the Netflix series *Dirty Money* from chapter 5? Well, the Panama Papers (2016),[6] Paradise Papers (2017),[7] and Pandora Papers (2021)[8] show that the offshore money machine operates in every corner of the planet, including the world's largest democracies—and the ultimate beneficial owners* come from more than 200 countries and territories, with the largest contingents from Russia, the UK, Argentina, and China. The key players in the system include elite institutions—multinational banks, law firms, and accounting practices—headquartered in the US and Europe. The leaked papers mentioned above offer merely a glimpse (35 current and former world leaders, and more than 330 politicians and public officials in 91 countries and territories)[9] of the tip of a massive iceberg that we're slowly beginning to discover—yet another sign of how badly our economic system has been distorted.

In 2008, free markets failed, and because industries within those markets were considered too big to fail, governments bailed them out, rescuing the wealthy and giving them even more market power. But as we saw earlier in chapter 3, markets are not free—all the profits went to a minority while the losses were left to the taxpayers.

Given that bailout funds didn't come directly from our individual pockets, it is difficult for the wider population to comprehend that this is what actually happened, but two significant impacts are worth naming. One, the actual dollars and cents in our bank accounts or cash in our hands dropped in value, reducing our buying power, especially to buy assets. And two, our governments were left with less to spend on social infrastructure like healthcare, education, and public transport, effectively diminishing investments for our future. Fifteen years later, the effects of those policies have come home to roost.

But governments didn't stop at diminished investments for our future. In many countries, austerity measures that were put in place

---

* Ultimate beneficial owner: the person who ultimately owns or controls or benefits from an asset; for example, a property or company. The beneficial owner may be different from the legal owner, often through a complex web of shell companies. This setup is especially used by political figures because it can be used to keep politically unpopular or even illicit activities from public view.

to cut existing government expenditure took even more out of our pockets than the bailouts themselves. In addition to austerity and the specific impacts of the 2008 bailouts, we've also begun to realize that the government deregulation revolution of the 1980s and 1990s went too far. The profession of economics, which almost certainly ignored market failures in the past, is now scrambling to find alternatives to the simple laissez-faire message propagated by thinkers such as Milton Friedman and Friedrich Hayek, which led to the neoliberalism and deregulation of the '80s and '90s. Luckily, many economists are starting to realize that true inclusion puts people first, which is what the current models are missing.

Financial deregulation is responsible in part[*] for both the Great Recession that occurred from late 2007 to 2009 and the resulting Global Financial Crisis that continues to haunt us today. With the exception of the Nordic countries, who proactively reskilled workers, free trade might be considered another example of detrimental government deregulation worldwide. Economists are only now realizing how many American workers were affected by Chinese import competition, especially without investments to retrain Western workforces.

There is a broad realization that government is more important, and essential, than neoliberalists believed, so much so that after decades in retreat, governments in some parts of the world have started to step up, including in the EU. From new regulation covering competition policy, climate, worker rights, and much more, to a renewed zeal for industrial policy, some governments around the world are standing up to the private sector and regulating in the interest of citizens. Government is back in business, or so it seems at least in some countries.

Yet when it comes to regulation, if one government were to tighten their regulations in isolation, it might disadvantage them, at least at

---

* The other part is human greed.

Luckily, many economists are starting to realize that true inclusion puts people first, which is what the current models are missing.

first. Global cooperation is desperately needed, and little of it is happening. But as we head from a unipolar world (one ostensibly ruled by the US and its allies) to a bipolar world (with the G7 countries of the US and friends on one side, and China and its allies on the other), there are likely to be more challenges ahead.

Whoever goes first, governments are going to have a big role to play going forward. To create inclusive economies, there is already an urgent need for them to step up and fund innovation, mandate clean energy, and support their economies more broadly with policies that will benefit those other than just the wealthy. Azeem Azhar, entrepreneur and creator of the influential Exponential View newsletter, predicted that the year 2023 would be a watershed for a new doctrine he calls "catalytic government."* He explains that rather than traditional interventions, catalytic policy interventions will incentivize the private sector to focus on accelerating key strategic areas—green energy transition, computing power (semiconductors), etc.—without government getting in the way. He went on to say:

> *Catalytic governments, however, will be opinionated. They will set industrial, technological, and national security priorities. But they will use a wide variety of tools to encourage and support businesses to meet those priorities. The government will seek to shape outcomes, not leave it to the market.*[10]

If you're wondering why governments should intervene at all, note that government is important for spending, regulating, and innovating—and let's not forget much of the innovation we have today can be traced back to government funding (e.g., semiconductors, GPS

---

* A catalytic government refers to a governmental approach that functions as a catalyst for positive change, progress, and development within a society or economy. In this context, the government takes on a proactive role in initiating and supporting policies and projects that stimulate growth, innovation, and overall improvement.

technology, and the internet). Azhar says, "The risks of leaving things to the market—where the industry oversupplied us with dating apps and 10-minute delivery services—are too great." And he predicts that governments will not seek to replace the role of research or industry in these activities; rather, they will seek to support and accelerate them. For example, President Biden's Inflation Reduction Act is expected to stimulate nine million new jobs over the next decade.[11] The UK government announced ambitious plans including a multibillion-dollar program "Powering Up Britain" and expects to create two million new long-term good quality green jobs by 2030.[12] The EU aims to make Europe the first climate-neutral continent by 2050 and is expected to create an additional 2.5 million jobs by 2030.[13] And globally, the C40 cities initiative is spearheading the creation of 50 million good, green jobs by the end of the decade.[14] Overall, most jobs will be in the private sector, though not all of the jobs created will be net new employment as some workers get hired away from other jobs that may disappear due to the transition.

And there is hope that catalytic government policies will shift the balance from large corporations to local communities. Here's Azhar again:

> Because it has less faith in unbridled finance and more faith in the interaction of human and technological capital, catalytic government will end up nurturing local communities over anonymous global supply chains.

With unprecedented investments into growing sectors like clean energy, clean manufacturing, and energy-efficient buildings, governments can stimulate economic growth and innovation. And perhaps this increased economic output will ultimately help governments do even more for their citizens.

£ € $

After several decades when general welfare increased, over the last two decades the 1 percent have left the rest of us behind. Most of this is attributed to choices made by governments, which begs the question: What if we made different policies? Despite prevailing narratives, there are genuine pathways for inclusive economics to include everyone. One consideration that catalytic governments could make is Universal Basic Services, or UBS. Unlike the more widely discussed Universal Basic Income (UBI), UBS denotes a wide range of free public services enabling every citizen to meet their basic needs and achieve certain levels of security, opportunity, and participation.

The core principles of UBS are:

- Universal: guaranteed entitlement according to need, not one's ability to pay.
- Basic: sufficient rather than minimal, enabling people to meet their basic needs, participate in society, and flourish.
- Services: collectively generated activities that serve the public interest.

UBS typically are a collection of seven free public services that enable every citizen to live a larger life by ensuring access to safety, opportunity, and participation. These are shelter, food, healthcare, education, transportation, information, and legal services.

Drawing on Maslow's famous hierarchy of needs,* universal access to basic services is one way to guarantee a minimum standard of living. By meeting people's physiological needs (food, water, shelter), and providing them with safety and security, we provide a strong foundation for self-esteem and community building. A platform of basic services makes real the promise that a basic income pretends to deliver. Further, advocates for UBS highlight that focusing on more comprehensive provision of services rather than only giving cash handouts preserves a strong incentive for citizens to work, while the state takes care of those who cannot work.

If we were to give everyone a UBI, would we need UBS? Advocates for UBS argue that for certain goods, direct provision by the state has advantages that cash transfers or UBI cannot compete with. One reason is that cash transfers may not be enough to cover needs. The amount of health or social care someone needs varies widely over the course of one's life and from person to person in ways that are unpredictable. Given this, if everyone were given an equal cash payment, the outcome would be unequal, as those with high needs would be unable to cover the cost of their care.

As we saw in chapter 1, the NHS isn't without its flaws and is in need of major reform to make it more efficient, but one has only to look at the US healthcare system to see the dangers of for-profit private provision. President Obama attempted to tackle the issues of unequal needs by providing more universal and subsidized access to insurance with the introduction of the Affordable Care Act, colloquially known as Obamacare. A decade later, it is now embedded in the healthcare system, roughly halving the uninsured share of the population, especially by preventing premiums from going up due to preexisting

---

* Maslow's "Hierarchy of Needs" is a psychological theory proposed by Abraham Maslow in 1943. It is a framework that categorizes human needs in a hierarchical manner, representing the progression of human motivation and development.

conditions and addressing affordability for freelance workers. However, Obamacare did not change the structural ownership at the heart of healthcare. As a result, resources are channeled toward where the money is rather than toward the needs.

When healthcare is provided for profit, there are huge incentives at play. Hospitals overtreat or prioritize the most lucrative treatments, and stick insurance companies with the bill. Of course, insurance companies are for-profit too and so they price it into premiums, which is why health insurance remains so expensive in the US.

In the post-war era, many countries, including the US (in spite of its resistance to universal healthcare) moved toward what was previously known as the welfare state. In the UK, for example:

- The NHS was born in 1948—providing free universal healthcare. Prior to the NHS, patients were generally required to pay for their healthcare. Free treatment was sometimes available from charitable voluntary hospitals.
- Concessionary travel schemes were introduced to provide free travel on public transport for kids under 11, residents of cities who were aged 60 and over (now 66), or those who have a disability.
- Social housing (also known in the US as low-income or affordable housing) boomed in the '50s and '60s, with mixed socioeconomic housing throughout the country—even today, social housing exists in Chelsea right next to the billionaires' row, though as you would expect, much has changed in the last few decades. Social house building in England is at its lowest rate in decades. Since 1991, there has been an average annual net loss of 24,000 social homes, resulting in 1.4 million fewer households in social housing than there were in 1980.
- Free education was introduced in the late 19th century and remains free for primary and secondary state schools today. Up

until 1998, it was free to go to university too. Now there's a fixed fee of around $11,000 per year for all courses.

• Food banks and legal aid services are available to citizens around the country, provided by both local councils and charities.

The problem in the UK is that, other than the NHS and the state school system, none of the other basic services are universal. The NHS is the pride of the nation and there is no stigma attached to using it, and by and large that is true for state schools too. But that's not the case with the other services, which are means tested, difficult to access, and signal that you can't afford something independently. Equally, many who desperately need these services are ashamed to request them or don't know how to.

A closer look at funding to the NHS shows that since 1979–1980, the budget has grown fourfold in real terms and has doubled its share of the GDP. However, at the same time the population has grown by 10.6 million, spending per person has not grown as fast as the total spend. And it's not only the population headcount that has changed. So too has the demographic structure. In particular, the number of older people has grown, both in absolute terms and also as a proportion of the total population.[15]

Why can't a rich country like the UK fund the NHS adequately? It comes down to policy. The Conservative government came to power in 2010—believing in a smaller government, lower taxes, and less government spending—and introduced austerity measures that reduced the capacity of the NHS over the following decade. Real terms spending increases per head averaged just 0.4 percent a year and included four years in which spending per head actually fell. It was a period of stagnation in terms of the resources available to the NHS to fund improvements in healthcare quality. [16]

TIME PERIOD, POLITICAL PARTY	AVERAGE ANNUAL CHANGE IN PER CAPITA HEALTH SPENDING (ADJUSTED)
1979–1997, Conservatives	2.03%
1997–2010, Labour	5.67%
2010–2015, Conservatives/Liberal Democrats coalition	-0.07%
2015–2021, Conservatives	-0.03%
2021–2024, Conservatives – committed spend	2.05%

CHANGES IN UK HEALTH SPENDING PER CAPITA, ADJUSTED FOR DEMOGRAPHIC CHANGES[17]

It should come as no surprise that the Conservatives hollowed out the NHS. But it was even worse than expected. The Boris Johnson Brexit bus lie[*18] that the NHS would get an extra £350 million a week was one of the most contentious issues of the 2016 EU referendum campaign. Obviously, none of that money went where it was said it would. We went from clapping for the NHS during the pandemic to unprecedented strikes by junior doctors and nurses due to the cost-of-living crisis post-pandemic—causing over half a million patient appointments to be rescheduled.

After years of underinvestment, the Conservatives have finally committed to increase spending by £13.2 billion in cash, although rising

---

* For those outside the UK, during the Brexit campaign Boris Johnson toured in a bus emblazoned with large lettering claiming, "We send the EU £350 million a week" followed by "let's fund our NHS instead."

prices will cut this to around £2.4 billion.[19] In 2023, the opposition leader Keir Starmer unveiled Labour's mission to create an NHS fit for the future. We'll just have to wait and see how that effects how people vote. But even so, as we saw at the end of chapter 4, restricting our responsibility to just the ballot box and leaving the rest to even the most progressive government isn't going to solve our problems.

One possible reason we don't have UBS, at least in the UK, is that businesses (and the wealthy) don't want to pay for it. Not just in taxes—that part is understandable—but much more in terms of wages. When people are desperate to make ends meet, to pay bills, and have a roof over their heads, they tend to accept less. As we will see in the next chapter, people are not paid what they are worth—they are paid what they have the power to negotiate. The more basic services people have access to, the more power they have to negotiate, and that's a big concern for businesses that are solely focused on profits and maximizing shareholder returns.

With this singular focus, big business and their lobbyists have succeeded in influencing governments who have continued to provide favorable policies to the private sector. For example, Walmart, the largest employer in the world, with 2.3 million employees,[20] pays most of its workers so poorly that they need further support from federal aid just to survive, while Walmart makes record profits. And it's not just Walmart: Amazon, Kroger, Dollar General, and other food service and retail giants are accomplices too, costing taxpayers tens of billions of dollars every year. Overall, 70 percent of the 21 million federal aid beneficiaries in the US work full time.[21]

£ € $

As technology continues to define and expand employment opportunities, globalization, and new definitions of growth and access in the

"There is enough for everyone's need but not enough for everyone's greed."
—Mahatma Gandhi

information age, it is critical for our economic system to be able to reward people's contributions appropriately. And, as with most things, shifts happen gradually. Thankfully, movement toward inclusive economics has already begun.

In 2019, Salesforce founder and CEO Marc Benioff wrote in *The New York Times* why we need a new capitalism.[22] He rightly points out that the current system has led to profound wealth and income inequality. To fix it, we need businesses and executives to value purpose alongside profit. Profits are important, but so is society. The world is hungry, not because there is no food, but because those who need it are not getting it. One way or the other, those who have the power and the means have not cared enough to do something about it. If our quest for greater profits leaves our world worse off than before, then all we will have taught our children is the power of greed. As long as each of us continues to think greed is good, no change will be possible. As Mahatma Gandhi said, "There is enough for everyone's need but not enough for everyone's greed."

The move from shareholder capitalism to stakeholder capitalism is promising. Stakeholder capitalism is a term that was coined in 2019 by Business Roundtable as they finally realized the need to consider employees and other stakeholders and not just shareholders. B Corp certified companies* are also leading the way, with some B Corps pledging to give away (and actually giving away) 50 percent of their profits to charity. These organizations strive not only for profits, but for the betterment of the world around them. And let's not forget cooperative enterprises and employee-owned businesses, which have been around in successful capacities for the last 180 years.

This is about more than having a state versus market-led approach. For me, it isn't about whether the state should have more or less control

---

* B Corp is a type of business entity that is legally structured to prioritize social and environmental goals alongside financial profits.

over spending, or own more of a corporation's or country's assets. I believe it's about how each one of us participates in our economic system, and how together we can shift the rewards from people who control the capital to people who create value through their productivity. We need to restore the balance, and inclusive economics rewards both people and capital.

Buckminster Fuller once said: "You never change things by fighting the existing reality. To change something, build a new model that makes the existing model obsolete." He's right—as demographics change, political and economic systems will change. 2016 was the last US election when baby boomers were the majority. Over time, I believe we will have a new economic system in the same way that neoliberalism once came into force.

If not, I see us heading toward some form of anarchy or dystopia. The people who control the capital have become so powerful that they have gained both regulatory capture and industry capture. And their greed, as all greed, knows no limits. Those in power—and I don't mean politicians, though let's not exclude them—simply can't help themselves from exploiting the rest of the world.

Yet just as there will always be people who smoke cigarettes in spite of the negative impacts, there will always be some who subscribe to megaprofit capitalism that treats people as commodities and commodities as infinitely extractable. That doesn't mean we have to join or support them. It is said that over 80 percent of the world's economy is controlled by fewer than 2,500 people. That's 0.00003 percent—and yes, you read that correctly, with four zeros after the decimal. If even a 10 percent change happens in the hearts of those 2,500, the entire world will change.

That is a hopeful aspiration—but if all we do is hope for the powerful to be less greedy, we're implicit as well. By continuing to worship the

"You never change things by fighting the existing reality. To change something, build a new model that makes the existing model obsolete."
—*Buckminster Fuller*

rich and attempting to emulate them in our wealth-building gambles, we're perpetuating the system they thrive on. Remember, the government is for the people, by the people, and of the people. If the people's consciousness is low, we get a government with a low consciousness in return. The same goes for businesses.

With an increase in consciousness, some people are willing to earn less to do more meaningful work, as discussed in chapter 5. But even as scandal after scandal breaks, movements like #OccupyWallStreet, #DeleteFacebook, #DeleteUber, #BoycottAmazon, and #AmazonStrike often gain early momentum, then turn out to be short-lived. The vortex that is our current economic system is powerful and will require a much stronger collective movement that can endure long enough to force it to reach a tipping point.

Raising our own consciousness is the only change we can actually enact—but once we do, our opinion of wealth and power automatically changes too, and with it, the way we sustain or transform the economic systems we participate in, toward an inclusive economy.

The next chapter shows us that transformation is possible by starting small.

Chapter 8
Powe

ed by People

In 1975, economist E. F. Schumacher's book, *Small Is Beautiful: A Study of Economics as if People Mattered,* challenged the 20th century's intoxication with "giantism," or the idea that bigger is better. Schumacher believed creating bigger markets and bigger political entities would lead to a dehumanization of people and the economic systems that ordered their lives, warning that they would ultimately begin making decisions on the basis of profitability rather than human need.

Schumacher predicted the rise of depression, anxiety, panic attacks, and stress that we see now and countered it all with the repeating message that "small is beautiful." And, he noted, a return to human scale—centering human needs and human relationships—would lead to the ethical response of stewardship of the environment. In his view, people-centered economics would enable environmental and human sustainability.[1]

Today, small has become cool, but only as part of a branding strategy that masks our ongoing concentration of political and economic power. Over time, mergers and acquisitions in industry after industry inevitably happened in the name of efficiency with the benefits largely returning to shareholders rather than workers—many of whom face the axe when companies merge. And at the moment, the model is deeply woven into society—everything eventually builds to something bigger. It seems that giantism has triumphed. Why? Because "greed is good," of course!

Take the simple example of an average working environment: those who take on more responsibility get paid more. People who are really good at what they do get promoted as a reward for doing their job well, often moving into a managerial position. Now they no longer do the work they were so good at, but rather oversee others as they do it. It's not all bad—there is some merit to this, as the person gets to pass on skills and experience to others in a cycle they probably benefited from as well. Some are natural managers too, making it a good fit for everyone. But what about those who aren't suited to managing people or simply don't want to do it? In professional services and a few other industries, new tracks have been formed to allow specialists to progress in their career without saddling them with an army of direct reports. But overall, this is the only way up the ladder—and since it moves automatically, the ladder functions more like an escalator.

The idea is that *managing* more creates more value, which justifies more compensation. We saw this thinking take hold in the 1990s, when CEO and executive pay skyrocketed. In the US, top-level pay is often 300 times more than that of the average employee, though clearly a CEO cannot be 300 times more productive. Value creation—which is the process of turning labor and resources into something that meets the needs of others—is driven by people. Financial capital is necessary, of course, and it is why inclusive economics includes growth as a pillar. But when we put too much emphasis on capital and growth, too much power is transferred to those who control the major capital flows.

The disproportionate rewards system for "investors" and senior/executive management has been further exacerbated by senior management's remuneration becoming linked to the share price, bringing investors and management into alignment. As a result, benefits go to investors and management, while workers feel the consequences of cost cutting in the name of efficiency and profitability.

White-collar workers reap the rewards of this perception as well, while blue-collar workers, and often gig workers, are paid minimum wage—or less than minimum wage if there isn't enough work for them.

Last year, my wife and I had window blinds installed in our house. We live in the UK, where the sun rises early and sets late for half the year, and anyone with young kids knows the value of good blinds. The blinds took months to arrive—made to measure for each of our existing windows before being manufactured in China. When they finally got here, a person came and spent the whole day installing them—including eating lunch in his van around 4:00 p.m. He did a good job, but because there was an issue with one of the blinds, the owner of the business visited to have a look.

The owner arrived in a rather swanky pickup truck, creating the appearance that his business was doing very well. Additionally, because we had to pay a 50 percent deposit (presumably to cover the cost of the blinds) it didn't seem like a capital-intensive business. Of course, the owner is responsible for sales and marketing—he has a slick website with videos and testimonials that convinced us to buy. But it left me wondering who made more money: the installer for a day's work, or the owner who arranged for the blinds to be ordered and shipped from China and double-checked the work once it was done. My guess is the owner made much more. He also likely has three or four installers working for him, multiplying his income even further, while each installer—doing the actual work—just gets by.

When work like this—installation, delivery, repair—is classified as self-employed, there isn't any requirement for the businesses who engage the worker's services to pay them for all of their time. Ride-sharing platforms, for example, don't pay their drivers for wait time, or even the time it takes or the fuel it costs them to drive to a pickup point.

It gets worse for those in the creative industry. Spotify pays the average musician around just $0.003 per song stream. A friend of mine explained to me how the $10 subscription you pay each month gets divided: first a big chunk to Spotify, let's call it $4, then the rest to artists based on a percentage of how many times a song plays. If Ed Sheeran owns 1 percent of all the music played on Spotify, then he gets 1 percent of $6 ($0.06) from every premium user's subscription whether they listened to Ed Sheeran or not. And we know that the majority of that goes to the record labels. It's no wonder that Taylor Swift pulled her entire catalog off Spotify and rival services in 2014, saying, "I'm not willing to contribute my life's work to an experiment that I don't feel fairly compensates the writers, producers, artists, and creators of this music."[2]

Swift finally ended her three-year boycott of streaming service over royalties, returning to streaming services to "thank her fans" for her album *1989* passing 10 million in sales. But who really knows what happened behind the scenes? A year after that decision, she signed a new deal with Universal that included remarkable personal terms for herself.

But it is the power the record labels hold (the big three control 70 percent of the market) that makes artists uniquely vulnerable to this kind of exploitation. These labels have the ability to turn you into a mega star or crush your dreams. You can make decisions on principle if you're Taylor Swift, but what about struggling artists? If they aren't earning enough, it may have nothing to do with how good they are, but rather the fact that the platform on which they publish (or self-publish) their music isn't paying them their fair share. And sadly, research in 2019 shows that exploitation is seen as more acceptable if workers are passionate about what they do.[3]

Despite all of the democratization offered to artists—anyone can release a song (or publish a book) these days—the streaming platforms put the record labels back in business. Everyday 100,000 new songs are uploaded, and unless you're signed to a record label, it's incredibly hard to get enough visibility to make it through the noise.

All this is made possible by what Cory Doctorow and Rebecca Giblin call "chokepoint capitalism" in their eponymous book *Chokepoint Capitalism: How Big Tech and Big Content Captured Creative Labor Markets and How We'll Win Them Back*.[4] Doctorow and Giblin go into great detail to show how exploitative businesses create insurmountable barriers to competition that enable them to capture value that should rightfully go to others. Reinforcing a theme we've seen over and over in this book, Doctorow and Giblin say, "Competition is supposed to be fundamental to capitalism. Over the last four decades though, greedy robber barons have worked out how to lock in customers and suppliers, eliminate competitors, and shake down everyone for more than their fair share."[5]

Chokepoints are not unique to the creative industries. Lots of companies try to create the conditions that will allow them to take a disproportionate share of the value of other people's labor.

In his utopian novel *Another Now: Dispatches from an Alternative Present*, former Greek finance minister Yanis Varoufakis argues that all people working in a given business should be treated equally because without people you simply can't produce anything. In his example, two people start a café and hire a server. The waitress then has an equal share in the business, with all three of them owning a third each. Similarly, in a factory, every worker *and* the management would have equal ownership.[6]

In essence, he is describing a cooperative.

And his argument is not wrong. Without people, not a single business on this planet would survive. Farmers grow crops, workers build goods, and intangible products like computer code and creative ideas are all necessities and all inextricable from the people who create them. We haven't yet reached a state of autonomous artificial intelligence to prove otherwise—though that might be coming soon. And while corporations believe that no one on the production line is irreplaceable, the same is true on a corporate level. Steve Jobs's untimely passing is a clear example that a single person leaving a business doesn't bring about its downfall, and they likely shouldn't be compensated as though that is the case. That said, founders are critical to the success of startups and small businesses. Going back to the café example above, let's assume that of the two people who start the café, one is the chief and the other looks after the marketing, finance, and administrative aspects of the business. If the server left the business, they would find it easier to find another, as compared to having to replace one of the founders. Steve Jobs was critical to Apple's success in their early days, and also, as it turned out, after this return to the company when it was struggling—11 years after he had been ousted. Perhaps he would have created even more value if he were around today, but Tim Cook seems to be doing just fine.

In the last 60 years, US GDP per capita has more than doubled, and productivity has increased sevenfold. But in the same period, pay for workers went up by less than a fifth of the increase in productivity. In the vast majority of businesses, the people who do the heavy lifting don't get their share of the upside, and that's because opportunities remain exclusive by design rather than inclusive and open to everyone.

Would it harm businesses to disburse the rewards more evenly? For argument's sake, let's say Uber did give all their drivers 10 percent shares—would it matter to their existing shareholders to have $98 billion instead of $112 billion? The same question applies for Amazon and all other gig economy businesses: Why do those who provide the capital get to take all the spoils?

The people at the bottom who create the initial value see very little of it in return while those who are further up the chain extract the majority. No doubt the supply chain is important, or the farmer's produce would rot on the farm—but is it worth the 80 percent the chain takes while the farmer gets by on the little that's left?

£ € $

Society has a warped view of people's contribution and value because our economic system treats people as a commodity. And because we are treated as a commodity, here's what happens when supply/demand changes.

Historically, societies have needed more people to be educated and skilled in order to grow—but as more of the masses reached higher levels of education in the last three decades than ever before, job opportunities simply did not grow at the same pace. As a result, competition for the limited number of available jobs grew, and companies took advantage of that scarcity by paying as little as possible to the competing workers, all in the name of maximizing value to shareholders. Across the globe, millennial students took the brunt of this burden, leaving them frustrated with their student loan payments for degrees they can't use or jobs that don't pay enough to cover their loan payments. This was even worse for those who graduated during the global financial crisis and, more recently, during the pandemic.

Women have also had a historically difficult time in the workplace. Misogyny and male chauvinism have been major contributing factors, but ultimately it is profit seeking that continually gives women the raw end of the deal. According to the U.S. Census Bureau, in 1960 a woman made 60 cents for every dollar made by a man. Forty years later, in 2000, that gap had been narrowed by just 10 cents. It has taken two decades more to shave another dime off the gap. Today, women still make 20 percent less on average than their male counterparts, and the gender pay gap is not expected to close completely for another 125 years. Do we really need more than a century to recognize that women who are doing the same job as men should be paid an equal wage?

The problem isn't logical because perception is the real culprit. The reality, as a McKinsey & Company study showed, is that companies with more gender diversity on their executive teams do better—they are 21 percent more likely to outperform less diverse teams in terms of profitability.[7]

In 2015, Salesforce founder and CEO Marc Benioff—among a rare breed of billionaires who actually want to be taxed more—says he initially didn't believe any gender-based pay disparities were pervasive when he was confronted by his employee success chief. He had been working hard at this problem for three solid years, starting in 2012 when he began to notice, with horror, that when he called a meeting, the number of women in the room was often close to zero. He soon discovered that less than 29 percent of Salesforce's total employees were women, and they made up only 14 percent at the leadership level. With a higher consciousness than most of his peers, Benioff was, and is, much more interested in general welfare, starting at but not limited to Salesforce. As a result, his decision to close the gender pay gap at Salesforce was a no brainer.

It wasn't an easy process or a cheap one: it took three pay assessments and cost a total of $8.7 million per year to address differences in pay based on gender, race, and ethnicity. But the payoff was incalculable, with benefits that will continue to accrue for years—increased employee morale and satisfaction translating to profitability gains as highlighted by the McKinsey & Company study. In addition, for two years in a row after this effort, Salesforce landed the number one spot on *Fortune*'s list of best companies to work for, as well as the top spot on *People magazine's* list of "Companies That Care"—good PR no doubt, but more importantly, it also resulted in attracting the best talent and more customers who want to do business with an ethically run company.

Post-pandemic, more businesses are waking up to the fact that they can't treat people like commodities. Although it remains to be seen how deep it goes—are they only being friendly to employees when they need them? What will happen when times of surplus return?

£ € $

The late 2000s saw the emergence of the "sharing economy," defined as an economic system in which personal assets like a car, house, etc. are shared between private individuals, either freely or for a fee, typically by means of the internet. When it first started, it was much more personal than it is now. When it was small, it felt like more than a transaction. Guests would live with their hosts (in their spare bedroom or even on a couch in the living room) and often get more than just accommodation. Relationships were built and real cultural exchanges took place. Hosts could differentiate themselves with their personality. But as the industry grew, all that changed. Now the majority of hosts typically do not live in the same property as their guests. As the platforms became bigger, they attracted different clientele too. These visitors wanted to be left alone. For families going on holiday, renting an entire home rather than staying at a hotel or resort is a different, often preferable vibe.

Smartphones enabled this kind of networking at an unprecedented level, and the idea of earning extra cash from your possessions when you aren't using them quickly caught on. Platforms like Uber and Airbnb provided the first opportunities that, at the beginning, benefited people on both sides of the trade. People began renting out spare rooms or using their car to make extra income on the side.

Workers who commuted into cities would pick up people on their way, do their day job, then turn on their Uber app to drive people back in the evening.

But even as individuals answered the call to share their resources, the platforms that enabled sharing couldn't sustain themselves (as defined by giantism) purely on side hustles. They needed to be more reliable, which required people who could work full time. To work full time, people began leasing cars, renting homes, and driving with the hope of making a living rather than getting better utility from assets they already owned.

Strategist Louisa Heinrich wrote about this phenomenon in a 2015 post she titled "Sharing, Shmaring." She said this (my comment in brackets):

> Most of the businesses lumped together underneath the "sharing economy" moniker have nothing to do with sharing. Sharing is free, sharing is noncommercial. Sharing might stretch to collective ownership or swapping used goods, but it definitely doesn't mean profit [especially when the profits aren't shared with the gig workers]. When we tell our kids to share their toys, we're not telling them to charge Jimmy by the hour to play with their Lego. Whereas Airbnb, Relay-Rides, TaskRabbit et al. are very commercial indeed. Labeling them with the word "sharing" misses the critical point that these businesses are proving: humans like to do business with other humans.[8]

As with so many other industries, it soon became apparent that the very people who helped build these platforms to astonishingly high valuations—often in the tens of billions—were being squeezed. Uber became the largest taxi company that doesn't own a single taxi; without people to drive their personal cars, the business itself wouldn't exist, much less at the level it does now. Valued at $112 billion in April 2021, they have fought tooth and nail to classify their drivers as "partners" and not employees. I'm not saying their drivers should be employees, but what I am saying is that their drivers should partake in the company's overall wealth creation—given they are such a key success factor.

Plenty of reports also cited anecdotal evidence that these platforms are improving financial health for gig workers, touting them as success stories—and legitimizing questionable practices. It is easy to find three or five stories of gig workers who are grateful: they have an income when they previously didn't, while some are able to supplement existing income or earn money while defining their own hours. Some have cars for the first time in their life and they can use them for their family when not working—though it should be noted that this "benefit" contradicts the origins of the so-called sharing economy.

There are, of course, wild success stories, where some early drivers made so much money that they now have a fleet of cars on the platform with other drivers driving for them—much like a pyramid scheme, where those who get in early earn from the efforts of those who get in later.

Gig workers report a feeling of independence that comes from not having to report to a manager the way they had to at other jobs. One driver told me that if he felt tired, he could switch off the app and have a nap and nobody would question him. But these platforms have other ways of getting their so-called partners to stay on the platform. They run promotions or challenges that "incentivize" more working hours. An example: 50 trips in three days gives you a cash bonus over and above the money you make for those trips and customer tips.

For every success story, however, there are plenty others about how much gig workers struggle under financial pressure, trying to make ends meet. Some share a car with another driver, each driving for 12 hours so that the car is utilized fully. But when the car breaks down, both of them temporarily lose their income and have to foot the bill to fix the car. Others drive for up to 16 hours a day and sleep in their cars on the off hours—platforms are cracking down on this, but not very effectively, as drivers can work for multiple platforms.

When the pandemic hit, I was venture building for Catalyst Fund, a startup accelerator that helped inclusive fintech startups reach product-market fit.* The startup we were helping was providing microloans to gig workers. The first step in this process is to validate the product offering, so a colleague and I began doing user research through interviews with gig workers in India to understand their financial lives so they would be better served with financial products from a range of different delivery platforms. We spoke to Uber drivers, food bicycle delivery riders, and grocery delivery riders.

For these people, gig work wasn't a side hustle. It was their full-time job.

Two stories really stuck with me—the first came from April 2020, when India was in a strict lockdown. All restaurants were closed and ride-sharing companies went with them. Hari had been working with an online supermarket for two years. Like Hari, the only gig workers who still had work were grocery delivery workers—and those platforms were hiring, lapping up lucky workers who could step into new openings. Hari explained to us that demand for those gigs skyrocketed, alongside two things: the grocery delivery platforms reduced commissions by 20 percent, and the basket size of each order increased due to people buying more than just one-off items via delivery. That left delivery riders, like Hari, carrying big bulky bags of groceries on their bikes while being paid less. What's more, now that there were

---

* Product-market fit (PMF) is a concept in business and entrepreneurship that signifies the alignment between a company's product or service and the needs and preferences of its target market.

more riders on the platform, each gig worker got fewer trips—a theme we kept hearing as we spoke to more and more gig workers. Hari grew frustrated and eventually quit his job, moving back to his village.

The second was a man, let's call him Rahman, who was married with two kids, aged one and two years old. He lived 20 kilometers away from the Indian city of Hyderabad. To save time and the cost of fuel, he lived in a hostel for six days a week, going home just one day a week. For the year prior, his father had been handicapped—one hand and leg were paralyzed. While his mother took care of his father, Rahman and his brother paid for his father's medical expenses, making them the two income earners in the family. While his small salary (stipend) stayed the same during the pandemic, his main source of income—the commission he received based on deliveries—was reduced as he went from 70-plus deliveries per day to fewer than 30. He had no savings, and whatever he was able to earn went toward meeting basic needs. He was unable to take his father to large hospitals, which had what he needed but were too expensive.

Rahman's big worries centered around not having enough money. He told me, "I can't move ahead, and I have to step back. Kids ask for things I can't give them." He was also worried about his phone, as his work was tied to his phone. If it broke, that would be a month's worth of salary that he'd need to put in to repair or replace it. Similarly, he hoped that his vehicle wouldn't give him trouble, and he tried to remain healthy so he could keep working. He was 33 years old and studying to become a lawyer, but with three years completed out of a five-year program, he couldn't complete his education because he couldn't pay his fees. He tried to get a loan but couldn't. Even if he could attend classes, he'd lose his job if he missed that much work, which meant he wouldn't be able to attend to his parents and family.

The truth that we uncovered in our interviews was that gig working platforms are, and always were, a race to the bottom. The danger in this scenario is that the supply side is free for the platform. A gig worker only earns when they are on a gig rather than being paid a fixed salary regardless of whether there is enough work for them. Gig workers absorb their own costs—of time waiting, driving to pick up a passenger, and vehicle maintenance, and they only get paid from the time they pick up a customer until they drop them off. This means the platform can have an oversupply of gig workers without additional cost. In fact, that's a good thing for platforms, because it means the customer is even more likely to get a cab in two minutes or less.

That doesn't mean their costs are fixed. DoorDash, a platform that offers delivered food and other couriered orders, offers its dashers increasing amounts based on "takers"—a delivery might start at $3.50, and if no one accepts, it goes up to $3.75, $4.00, $4.50, etc. But what little incentive platforms pay for more work barely scrapes the surface of the returns they're getting, and it doesn't actually increase the earnings of the worker. You might only get one trip an hour, making the "incentive" an effective wage of $4.00 per hour. Dashers did organize themselves, saying they wouldn't accept a trip for less than $7.50—but DoorDash was able to add more dashers to its platform and eventually, out of desperation, dashers had to accept lower bids or risk getting nothing.

If gig workers were paid appropriately for their time, platforms would have to manage how many workers they had on their platform at a given time to balance it with the demand from customers. Gig workers would earn a fairer wage, but wait times would go up for the customer. So the platforms got smart—they structured commissions in such a way that the more you worked for them in a day/week/month, the more commissions you earned. So not only were the workers getting the same terms across the board, but the rewards for working two platforms diminished your commissions on both platforms, forcing you to choose one.

Meanwhile, the algorithm prioritizes new joiners with the objective of hooking them. Gig workers are lured onto the platform with lots of trips, bonuses, and other incentives, but the frequency of trips inevitably decreases as the algorithm prioritizes new joiners with the objective of hooking them. Slowly, the incentives go away. Almost universally, workers are left working longer hours to make the money they used to make while founders, investors, and corporate employees make outsized returns.

£ € $

We're told that the price of something is always equal to its value, and that is used to justify some jobs (like cleaning toilets at McDonalds) paying less than a living wage. As we saw earlier in this chapter, it also implies that if you earn $50,000 a year and someone else earns $15 million a year, it's because they produce 300 times as much value as you.

This must be a very comforting assumption if you're a CEO paying yourself $15 million a year while paying your workers poverty wages. But it is utter nonsense. CEOs and senior executives are so highly paid because, relatively speaking, there are so few of them—they are in short supply and high demand.

The decreasing proportion of wages on GDP is not because workers have become less productive, but because employers have become more powerful. Labor unions were formed to collectively negotiate for the larger supply of blue-collar and gig workers, but apparently this was "bad" for the economy. The claim is that unions allegedly distort labor market outcomes due to the increase in compensation above competitive levels. As a result, the average employee needs to work more than a month to earn what the CEO earns in one hour.[9]

As Nick Hanauer says, "People are not paid what they are worth—they are paid what they have the power to negotiate."

Ever since we got off the gold standard, Western central banks have been able to print money at will. The days of scarce capital are long gone, but that capital is only freely available to a certain segment of society. This is primarily because of the incorrect belief that only the wealthy have the ability and willingness to eventually repay. Banks have the power to decide who to lend to, hedging their distribution in the name of risk. In his quest for fair worker treatment, economist and former Greek finance minister Yanis Varoufakis has called for the Bank of England (the British central bank, similar to the Federal Reserve in the US) to give everyone a free bank account—if they did so, he believes, they would be far better placed to regulate the money supply in the public interest, and the change would be noticeable overnight.

The whole banking system was set up the way it is partly because in the past there was no way any central bank could give every citizen a bank account. But with current and growing technologies, that is no longer a hinderance. Today, we primarily use our bank accounts as a store of value to make payments. Although banks are in the business of lending, they benefit greatly from being the custodian of our funds and, more importantly, being in the middle of every transaction we make. If payments and a store of value were to become separate from banks, they would be left with only one business—lending—and they would have to reinvent themselves to do that job properly, without subsidies from the payments business. Simply giving everyone a bank account at the central bank would decouple the payments systems from commercial banks. This would require banks to get serious about doing business with everyone rather than simply serving the rich while holding monopolies on the movement of our money and enjoying the superprofits that the monopoly creates.

"People are not paid what they are worth— they are paid what they have the power to negotiate."
—Nick Hanauer

In the not-too-distant future, further advances in technology will completely change the way all of society accesses capital. But access does still come with risks. In the wrong hands, such technology has the power to cause havoc. For example, programmable Central Bank Digital Currency (CBDC),* while offering benefits like efficient monetary policy implementation, also poses several risks including concerns about privacy and surveillance, excessive control by central banks, cybersecurity vulnerabilities, disruption to financial systems, inequality due to digital access, and loss of anonymity. You can imagine what an authoritarian government might do with this kind of centralized digital banking.

Another illusion of free market economics: it tells us that demand and supply always set the price—the problem is, businesses often control the demand and the supply. The OPEC oil cartel is a stark example. They meet twice yearly to set oil production quotas for each of their 13 member countries. When they and the oil industry were caught wrong-footed at the start of the pandemic in April 2020, the price of oil went to zero and then dipped into the negative. Then, in mid-2021, once the global economy started to recover, the price of oil began steadily creeping upward due to a combination of reduction in supply to meet the reduced demand due to the pandemic and subsequent lockdowns and the inability to increase supply quickly. Oil companies around the world knew that keeping the supply low made them all more money, and after such a drastic dip in price the year before, they made little effort to increase the supply for fear of the price decreasing. And all of this happened before the war in Ukraine broke out, sending prices through the roof. Oil companies have been reporting superprofits from the first quarter of 2022 onward.

---

* Programmable Central Bank Digital Currency (CBDC) is a type of digital currency with programmable features issued by central banks.

Even more recently, in April 2023, OPEC announced a surprise oil production cut of more than 1 million barrels a day, abandoning previous assurances that it would hold supply steady. Oil prices in March 2023 fell toward $70 a barrel, the lowest in 15 months, on concern that a global banking crisis would negatively hit demand.[10] So OPEC decided to get ahead and cut oil production to boost the price, resulting in oil rallying the most in more than a year—to $85 a barrel—after the unexpected announcement, delivering a fresh inflationary jolt to the world economy.

The power that large corporations wield has steadily entrenched itself into our sense of normalcy over the last five decades, massively increasing the inequality gap worldwide. OPEC is one example, but monopolies or oligopolies do this to a large extent.

When it comes to people, the supply of workers and demand for work is meant to set wages and working conditions. Before the pandemic, this power sat with businesses, which is why restaurant servers were paid $2.50/hour in many areas of the US. Post-pandemic, there has been a shift as people realize they don't need to do those jobs, which has resulted in some industries having difficulty attracting workers, forcing a little bit of a wage increase.

Population growth, especially in developing countries and where migration is high, has left no shortage of people who can do basic jobs—creating an increase in supply of people. In countries where there isn't a minimum wage and where labor laws are weak, businesses take advantage of their market power to atrocious effects. While the extent of the mistreatment varies, the problem is just as relevant in the developed world as it is elsewhere: low-skilled workers are generally treated poorly, and opportunities are so few that people have no choice but to work in whatever treacherous conditions they're left with. No one would choose to wear adult diapers to not have to take bathroom breaks on the factory floor or to urinate in a bottle in their delivery truck. But many companies don't have any qualms about putting their workers under increasing pressure with little regard for their humanity, simply because they can.

After the pandemic took away so many people's jobs, a cost-of-living crisis emerged and was exacerbated by the war in Ukraine. Supply for *everything* shrank by 20–25 percent across the board during the pandemic due to lockdowns, even as demand quickly returned. Pre-pandemic, there were 70,000 staff in the entire airline industry in the UK. When the economy started opening up in 2021, it was closer to 40,000, even as travel hit high demand once more. The industry that happily once sold excess tickets into the future simply couldn't recruit fast enough, as many trained professionals either retired or found other jobs. For example, front desk staff at airlines—those people who check you into your flights—found jobs as cashiers at supermarkets that paid better than their airline jobs. Over the last decade, inflation had been kept in check as supply and demand grew together by a few percentage points every year. But after the supply shrank and the demand returned, prices skyrocketed.

Similarly, after countries ended their lockdown, the price of wholesale natural gas went up nearly 300 percent in six months from March to October 2021.[11] This increased the prices of energy, which affected more than the direct purchase of natural gas for things like home heating. The price of fresh food shot up as well, since industrial refrigeration uses commercial CO_2, which comes from natural gas. (And don't forget that the price of oil was steadily increasing during this time for the same reason: not enough supply). Further, the pandemic left the shipping industry and supply chains in a mess—containers were in the wrong places, fewer crew members were available, and COVID checks increased shipping times, which decreased overall capacity. The combination of factors had a ripple effect throughout the world economy.[12]

In the UK, an NHS health worker and father-to-be told BBC Scotland that he was forced out of his family home by "eye watering" rent increases. Cost-of-living pressures meant the couple, whose first child was due in October 2022, could not afford the rent, and the stress of worrying about the roof over his head took a toll on his mental health. He said this:

> After living in the flat for three years we considered it our home. When the rent increase took place, it meant we had to move out of the flat. I found myself having panic attacks when there were threats. I was signed off work for two weeks and given medication. It was a very difficult situation to find yourself in. There was no way we could pay 21 percent more than we were paying before when the rent was already too high.[13]

Sadly, the vast majority of society is living in this kind of survival mode (and its partner, scarcity mentality)—including wealthy folks, who are all talking about the increase in energy costs at dinner parties.

In the past, labor unions have been effective, but their power to negotiate better terms for their members has been eroded thanks to lobbyist-generated government anti-striking policies, outsourcing, and automation. Workers' rights need to be modernized now more than ever—with gig workers demonstrating that need perhaps more than anyone. Those who work for large platforms are, in essence, full-time workers, but without any full-time benefits..

£ € $

As our consciousness is raised we will move away from value extraction to value creation to realize not only that we have power, but that we are powering far more than industry. We will begin to think about who and what our work does in the world. And as more and more of us make micro-changes in our lives to enable us to look beyond our ability to just survive—to create our own abundance rather than gambling our lives away to the rich—the more we all will thrive. Progressive executives are leading the way, as are Gen Zers who are entering the workforce and not settling for "that's how it has always been."

It's as though Maslow's hierarchy of needs has been placed onto a new foundation, where our survival relies on us coming together—and it turns out that concept existed long before Maslow. For example, I came across the Blackfoot model,* a way of life that offers an alternative resulting in a community that leaves no one behind. It has three layers: Self-Actualization, Community Actualization, and Cultural Perpetuity.

There are two big differences between the models: Maslow focuses on the individual, while the Blackfoot model focuses on caring for the community and keeping culture thriving. Self-actualization is the base of the Blackfoot model, while for Maslow it's the pinnacle of human achievement.[†]

Maslow spent six weeks with the Blackfoot (Siksiká) people in Canada. What he discovered was astounding levels of cooperation, minimal inequality, restorative justice, full bellies, and high levels of life satisfaction. In their paradigm, people are born into a community whose primary job is to keep them safe and ensure they can meet their basic needs so that they can express their gifts in service of their world.

These concepts of community care are more relevant and needed than ever—and there is evidence that they are taking seed. One example is social entrepreneur Teju Ravilochan who, inspired by his research into Indigenous communities, founded the nonprofit GatherFor, whose

---

* The Siksika Nation (Blackfoot: Siksiká; syllabics ᓱᖨᖚᖧ) is a First Nation in southern Alberta, Canada.

† Maslow eventually added "transcendence" to the top of his hierarchy, above self-actualization.

aim is to make neighborhoods feel like a family where neighbors show up for one another unconditionally, no matter what. The following words from Ravilochan encompass not only the importance of relearning Maslow, but also relearning ourselves:

> *This is our moment to step out of our lonely struggle to fend for ourselves, a story maintained by those winning in the status quo. This is our moment not to create something new, but to return to an ancient way of being, known to the Blackfoot, the Lakota, the Natives of the Cheyenne River Territory, and other First Nations. It's a story that leaves no one without family: a story in which we begin by offering each other belonging, and continue by teaching our descendants how we lived:* **together.**[14]

We don't have to invent new ways of being—not before going back to recover what years of colonization and capitalism have extracted from our sense of community. Together, we are the power that every major system requires in order to run, and we can be the power that changes each system as well. But first, we need to relearn how to see each other as cooperative partners, not competitors.

Part III

The Scop Impa

e of
ct

Chapter 9
Reimaginin

ɡ Community

Buckminster Fuller, the visionary and techno-optimist, famously said that for the first time in history, we have the opportunity to support and accommodate all humanity at a substantially more advanced standard of living than any humans have ever experienced.

This was 40 years ago.

While the standard of living has improved for some, I have a feeling Fuller wouldn't be so optimistic now. Instead, we're contemplating what economist and former Greek finance minister Yanis Varoufakis calls "techno-feudalism." Why? Because the hierarchy behind feudalism hasn't changed much since the 15th century.

The feudal system was once the dominant social and economic system in medieval Europe. In this system the nobility held lands from the Crown in exchange for military service. Vassals* in turn acted as tenants of the nobles. Peasants (called villeins or serfs) were obliged to live on their lord's land and give him homage, labor, and a share of the produce in exchange for presumed military protection. Villeins had more rights and social status than those in slavery, but were under a number of legal restrictions that also differentiated them from the

---

* A person in a subordinate position to another.

freeman. For instance, villeins could not leave without their lord's permission.

Today, nobility has been replaced by billionaires, vassals by white-collar corporate employees, and villeins and serfs by blue-collar workers. And the link between value creation and wealth creation is just as broken. Blue-collar and service industry workers, especially gig workers, get the same raw deal as serfs—they work their butts off just to make ends meet, while those further up enjoy outsized benefits of their efforts. Of course, nobility in the past only became so via inheritance, and although rags to riches stories are few and far between and most come into that sort of money through their family, you can *technically* become a billionaire from proverbial nothing today.

As mentioned in the previous chapter, Yanis Varoufakis's book *Another Now* presents a radical and subversive answer to techno-feudalism, exploring what a fair and equal society could look like:

> *Imagine it is now 2025 and that years earlier, in the wake of the world financial crisis of 2008, a new post-Capitalist society had been born. One where a global hi-tech uprising has birthed a post-capitalist world in which work, money, land, digital networks and politics have been truly democratized.*[1]

Varoufakis presents his vision in a dramatic and tantalizing glimpse of a brave new world where the principles of democracy, equality, and justice are truly served. Through the eyes of three characters—a libertarian ex-banker, a Marxist-feminist, and a maverick technologist—we see the genesis of a world without commercial banks or stock markets, where companies are owned equally by all staff, basic income is guaranteed, global imbalances and climate change cancel each other out, and housing is socialized. Contrast this against the poverty trap we have created—where the poorer you are, the more you have to pay—and you can see why it took science fiction for him to offer us his ideals.

Varoufakis presents two ingredients for this near-future shift: the first is the end of tradable shares, and the second is a version of UBI that is not funded by taxes.

Tradable shares allow someone like Rupert Murdoch to buy the shares of any newspaper in the world, which Varoufakis describes as an absurd situation that turns the media into a personal mouthpiece. And he's right. As we saw in an earlier chapter, serious decisions are not made in the US Congress, the UK Houses of Parliament, or German Bundestag, but are instead made among the boards of directors and at annual general meetings of the most powerful companies, such as Goldman Sachs,*[2] Microsoft, or Volkswagen. Our world is controlled by corporations via lobbyists. In *Another Now*, people-friendly banks and markets are established inside of a counter-reality of benign markets, benign banks, and special funds that guarantee the welfare of everybody.

The other big change Varoufakis makes a case for is UBI. His argument is strong, but the problem I've always had with UBI is the fact that society does need people to be productive. Under UBI, people who love their jobs would likely still work and earn additional income, but a lot of menial jobs that need to be done would only get done if they were extremely well paid.

I'll give you an example. Let's say everyone gets $1,200 per month. That is roughly what a person makes working full time making minimum

---

* In July 2009, *Rolling Stone* journalist Matt Taibbi pointed out that Goldman Sachs has a pervasive presence, stating, "The first thing you need to know about Goldman Sachs is that it's everywhere." Whether this makes the bank comparable to a "vampire squid," as Taibbi famously described it, is open to debate, but the fact that Goldman Sachs is widely prevalent is difficult to dispute.

wage in the US (this is before taxes are taken out and, by the way, still below the federal poverty level). How many jobs that nobody wants to do in the first place bring in that kind of income? For example, no one is cleaning toilets in McDonalds for the joy of it—they do so because they don't have a choice. If they no longer need the money, why stay? If even 20 percent of low-skilled employees quit the workforce, companies would need to pay many times more to attract people to roles no one wants, and they'd build that expense into the cost of visiting McDonalds. That kind of inflation never stays in one sector, either—so it's feasible to believe that the general cost of living could increase to $1,200 more than before the UBI, in effect canceling out any benefit it created.

I want to clarify that I don't think UBI is a bad idea. It would certainly facilitate the five principles of inclusive economics. But while we explore UBI more broadly, I believe there is a role for both UBS and universal and targeted cash payments in a progressive welfare system, which I discuss in chapter 11.

When we have robots doing all the jobs people don't want to do—ironically, one of the "fears" we have about our changing world—UBI can work. In a future world where all the basics are taken care of by robots, humans will be able to enjoy retirement at a young age, and leisure and relaxation without many of the life pressures we live with today.

The result of the two ingredients creates a third outcome in *Another Now*: all the real estate is owned by communities, and everyone rents their homes using their UBI. This levels real estate wealth and removes private rent, as the rent that is collected by communities is used for each community.

The society represented in *Another Now* is not perfect. However, it is decidedly better than *our now*.

If our current trajectory remains unchecked, we have to be careful we don't end up like the movie *WALL·E*, where rampant consumerism, corporate greed, and environmental neglect have turned planet Earth into a garbage-strewn wasteland where humanity is nowhere to be found. In that world, the planet still has hope, but humans gave up on it seven centuries earlier, when megacorporation Buy-n-Large (BnL) evacuated the planet onto giant starliners. Sound familiar? We have a crop of billionaires—Bezos, Branson, and Musk—who all have space ambitions. They claim to have been fascinated by the idea of space travel ever since their childhood. Now, as businesspeople, they also see a tremendous opportunity to make money by exploiting resources in space, perhaps because they can't see any way we can save our planet. If they had their way, less than 0.01 percent of the world's population would make it onto their "starliners," with no plan for the rest of us and our beautiful planet.

I can't accept escape for the few as our only future, especially as someone who thinks the idea of colonizing other planets or solar systems is ridiculous. Humanity has found a way to beat every previous perceived existential threat—starvation by overpopulation,* two World Wars, the Cuban missile crisis, etc. Even though we can't trust our current leadership to take us toward something that is not *WALL·E*, just like in *Another Now* or the many revolutions in the past, humanity *will* intervene. And I believe the rescue is most likely to come from the younger generations in the form of community.

£ € $

---

* There is more than enough food to go around (if we're willing to distribute it) and now we have the reverse problem in advanced economies, where due to aging, populations are shrinking.

In chapter 3, I discussed the privatization of profits and socialization of losses. While these phenomena came out of the global financial crisis, shareholder capitalism—in which a disproportionate amount of value goes to shareholders—was born decades before, slowly growing into the monster it is today. Ask any publicly traded company what their priority is, and they'll say it's to maximize shareholder value. That's like a coach prioritizing the needs of the fans over the needs of the players. Entertainment is important, but are they really going to build a winning team with that model?

While leaders have recognized the problem, some are just paying lip service, and over time it is becoming clear who is "trying" to change and who is actually doing the work to make changes.

In August 2019, Business Roundtable, a nonprofit lobbying association whose members are CEOs of 181 of the largest, most profitable, and most influential companies in America, coined the term stakeholder capitalism—a commitment to move toward a more inclusive model of capitalism and pay their workers "fairly." You could say they finally realized the need to include employees and other stakeholders beyond shareholders, as the long-dominant model of shareholder capitalism is proving to be unsustainable. Shortly after their announcement, the COVID-19 pandemic put these corporate commitments to the test. The result: big companies have spent five times more on shareholders than employees in the pandemic. Some examples from a 2022 Brookings Report put this in perspective:

Lowe's pays its median employee $24,600. In the pandemic it made $12.6 billion in profit and put $13 billion into stock buybacks. If it had given that money to employees, they would make $61,100.

Their main competitor? Home Depot pays a median of $27,400. In the pandemic it made $23.7 billion in profit and put $10.3 billion into stock buybacks. If it had given that money to employees, they would make $48,000.

How about Target? It pays $24,500. It made $9.6 billion in profit and put $5 billion into stock buybacks. If that money went to employees, they would make $36,800.

Best Buy? Median pay: $30,500. Profit: $3.8 billion. Stock buybacks: $2 billion. If it had given that money to employees, they would have made $50,000.

Dollar General workers make $16,700. The company made a $3.8 billion profit and spent $4.5 billion on stock buybacks. If that money went to workers, they would have made $35,400.

The list goes on. When things are going well, big companies give money to shareholders and execs. When things are going poorly, companies cut worker pay and jobs.[3]

No surprise, given the stakeholders the Business Roundtable represents.

Overall, the Brookings report highlights that company shareholders grew $1.5 trillion richer while workers got less than 2 percent of that benefit. Far from curbing inequality, the modest gains to workers were dwarfed by the gains to already wealthy shareholders, including executives and billionaires.[4]

The CEOs that belong to the Business Roundtable can learn from examples like yogurt maker Chobani, whose employees were told in 2016 that collectively they could eventually own about 10 percent of the rapidly expanding company. Transferring wealth from the owner to the employees in this way is a grand gesture, and it reflects a rising trend in employee ownership grants. Hamdi Ulukaya, Chobani's founder and majority owner, told employees to think of the grants as a pledge to expand the company even more.

Ulukaya had already been outspoken about corporate civic duty: 10 percent of Chobani profits goes to charity. One-third of its workforce is made up of refugees. And an employee ownership grant was always part of Ulukaya's dream plan. Still, his announcement came as a surprise to almost all employees. "We used to work together; now we are partners," Ulukaya told workers. "We built something; now we're sharing it."[5]

Similarly, Ricardo Semler, CEO of Brazilian company Semco Partners, believes that "growth and profit are a product of how people work together." He championed radical, employee-friendly corporate democracy, becoming famous for creating better workplaces and fostering a culture that encourages people to question why we do things the way we do and by devolving power to employees. In short, that's how he created companies where productivity and employee satisfaction go hand in hand. From 2010 to 2020, the company's sales increased by 600 percent and profitability by 500 percent. Equally impressive, with a current backlog of more than 2,000 job applications, Semco has had less than 1 percent turnover among its 3,000 employees in the last six years.[6] Ricardo built the Semco Style Institute based on his solid foundation and has since shared it with companies across the world. He has a huge fan following called "semlerists" in Japan who have started 120 companies based on his principles.

These are two examples out of hundreds, perhaps even thousands— but they are still exceptions. Over the years, many companies have used Employee Stock Ownership Plans (ESOPs) to give some of their employees shares in the company, usually C-level or senior management staff. But why not all employees? Giving shares to employees anchors them to the company. The "job for life" of the past was a reciprocal dynamic, where companies rewarded longtime employees with pensions and people had a strong loyalty to the company they worked for in response. Over the past two or three decades—not coincidentally at the same time that profits have been prioritized over people—this relationship has changed. Now, it really is a dog-eat-dog world. It is easier to get a pay increase by jumping jobs than it is to negotiate with the company you work for. So the merry-go-round turns, with people jumping from one job to the next expecting something better, with employers in a constant hiring churn. The short-term benefits are in favor of the employee, but the long term is rarely beneficial for anyone.

Anchoring employees to a company has two major benefits: one for the employer and one for the employee. First, the feeling of ownership changes the way people work, often making them far more productive, compassionate, and caring. Second, employees get to participate in the value they create through the stock market. For startups that aim to go public, employees who worked hard to get the company to that point also reap the rewards—the financial upside goes to the people who "produced the value," not just the venture capital investors who got in at the ground floor.

Another approach to further an inclusive economy through the business world is the B Corp movement. Benefit corporations, or public-benefit corporations, are for-profit but with positive impact. More and more ethical companies are popping up as part of the B Corp movement.* B Corp certified companies strive not only for profits, but for the betterment of the world around them. This includes their employees and their customers, as well as society at large and the environment—both locally and globally.

---

* The "B" in B Corp is open to interpretation. It was originally derived from "benefit corporation," a type of US corporate structure, but B Corp means many things to many people. B can mean "better"—so "better corporation"—which is what companies with B Corp status are aiming to be.

Who Gives A Crap is a great example of a B Corp that does good and makes a profit. They make toilet paper that isn't from trees and doesn't contain any nasties (inks, dyes, or scents), and they donate 50 percent of their profits to building toilets for the 2 billion people who don't have access to one. So far, they have donated over $6.1 million. If you use toilet paper (and you also, in fact, "give a crap,") you know who you need to start wiping with.

Who Gives A Crap is part of the larger B Corp trend that began over a decade ago. Early pioneers Buy1Give1 (B1G1) kickstarted a giving engine in 2007 that enables "buy one, give one" generosity and has created 250 million giving impacts. For the supporting businesses, there's the ability to say, "Every time you buy a cup of our coffee, a needy child gets a meal"—or whatever the case may be—and to work that generosity into their corporate storytelling.

Similarly, after a trip to Argentina in 2006, Blake Mycoskie became the "chief shoe giver" and founder of TOMS Shoes, investing $300,000 of his own money in the company. TOMS pledged to donate one pair of shoes for every one sold, and now expands the "One-For-One" campaign to support water, sight, birth, and anti-bullying initiatives. Through the TOMS brand, Mycoskie has raised awareness about issues like global poverty and health. As of 2019, the organization has provided people in developing countries with 95 million pairs of shoes and more than 722,000 weeks of safe water. Moreover, the TOMS Sight Giving Program has helped to restore sight in more than 780,000 individuals by giving recipients prescriptive glasses or surgery.[7, 8]

In order to use the B Corp badge, companies need to be certified by scoring at least 80 out of 200 on the B Impact Assessment. As part of the process, companies need to change their corporate governance structure to be accountable to all stakeholders, not just shareholders, making directors personally responsible for upholding their pledges. Companies recertify every three years or after a Change of Control (of company ownership) or Initial Public Offering to continue using the B Corp badge.

Did you know that bread is one of the most wasted foods in the UK? About 280,000 tons of bread are wasted in the UK every year—that's approximately 44 percent of all bread produced. Enter Tristram Stuart, a campaigner on the environmental and social impacts of food production. After meeting the brewers behind the Brussels Beer Project, who used bread in their "Babylone" beer (a nod to beer's origins of being brewed with bread), Stuart proceeded to found Toast in 2016, a company that uses surplus bread to brew beer. With bread wasted at a colossal scale, here was a circular economy solution to reduce waste, engage drinkers, and raise funds for charity. By brewing quality beers and engaging people in conversation, Toast nudges positive action for the planet. Aside from reusing waste and donating to charity—100 percent of distributable profits (or 1 percent of revenue, whichever is greater) goes to charity—what I found fascinating is Toast's Equity for Good model, which gets shareholders to commit to reinvesting any capital gains from Toast into social impact businesses and funds, ensuring the value created is invested for good. In 2022, Toast raised over $2.4 million from investors including the National Geographic Society, Heineken International, and sustainable business leader Paul Polman.

In 2021, Coutts Bank in the UK secured the sought-after B Corp status, which attests that the bank upholds certain social and environmental performance standards. The announcement came as Coutts attempted to boost its reputation after scandals in recent years. However, it was met with dismay by many in the B Corp community, given the 329-year-old private bank's checkered history.

In December 2022, Scottish company BrewDog lost its ethical B Corp certificate after a BBC film and open letter from workers revealed a culture of fear at the self-styled punk brewery. Turns out, not all B Corps are good actors, in spite of strict certification criteria.

At the end of 2022, there were over 6,000 Certified B Corporations in more than 80 countries and over 150 industries. And since the pandemic induced an increase in consciousness over the planet, there has been a huge rise in companies getting B Corp certified, with even more prioritizing their efforts to becoming a B Corp. This has led the B Corp to propose key changes that will include requirements on approximately 10 specific topics spanning environmental, governance-related, and social impact, which companies would need to meet in addition to using the B Impact Assessment as an impact management tool. With the increased interest, it remains to be seen if the B Corp status can continue to hold its reputational value or if it will get diluted over time. Will those who are trying to disguise their profit-seeking motives prevail, or will B Corp achieve its mission to transform the global economy to benefit all people, communities, and the planet?

It's important to reiterate that profits alone aren't bad. It's superprofits, or the search for superprofits, that lead to bad outcomes for stakeholders other than executives and shareholders. The point I want to make by highlighting the stories of Chobani, Who Gives A Crap, TOMS Shoes, and Toast is that it takes people who are more conscious to commit to giving away those profits as well as more conscious consumers who will find their stories compelling. People on both sides of B Corp success have realized that there is more to life than money. If that message spoke to everyone, then a lot more people and companies would follow suit—and hopefully, one day, we will get there.

£ € $

B Corps are for-profits with purpose—but co-ops are the original purpose-driven entities. In fact, there have been examples of cooperative endeavors throughout history, but the modern cooperative movement traces its roots back to Rochdale, England. In 19th century Europe, primarily in Britain and France, the cooperative movement became a response to the industrial revolution and the economic transformations that were threatening the livelihoods of many workers. Despite some initial success and a lot of failure, the basis for the modern cooperative movement wasn't established until 1844, when a cooperative society established the "Rochdale Principles."

At their core, the Rochdale Principles advocated for democratic control (one member, one vote), open membership, limited interest on capital, and distribution of surplus in proportion to a member's contribution to the society.

From this foundation, the cooperative movement continued to develop in the background of the industrial revolution until a new wave of consumer co-ops began in the late 1960s and 1970s. Born out of the ideas and philosophies of the 1960s counterculture, cooperative stores were opened by young, idealistic members who differentiated their organizations on the basis of trust. The fact that co-ops were known for providing high-quality, unadulterated goods meant you could trust the co-op, versus the average traders whose profit-based incentives didn't always provide the best quality or unadulterated goods to their customers.

In the years that followed, cooperatives continued to pop up across industries, defined as anything that can be owned by workers, customers, or members. The most successful example is The Vanguard Group. From its start in 1975, Vanguard has stood out as a very different kind of investment firm founded on a simple but revolutionary idea: that a mutual fund company should not have outside owners.

Founder John C. Bogle was a hard-nosed skeptic of Wall Street's investor culture. In college, Bogle studied the markets and realized that the vast majority of funds failed to deliver benchmark returns after costs. As a result, he thought most investment advisors were bilking customers with fees and were riddled with conflicts of interest, and that people claiming they could beat the market were basically snake-oil salesmen. Therefore, he structured Vanguard as a customer-owned mutual fund company with no outside owners seeking profits. This framework enabled Vanguard to put its clients first while continually lowering investment costs.

Low costs have been an important factor in the consistently strong performance of Vanguard's funds over time. Those costs could only be achieved because the shareholders are all clients, and the best way to return profits to the shareholders is to lower fees, especially as the company grows and achieves further efficiencies. In any other corporate structure, efficiencies and growth would have translated as profits to a select group of shareholders, as we have seen with other investment funds.

Vanguard's assets under management rose from less than $1 trillion in early 2009 to $7.2 trillion by December 2022, making them one of the world's largest and most trusted investment management companies worldwide. Vanguard is widely recognized as a leader in low-cost investing and a steadfast advocate for the interests of all investors—now numbering in the millions. Further, because Vanguard can't be acquired by an outside entity, its clients can be confident that it will remain the same unique company, focused solely on their clients' interests, in the years ahead.

This security has given Vanguard the luxury of thinking very, very long term: no quarterly profit metrics or earnings management to beat the Street's expectations, no outside owners who expect traditional equity return performance (8–10 percent), and no pesky hedge funds looking to stir up management to "unlock value" on behalf of themselves and their limited partners.

Building Vanguard was tough going at first, and investment fund managers ridiculed Bogle and his "folly," believing that investors would never settle for market returns. But a few decades later, Warren Buffett, Chairman and CEO of Berkshire Hathaway, shared these words about Bogle in his widely read annual letter to shareholders in 2017:

> *If a statue is ever erected to honor the person who has done the most for American investors, the hands down choice should be Jack Bogle. For decades, Jack has urged investors to invest in ultra-low-cost index funds. In his crusade, he amassed only a tiny percentage of the wealth that has typically flowed to managers who have promised their investors large rewards while delivering them nothing—or, as in our bet,*[*9] *less than nothing—of added value. In his early years, Jack was frequently mocked by the investment-management industry. Today, however, he has the satisfaction of knowing that he helped millions of investors realize far better returns on their savings than they otherwise would have earned. He is a hero to them and to me.*
>
> *Jack did more for American investors as a whole than any individual I've known. A lot of Wall Street is devoted to charging a lot for nothing. He charged nothing to accomplish a huge amount.*

In the 21st century, customer-owned cooperatives like Vanguard—owned by everyone who uses their services—can bypass the conflict of interest that all for-profit businesses have. This customer-centric focus is paralleled by another great experiment in employee-focused leadership across the pond—over 100 years ago, in 1918, an English

---

* Warren Buffett's famous bet with a hedge fund manager, which concluded in 2017, was a wager on the performance of passive index funds versus actively managed funds. Buffett, a proponent of passive investing, challenged the hedge fund manager, Ted Seides, to choose five hedge funds that would outperform an S&P 500 index fund over a 10-year period.

By the end of the bet in 2017, the S&P 500 index fund Buffett chose had significantly outperformed the basket of hedge funds chosen by Seides. This outcome served as a notable example of the argument for passive investing and the importance of low fees in long-term investment strategies.

businessman named John Spedan Lewis found a better way of doing business by including staff in decision-making on how the business would be run. The John Lewis Partnership (JLP) still exists in the UK today because of this unique vision of industrial democracy—where employees share profit, knowledge, and power.

In all the research I've done, Lewis is only one of a handful of people who thought this way and did something about it. He set out principles for how the company should operate and produced a written constitution to help employees (he called them partners) understand their rights and responsibilities as co-owners. Lewis wanted to create a way of doing business that was both commercial, allowing it to move quickly and stay ahead in a highly competitive industry, and democratic, giving every partner a voice in the business they co-own. This combination, so ahead of its time, continues to make JLP the leading retail brand they are today. I personally make it a priority to shop with them, knowing that the profits go to the people who power the business and not some greedy shareholders.

Couple this with John Scott, formerly the sole owner of what is today the Guardian Media Group, a British-based mass media company and publisher of *The Guardian* and *The Observer*. Scott was convinced the Inland Revenue tax authorities would claim full death duties in the event of his death, which would almost certainly mean the end of *The Manchester Guardian* newspaper (as it was known at the time) as an independent liberal newspaper—and with it, the legacy of his father, the paper's founder. His solution was radical.

In an act of extraordinary selflessness, in 1936 he renounced all financial benefits in the business for himself and his family by transferring all the ordinary shares in the company—a stake worth more than £1 million at the time—to a group of trustees. Thus, the Scott Trust became the owner of *The Manchester Guardian*. As former chair of the trust, Liz Forgan (2003–2016) puts it:

The Trust owes its existence to an extraordinary act of philanthropy by the Scott family. It must be one of the great acts of generosity by any family in recent memory.[10]

This is a unique structure that exists to secure the financial and editorial independence of *The Guardian* in perpetuity, as well as to safeguard the journalistic freedom and liberal values of *The Guardian*, leaving them free from commercial or political interference. I don't think there is another media outlet that is not owned by either the state or private shareholders. This gives them true editorial independence, though others claim to have that too—BBC, Reuters, *The Wall Street Journal*, etc.—not through their ownership structure, but by reputation. And of course, there is nothing that stops the current trustees from shifting their values away from the current mission—after all, they are human. Today, the Scott Trust Endowment Fund is worth over £1 billion.

Another example of a large and successful cooperative comes from the Basque country in Spain—the industrial Mondragon Cooperative Corporation. Mondragon Co-op was founded in 1956 under the oppressive conditions of fascist Franco Spain, thanks to the community-based democracy-building activities of a priest, José María Arizmendiarrieta. Mondragon has since become an extremely diverse network of cooperative enterprises, huge not only in Spain, but internationally too. It started with just six people. Today, there are more than 100,000 workers and dozens of co-ops within the corporation.

Mondragon does everything—manufacturing services, food production on farms, plus running their own bank and their own university. And the workers truly own and, more importantly, run everything. A rule at Mondragon keeps inevitable inequality to a minimum: the highest-paid worker cannot get more than eight and a half times what the lowest paid worker gets.

Whether it was Bogle's folly, Lewis's belief in industrial democracy, Scott's fear of death taxes, or Arizmendiarrieta's religious uprising—it is clear that you can build a great business without being in it to enrich shareholder wealth. Cooperatives are a valid and versatile way of spreading and sharing the upside with everyone who helped create it.

Yet we worship billionaires like Bezos, Buffet, and Branson who have done the opposite, keeping much of their wealth to themselves.

I grew up worshipping these billionaires because I wanted to emulate them. We all want to be rich! And in doing so, we lose our way. But as my consciousness increased, I made changes in my life and have found people with similar levels of consciousness who are focused on community. Together, I believe we will increase the consciousness of those around us and change our planet's perilous trajectory.

£ € $

In chapter 4, I shared that my wife and I stopped using Amazon Prime in July 2021. Amazon was in the news because of the way it treats its employees, especially delivery drivers and those working in their warehouses. What stuck with me about these stories—more than the pay, which is only slightly higher than minimum wage—was the pressure these people are under to make sure packages are delivered the next day.

As a household, we made the decision to stop buying Prime items in March 2021, and it took a few months after that to get used to the idea and take action. There were two reasons behind the delay. The first was that there wasn't an easy alternative to Amazon, where you can get virtually everything you need in one place with a seamless user experience. If you're not happy with your corner store, you can go to the next one, but Amazon doesn't have that kind of equivalent. The second reason for the delay was accepting that we'd have to pay more elsewhere.

Over those few months, I came to realize that wanting to pay as little as possible for a product or service is being selfish. Why? Because when we pay less, someone gets less. Who is that someone? Not usually the retailer who sold it to you, but the person who made the product in the first place, or in Amazon's case, the suppliers (who pay up to 50% in junk fees including Amazon's shipping costs) and the warehouse workers and delivery drivers who got it to you. By paying more for shipping and sometimes more for products, my wife and I are paying the true cost of production rather than benefiting from Amazon's practice of subsidizing shipping at the expense of their workers. And it's not just people who are exploited—our planet takes the hit too.

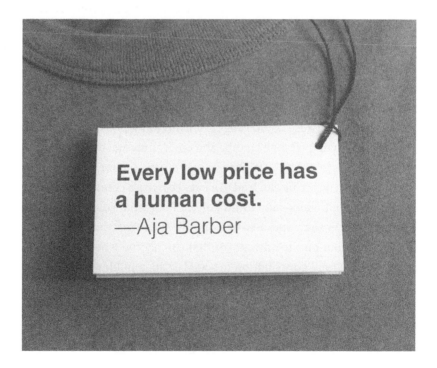

Every low price has a human cost.
—Aja Barber

Every gap in our economic system discussed so far is underpinned by the human compulsion to compete—first for survival, then for entertainment, then for excellence, and ultimately, as a measure of self-worth. In our ignorance, we buy the cheapest products available, regardless of the harm they do to people and planet, so we have what we think we need in order to "win." In their greed for profits, companies compete for our loyalty with lower prices, and the cycle continues. This culture is so strong that bargain hunting is a badge of honor—buying something you don't need because you got a great deal gives you a story you can tell at your next social gathering, instead of buying nothing or buying something you need for a fair price.

Even though we would all be better off contributing our resources and energy to our communities and wider society, the call to compete pulls us back. It is why we think we need superprofits to make a difference, why we try to keep up with the Joneses, and why we would fear for our survival if we were to refuse to participate in the economic system of the day.

Similarly, corporations should exist for the benefit of society. Sadly most corporations leverage what economists call negative externalities—business retaining its profits for shareholders while imposing the costs on society. These could range from anything like litter or noise pollution to driving climate change and environmental degradation—meaningful costs that an organization may create, but for which it may not be liable to pay. This can lead to a backlash from communities, the media, and politicians—and ultimately can put what you might call a business's "license to operate" in jeopardy. It can also lead organizations to miss out on the advantages that can accrue when creating a more positive total contribution to social or stakeholder value.

The fact is, consumers don't care about increasing shareholder value when they make their purchase decisions. Most only care about the price—but the price does not reflect negative externalities.

Some consumers do care about choosing products, services, and companies that they believe make a meaningful contribution to improving their lives; however, this comes at a premium, as in most cases consumers have to pay more for sustainable products. The prices of these products factor in negative externalities—this difference is known as the green premium.* As we've seen, the more our consciousness rises, the less the additional cost means to us. Many of us have started paying more and buying sustainable products and products that support a cause.† And that has created a demand, which has in turn led to the production of more new sustainable and cause-supporting products. In addition, as conscious millennials get into positions of power in large corporations, they are making changes to product lines and parts of the supply chain, collectively doing things to make a larger difference through their work.

Our demand for sustainable products is changing the way products are manufactured. As consumers, we can use our collective buying power to buy from these responsible businesses and inspire others to do the same. Individually, our decisions have a small but noticeable impact. When we come together to make decisions from our shared increase in consciousness, we can change the tides. And if you run a business of any size, you can join this global movement too.

£ € $

---

* Green premium refers to the difference in cost between a product that emits carbon and an alternative that doesn't. For example, the current average price of jet fuel is $2.22 per gallon. If an airline wanted to swap gasoline out for a zero-carbon advanced biofuel alternative, they'd have to pay $5.35 per gallon—a whopping 140 percent increase. That $3.13 difference is the green premium for gasoline.

† However, in the long run, the additional cost may not turn out to be substantial either—when we get out of the habit of constantly buying cheap, disposable stuff, we may actually save money by investing in good-quality, sustainable products that last.

This begs the question: Why aren't people starting up co-ops instead of pure profit startups? Sure, it comes with a lot of the same risks without the upside of big payoffs, but if you're not motivated solely by money, this is an option worth exploring.

In 2017, I joined Ignite, a remote startup accelerator based in the UK and the first co-op fund I had encountered in the startup world. Ignite asked all its portfolio companies to give 1 percent of their shares to the fund in exchange for one share for each founder. This meant that the community of founders could take part in each other's success, which made sense especially because the community generally plays such a big role in helping each other. It also proved to be a great self-selection tool—I was surprised by the number of founders who didn't want to give up 1 percent of their company. Ignite didn't want them. They viewed those founders as selfish and took their resistance as a sign that they might extract from the community and not reciprocate. In December 2022, the first startup exit* took place. Tristan Watson, one of Ignite's co-founders, messaged us saying, "Don't get too excited—no one will be buying Teslas, but it might cover a new laptop!" Each of us got £1,255—a decent Christmas bonus—and a nice way to say thank you for the support and the camaraderie.

Here's another option for startup founders: Founders Pledge, a London-based charitable initiative, in which entrepreneurs commit to donating a portion of their personal proceeds to charity when they sell their shares. Y Combinator (YC), the most famous startup accelerator in the world, adopted the scheme in 2016. Founders interested in giving back can commit to donate a meaningful percentage of their personal

---

* A startup exit refers to the process by which the founders, investors, or other stakeholders of a startup "exit" or realize their investment in the company, typically by selling their ownership stakes to a larger company, private equity firm, venture capital firm, or through an initial public offering (IPO). A successful exit is a significant milestone for startups and can provide financial returns and liquidity for the stakeholders involved.

proceeds to social causes following an exit. The current average is 11 percent, and over 500 entrepreneurs have taken the pledge. To increase its impact, Founders Pledge recently launched Pledge Ventures with a hope to supercharge "for good" projects in a new way. Pledge Ventures will donate 85 percent of carried interest and up to 50 percent of management fees back to Founders Pledge to fund operations, build up a long-term capital endowment, and "scale its impact." The difference is that for YC's founders participation is optional, while for Ignite's founders it's compulsory. However it gets done, an inclusive economy requires us to make impactful giving the norm, not the exception.

You often hear expressions like *cutthroat* and *hard as nails* to describe businesspeople whose success is attributed to their ruthlessness. The deeper problem is that, at this stage in history, competition is no longer helping us survive. In fact, it is the threat. And yet, traditional structures of business and investing are still operating on old assumptions. We're often asked, "What is your competitive advantage?" which assumes we want to *take*—market share, customers, attention—rather than co-create or collaborate on something new.

Building a startup is hard work, and for founders, the payout often just covers opportunity cost or what they would have earned over that period of time if they stayed in a salaried job. It's only those with the huge exits that we read about who make it big—and that represents an incredibly small percentage. My Ignite cohort had eight startups, and mine didn't make it across the line, along with four others. Of the remaining three, five years later, only one had an exit.

In his book *Collaborative Advantage: How Collaboration Beats Competition as a Strategy for Success,* strategic consultant and social entrepreneur Paul Skinner argues that we have now reached a turning point in history where creating competitive advantage may no longer be in the best interests of an organization. I couldn't agree with Skinner more when he says, "Collaborative advantage is about galvanizing people

"There's not a creature or even a particle in the universe that's self-sufficient. We're all dependent on everybody else."
—*Daniel Suelo*

from both inside and outside your organization around a common purpose, so that together you can achieve a scale of success which would be impossible from acting alone." I believe the concept of a collaborative advantage is so powerful that it could be more disruptive than even technological innovation, at least in this decade.

As minimalist Daniel Suelo says beautifully, "There's not a creature or even a particle in the universe that's self-sufficient. We're all dependent on everybody else." The co-op model is not for everyone, but there's no reason not to try something new, and there's every reason to step outside of the confines of a winner-takes-all mindset. A mix of corporations, B Corps, and co-ops would be a good way forward and out of our current economic model. So would a movement of people willing to rethink their spending, withdraw their participation in shareholder capitalism, and value people over capital.

Individually, we can only move from "winner takes all" to "everyone wins" by reaching a level of self-acceptance that turns our focus away from comparison and onto community. When we do so collectively, we can take the next step toward "everyone thrives"—twenty-two centuries after Julius Caesar's divide and conquer strategy was imprinted on our society.

This is the true antidote to the global threats we face: community collaboration, not competitive division. The power is in all of our hands. By coming together, we are empowered to do, be, and create something bigger than ourselves, for more than just ourselves.

Ready to get connected?

Chapter 10
Cooper

ting Globally

For millennia, people have formed and maintained communities to meet common needs, expanding over time into more and more complex forms such as religions and countries. Along the way, our selfishness—an innate human need that's just as self-protective as the need for community—complicated those relationships. We continued to form and seek out groups, but we lost the sense of trust and care for each other that we really needed.

Community is both a feeling and a set of relationships among people. Members of a community share a sense of trust, belonging, safety, and care for each other that we are hardwired to seek out. But community and selfishness are on two sides of the same spectrum. While we are healthiest somewhere in the middle of that spectrum, over the last two decades, we have experienced a subtle shift toward the negative end as we moved toward individualism and the idolization of media-sensationalized "winners." Without clocking that subtle shift when it happened, our focus and attention was quietly pulled away from the real people around us (our community) and onto lottery winners or reality TV personalities who came into seemingly sudden wealth and fame. This obsession with celebrity fed into the Matrix and depleted our sense of connection.

Yet for some of us, the pandemic offered a positive outcome from a horrible situation, bringing us together in a correction back toward community. Globally, we had to unite to survive, and in most parts of the world, people did their part by getting vaccinated and following public health mandates for masking and distancing. Regions that lacked the sense of community that would motivate this level of co-operation struggled to contain the spread of COVID-19 to the extent that others did.

Community is the antidote to our current economic system, but we can't forget that the new community is global. In some ways, this shouldn't come as a surprise. All big companies think globally. No high-valued company in any industry has ever limited itself by geography. Apple may have started in California, but their growth and influence has expanded far beyond a single state. Google didn't select a city and decide they would service just that area. And ByteDance, a Chinese company, has just presided over the incredible rise of Tik-Tok—passing one billion users in 2022 across the world.

Language has formed the foundation of our global interconnectedness. As a side effect of colonization—another horrible situation with world-changing consequences—English, Spanish, and French are all spoken in various parts of the world. This allowed technology, telecommunications, computers, and the internet to connect the world, each in turn. Global trade has flourished—exports today are more than 40 times higher than in 1913.[1]

Private companies first exploited the arbitrage of labor cost to make domestically sold products at internationally produced prices, then quickly realized they could also expand to sell their products and services all over the world. Governments, on the other hand, are literally stuck.

For centuries, governments have defined themselves by the geographic borders that they operate in. Their thinking is stuck nationally—or at best, regionally. In fact, Brexit moved the UK from regional integration to nationalistic, and the vast majority of the population are poorer as a result.

What I'm building toward here is a universally disliked but vital conversation—about taxes. Yes, in a global context.

Taxes are the fees we pay to be part of a community, no matter how poorly it is functioning. In fact, functionality is a spiral: the fewer taxes people pay, the less there is that can be done for the people who pay taxes. Governments need to collect taxes from their communities (citizens) in order to provide for them, and this is where problems arise. In a global community, who is a citizen? Governments are running on a clunky geography-based operating system that limits collection and provision, but the world runs on a newer, scalable operating system in which people and companies no longer function within one physical boundary. As such, "global citizens" or nomads and big companies can no longer be taxed properly. They're making money in the UK, which is lightly taxed in Ireland, then they are spending it in China or the far East, then investing it in something based in Dubai, and so on and so forth. The reason why tax arbitrage* exists is because each government is still operating within the notion that the world ends at their border.

This is already the case for high-net-worth individuals and corporations who move to the US in pursuit of lower state and local tax rates. Over 50 percent of publicly traded companies in the US are incorporated in the state of Delaware; in Europe, the majority of digital corporations are based out of Ireland. As long as governments operate separately, without any sort of global taxation policy, they will collectively lose.

---

* Tax arbitrage refers to the practice of taking advantage of differences in tax rates, laws, or regulations between different jurisdictions to minimize tax liabilities or maximize tax benefits.

In April 2021, Janet Yellen—President Joe Biden's treasury secretary and former head of the Federal Reserve—did call for countries to agree on a global minimum tax rate for large companies. Ms. Yellen said it would help "make sure the global economy thrives based on a more level playing field," and would help end a "30-year race to the bottom."[2] By July 2021, the finance ministers of the powerful G20 countries signed off on a tax crackdown, formally endorsed by heads of state like Biden and Macron in October 2021. The pact would establish a global minimum corporate tax of at least 15 percent to deter multinationals from artificially shifting their profits to international tax havens in order to evade payment obligations in their home countries. Some called for the rate to be increased to 25 percent as the 15 percent rate immediately put pressure on countries with higher rates to come down, closer to the global minimum. In any case, the breakthrough represents a major reversal of the rise of tax avoidance by the biggest multinational firms. After the agreement was struck, President Biden tweeted: "This is more than just a tax deal—it's diplomacy reshaping our global economy and delivering for our people."[3]

While this may seem like it came from nowhere, it didn't. Negotiators have been chipping away at this for years under the auspices of the Organization for Economic Cooperation and Development (OECD).* There had been a sense for a long time that this project was only a whisker away from the finish line and just needed a little push to get it across. What changed? The White House. President Biden and Yellen have broken with Washington's long-standing and bipartisan hostility to international tax overhauls to embrace the OECD's concept of a global minimum tax. This is half the OECD's agenda. Meanwhile, Mr. Biden and Ms. Yellen hoped a sufficiently high global minimum tax

---

* Working with over 100 countries, the OECD is a global policy forum that promotes policies to improve the economic and social well-being of people around the world.

would shield the American economy from the anticompetitive consequences of their plan to raise the corporate tax rate for US companies
from 21 percent to 28 percent.

To get there, Biden and Yellen are willing to make concessions on the
other half of OECD's agenda: a parallel proposal to upend how (and by
which governments) digital services companies such as Google, Meta/
Facebook, and Amazon are taxed. Under century-old global standards,
those companies are taxed on their profits by the governments where
the firms operate global or regional headquarters—places such as Delaware or Ireland. Many OECD members, especially in Europe, would
like to tax those companies on revenues in the countries where they
earn it. For a variety of complex diplomatic reasons, the two parts
of the agenda need to proceed at the same time to secure agreement
from all 130-plus countries participating in this scheme.

A separate proposal calls for an additional tax on the largest and most
profitable multinational enterprises—those with profit margins of at
least 10 percent. Officials want to apply that tax to at least 20 percent
of profit exceeding that 10 percent margin, but they continue to debate how the proceeds would be divided among countries around the
world. Developing economies, where a lot of the growth is found due
to their younger populations, are pushing to ensure that they will get
their fair share.

While the progress has been encouraging, all this effort is likely to be
ineffective as long as the root of the problem—the clunky operating
system—remains unaddressed.

The Corporate Tax Haven Index of 2021 highlights that a club of rich
nations (OECD), shaping international regulations on corporate taxation, bears responsibility for more than two-thirds of the global instances of corporate tax evasion. Dereje Alemayehu, the executive
coordinator of the Nobel Peace Prize-nominated Global Alliance for

Tax Justice, said the index's findings showed the biggest economies in the world were helping companies avoid paying $245 billion in taxes and "to trust the OECD in light of the index's findings today is like trusting a pack of wolves to build a fence around your chicken coop."[4]

What's more, critics argue that a global agreement on a minimum corporate tax rate between countries is no different from price-fixing collusion like we've seen with the OPEC oil cartel. If companies are not free to locate themselves (in tax havens), then the argument is that they are not freely conducting business. Further, the agreement only refers to the statutory rate, which differs from the effective rate that corporations actually pay. In the US, the 21 percent statutory corporate tax rate is an illusion manipulated by a plethora of tax lawyers and accountants, resulting in an effective rate around 8 percent. Similar differences between statutory and effective rates exist in other countries too—there are 362 perfectly acceptable ways to avoid taxes in the UK alone. According to *The Telegraph*, there are hundreds of different reliefs on all sorts of tax for those in the know.[5] This means that even if an agreement to adopt a global tax code is reached, an effective tax rate across the board is unlikely to be achieved.

As Deborah Orr, an award-winning journalist and author, rightly pointed out, "Google, Amazon and Apple haven't taught anyone in this country to read [at least not yet]. But even though an illiterate market wouldn't be so great for them, they avoid their taxes, because they can, because they are more powerful than governments."[6]

Let me state the obvious: taxation in capitalist countries massively favors the super-rich. Whether this is because of the belief that taxing the rich less creates jobs, or because the rich have used their power over the decades to influence governments, or because they have parked their money and assets in tax havens, the wealthy are not pulling their weight in what amounts to a community fund. Even for those who aren't in the 1 percent, the allure of tax relief is strong.

The more we make, the less we want to pay in taxes. But I wonder why that is. Do we intentionally think about the pros and cons of paying less in taxes, or do we just fall in line because that's how society works?

In April 2022, Akshata Murty, the wife of then UK Chancellor of the Exchequer and current prime minister Rishi Sunak, was caught up in controversy. She had claimed a non-domiciled tax status[*] in the UK, which exempted her from paying taxes on dividends received from overseas companies—in her case, approximately $15 million. The storm brewed for some time, until Murty finally relented and "did the right thing," saying she would pay UK taxes on her overseas income.

In my mind, the debate shouldn't have been about the chancellor's wife's tax status, but rather why this tax status even exists in the first place. Initially introduced two centuries ago to lure millionaires to live in the UK without having to pay a UK tax on their foreign income, the big idea was that the wealthy would spend money and make investments where they lived, thus boosting the UK economy—but if people only made investments where they live, tax havens wouldn't exist. Isn't it ironic that the world's leading tax havens are British Overseas Territories and crown dependencies—the Cayman Islands, the British Virgin Islands, and Bermuda—ahead of Switzerland, the Netherlands, and Luxembourg.[7] Here's Alex Cobham, the chief executive of the Tax Justice Network:

> A global tax system that loses over $427 billion a year is not a bro-
> ken system, it's a system programmed to fail. Under pressure from
> corporate giants and tax-haven powers like the Netherlands and the
> UK's network, our governments have programmed the global tax

---

[*] Non-domiciled tax status: those who have this status must still pay UK tax on UK earnings but do not need to pay UK tax on foreign income. They can give up their non-domiciled status at any time.

system to prioritize the desires of the wealthiest corporations and individuals over the needs of everybody else.[8]

Dr. Kojo Koram, author of *Uncommon Wealth: Britain and the Aftermath of Empire*, says it directly: "Britain's global role in the 21st century, as in the 19th, is to increase inequality."[9]

Zooming out, this isn't just about the non-domiciled tax status. Why do so many loopholes exist? Who do they benefit? Certainly not the common man. These intricate schemes were devised by and for the benefit of the super-rich. While some are compelled—by public relations efforts or by law—to "do the right thing," it seems that plenty of others are legally able to do the "wrong" thing.

And it is not just the super-rich who have benefited. The digital nomad trend continues to accelerate to something more lasting than a trend, and as it does, more and more people will benefit from tax arbitrage. Meet Sam, for example: he incorporated an online business in Estonia, paying very little tax in the process. He then moved to a tropical country and spends his time traveling around the world, chasing the sun. Sam considers himself a global citizen, but by legally reducing his tax bill, is he really contributing to the global community?

£ € $

An inclusive economy requires the level of sustainability that our planet also requires. Said another way: if we address all the issues around the current economic system but leave out the problem of climate change, we're still doomed. The climate crisis is a global problem that will affect every country in the world, and the solution needs to be global as well.

In 2004, at the invitation of the United Nations, a joint initiative with over a dozen leading global financial institutions published a report titled "Who Cares Wins: Connecting Financial Markets to a Changing World." The report popularized the term ESG (environmental, social, and governance) and made recommendations to better integrate environmental, social, and governance issues in analysis, asset management, and securities brokerage.

In less than 20 years, the ESG movement has grown from a Corporate Social Responsibility initiative launched by the United Nations into a global phenomenon representing more than $30 trillion in assets under management.[10] In the year 2019 alone, capital totaling $17.67 billion flowed into ESG-linked products, an almost 525 percent increase from 2015, according to Morningstar Inc. In addition, since 2020, there have been accelerating incentives from the United Nations to overlay ESG data with the Sustainable Development Goals (SDGs).

However, critics claim ESG-linked products have not had and are unlikely to have the intended impact of raising the cost of capital for polluting firms, and some people have accused the movement of greenwashing.* Further, both FTX and Silicon Valley Bank, who failed spectacularly, had high ESG scores, bringing into question the governance aspect of ESG, especially for FTX.

My point here is that relying on ESG isn't going to get us where we need to go. This is a question of our responsibility to the global community as well as our relationship to taxes: as long as we continue to burn our planet, we desperately need a global carbon tax to help curb the damage.

---

* Greenwashing refers to the practice of making false or misleading claims about the environmental and sustainability efforts of a company, product, service, or practice in order to appear more environmentally friendly or socially responsible than it actually is.

Carbon credit* exchange, despite its issues, is a start.† Millions of people have accessed clean energy thanks to subsidization from carbon credits. But incentives will only get us so far. Global warming and climate change are a direct consequence of carbon emissions, driven by our current economic system, in search of constant growth at any cost. We need to reach zero carbon emissions as quickly as possible, and the disincentivization of a carbon tax does three things toward that end: 1) it deters corporations from the status quo, 2) it reduces fossil fuel exploration, and 3) it funds the innovations needed to move away from fossil fuels.

Importantly, a global carbon tax would not only deter manufacturers from polluting, it would also increase the price of products that pollute the environment, bringing them to their true cost (and more in line with sustainable products) and reducing or even eliminating the green premium. This isn't an artificial price increase or a punitive tax (recall the "negative externalities" from the previous chapter?). The cost is already there, but corporations are currently deferring this cost to the planet, hidden from consumers. A carbon tax would only bring that cost back into the conversation when purchases are being made.

---

* A carbon credit is a generic term for any tradable certificate or permit representing the right to emit one ton of carbon dioxide or the equivalent amount of a different greenhouse gas [tCO_2e = tons (t) of carbon dioxide (CO_2) equivalent (e)]. One carbon credit is equal to one ton of carbon dioxide, or in some markets, carbon dioxide equivalent gases Carbon trading is an application of an emissions trading approach. Greenhouse gas emissions are capped and then markets are used to allocate the emissions among the group of regulated sources.

† Carbon credit trading and emissions reduction initiatives are happening globally, with various implementations that can be voluntary (companies buying carbon credits to advertise their commitment to sustainability, or individuals offsetting their travel emissions) or policy-driven (the Kyoto Protocol and the Paris Agreement are international agreements that encourage emission reduction efforts among participating countries).

But the rationale of a carbon tax isn't what's standing in our way—it's oil companies and big business, period.

Energy prices have been steadily increasing from the middle of 2021 to the time I'm writing this chapter. The increase began with global supply chain problems that made it more difficult to ship things around the world, oil and gas included. However, it is important to note that the total quantity of oil and gas around the world remained more or less the same pre-pandemic and 18 months later, and the price increases began before the Russia-Ukraine war began. Not to mention, in January 2022, oil companies posted record profits. When asked about the stark contrast of these profits compared to punishingly high bills faced by households already struggling with sky-high inflation, Shell's chief executive, Ben van Beurden, said the company could not "perform miracles" to bring oil and gas prices down, adding: "It is what it is."

This is daylight robbery—Varoufakis calls it the scam of the century. The price of both oil and gas are artificially set, but corporations are able to point to someone other than themselves because it's technically global markets that "set the price." For example, the UK produces enough energy for its own use, and the cost to produce this energy has only increased marginally. Yet, some 35 percent of energy is imported into the UK[11] and even what is produced at home is sold at global prices—why? Because private companies like Shell and British Petroleum can choose who they sell to, among anyone anywhere in the world. When TotalEnergies of France cut prices at the pump, van Beurden rejected suggestions that Shell should follow suit, saying Shell's philosophy was to price "on a competitive basis." In reality, Shell vowed a return for investors from its obscene profits by buying back $6 billion of shares over a period of three months.

Research in 2022 revealed that the oil and gas industry has delivered a staggering $3 billion in pure profits *every day* for the last 50 years.

The vast majority of that has been captured by petrostates[*] and fossil fuel companies—to the tune of $52 trillion since 1970. Author and professor Aviel Verbruggen says this level of profit only serves to "buy every politician, every system...It protects [producers] from political interference that may limit their activities and delay action on the climate crisis."[12]

Government responses trickled in. The UK announced a windfall tax[†] on energy firms, requiring them to pay an additional 25 percent tax (described as an energy profits levy). Six months later, it was increased to 35 percent and extended from 2025 to 2028. The UK hopes to raise $50 billion over six years. Other countries, like India, have introduced a windfall tax too. Hopefully the efforts are not full of holes. In the 12 months prior to this writing, Shell hadn't paid a single penny on the UK's proposed windfall tax.

The way forward would be to change the entire way governments tax corporations, from income to carbon emissions. A complete restructuring is the only way to properly address all the issues we face. Given the current state of politics, this might be a step too far—and given the wealthy holding the puppet strings for politics and governments, perhaps we shouldn't hold our breath. Instead, let's look at our role and what each of us can do.

£ € $

---

* Petrostates, short for petroleum states, refers to countries whose economies are heavily reliant on revenue generated from the production, export, and sale of petroleum products, particularly crude oil.

† A windfall tax is a one-off tax that is imposed on unexpected or unusually high profits or gains made by individuals, companies, or industries due to favorable circumstances, such as changes in market conditions or government policies.

The truth is, most of us dislike paying taxes. Growing up in India shaped my opinions on the matter in ways that have been difficult to reconcile. There is so much corruption and so little visible benefit that it is easy to believe you don't get much back for your taxes—better to minimize your tax burden and invest elsewhere. This is how the majority of people think, and I was no exception.

We often look at the infrastructure around us and what our day-to-day government services leave to be desired and feel that we're getting shortchanged. But ROI is the wrong way of looking at it. If no one paid taxes, how could the government function? Taxes create intangible benefits that we may never realize we enjoy: defense forces to protect us, emergency services for our hour of need, independent judicial systems to maintain balance, and more. Few are advocating for the elimination of taxes completely because none of these services would be possible without them. More would say they want to pay as little tax as possible—just enough to avoid living in a dystopia—as the bare minimum contribution for bare minimum survival.

The disconnect is clearest when it comes to the wealthiest among us who want the government to protect them, to maintain a well-functioning society, to build infrastructure that provides them with more opportunities, and to not restrict their earning potential through overbearing regulations. Yet, when it comes to paying for all of those benefits, they are notorious for minimizing the taxes they owe.

Let's not paint them all with the same brush; of course there are exceptions. In January 2022, over 100 of the world's richest people signed a letter titled "make us pay more taxes" and presented it to the World Economic Forum.* They called themselves the Patriotic

---

* In 2021, there were 2,755 billionaires in the world, and less than 4% wanted to be taxed more.

Millionaires and said that the ultrawealthy were not currently being forced to pay their share of the global economic recovery from the pandemic.[13]

The Patriotic Millionaires, together with Oxfam and other nonprofits, proposed a progressive wealth tax starting at 2 percent for those with more than $5 million and up to 5 percent for billionaires. Such a wealth tax could raise $2.52 trillion—enough globally to lift 2.3 billion people out of poverty and guarantee healthcare and social protection for individuals living in lower-income countries.

Similar to the Patriotic Millionaires, French superstar economist and author Thomas Piketty proposed a global wealth tax instead of a consumption tax as the way to go. Piketty laid out his vision for fixing global wealth inequality in his book, *Capital in the Twenty-First Century*:

> *It isn't good for the economy when the largest multinational corporations pay a lower effective tax rate than small- and medium-sized businesses. The middle class feels that they are paying more than the very rich. This is not good because at some point later on down the road if you want support for globalization, it's important that broad groups in the population feel that they are benefiting from it.*[14]

Piketty went on to say that billionaire Bill Gates said to him, "I love your book. I care a lot about inequality, but I don't want to pay more taxes."

And therein lies the problem.

We are stuck in layers of greed hidden in scarcity mindsets, tax evasion, and fear of wealth redistribution through taxes. Truly conscious individuals have the opportunity and responsibility to rethink a global taxation system that is more equitable and effective instead of bargain shopping for societal protection.

Here's the kicker: the Patriotic Millionaires only signed a letter. Nothing more. Frankly, it would be more powerful if they also parted with their money—put in an account held by The Patriotic Millionaires LLC, earmarked to pass on to the government. That would be leading by example. As Ricardo Semler, trailblazing CEO of Semco reminds us: "If you're giving back, you took too much!"[15]

Or what if, instead of getting zillionaires to contribute, we all pitched in a bit more? That same amount, $2.5 trillion, could be raised by taxing the top-earning billion people in the world an average of $2,500 each on a sliding scale. All of us giving back just a bit more would be every bit as powerful as relying on the few, with a more direct impact than we could create by only pressuring the rich or waiting to become rich ourselves.

If you're feeling discomfort at the suggestion that the middle contribute more, you're beginning to see the problem. We know the top pays next to nothing and the middle pays disproportionately and that taxes aren't the only answer to inequality. We also can't forget that there has been a staggering rise in billionaires' wealth since the start of the pandemic. As the world went into lockdown and the global economy faced its worst recession since World War II, the fortunes of the world's 10 richest individuals rose to $1.5 trillion—or $15,000 a second. If you don't take more than your fair share in the first place, you won't have to be "made" to give back as much.

In reality, only a small minority of people—from any economic background—see the letting go of money as a motivating factor in itself. These are typically people who dedicate their lives to religion and spirituality or similar altruistic causes. In some cases, people turn to philanthropy after much success in the business world, but not always. A lot of wealthy people do set up foundations, but it should be noted that these foundations also receive tax breaks—less money for the government, more for their philanthropic efforts. Without taking

"If you're giving back, you took too much!"
—*Ricardo Semler*

anything away from philanthropic efforts, tax breaks shouldn't be the only incentive to be generous. I'm all for philanthropy, but not while reducing the capacity of government.

For years, I focused heavily on tax minimization, and as a former chartered accountant, I was particularly good at it. A few factors contributed to my perspective shift. The first was opportunity cost—realizing that I could be spending time increasing my earnings rather than decreasing how much tax I paid (although, at the time, if the amount of money in question were bigger, I would have happily followed our friend Sam and set up an offshore company). Second, and more importantly, I was in year three of a process that was helping me let go of scarcity and adopt an abundance mindset. Only then could I accept government inefficiency, trusting that the government will do its best with my taxes, even though the waste will continue. Knowing that I'm wholeheartedly doing my bit is enough to make me feel free and at peace—a feeling that I wouldn't want to lose for any amount of money saved in taxes.

If we want to seize our responsibility to fully and generously participate in society, that includes shedding our old narratives about taxes. To do that, we have to face our old narratives about abundance—because desperately trying to make the bare minimum contribution has scarcity written all over it.

For me, the scarcity mindset was not just about taxes. I used to fight with companies too—for being billed the wrong amount or for compensation for mistakes, etc. I've learned to let go of all of it. Not getting bogged down in the fight for every last penny has really helped me feel happier and has reinforced my abundance mindset. I pay what comes to me, even if it is not fair or right, and I move on with my life. Of course, the totals in these instances are small, but it is often the small amounts that we get most upset over, fooling ourselves that it is the principle and not the money. But it's all part of a scarcity mindset.

In July 2020, I found myself in a situation that I thought was truly unfair. Four years prior, I had lent my former co-founder a large sum of money for a few months to finish the renovations of his house, which he had promised to repay soon after he remortgaged, but hadn't. That summer, he proposed injecting a similar sum into a business we owned equally, with an aim to dilute my share. It became clear he wanted control when he also asked me not to contribute, which would have kept our shareholding equal. Given the amount I had lent to him, he was effectively using my money to dilute my shareholding—a gross unfairness that I found particularly hard to swallow.

I spent hours fuming, writing emails that I sent and some that I didn't. I spoke to our third co-founder, who said he understood my feelings and that he would understand if I blocked the investment into the company. And why wouldn't he? The expected response is to protect what seems rightfully yours, even if it's only "on principle." We see it in demands for refunds when services aren't exactly up to par, business deals (like these) going south, and siblings spending years in court when their inheritance isn't as expected. At one time in my life, not that long before, I would have taken our co-founder's advice and used my veto to blow it all up. If I couldn't get fairness, nobody would. But the combination of a steady rise in my consciousness over time and a significant wake-up call in the midst of that circumstance changed my perspective.

A week into this situation, my parents got a severe case of COVID. My father has quite a few comorbidities, and my focus turned to them and my worry for their well-being. They did recover, but the convergence of events made me wonder: What if my former co-founder had done something I considered to be fair, but then one or both my parents passed away days later? The latter was far more significant to me, of course, though I had no real control over either situation. Why were my parents saved when other families were devastated by COVID's impacts? Did it have anything to do with fairness? Truly, nothing in life is "fair," making fairness or even justice a poor standard of measurement for an individual's choices.

When injustice is committed, not even a court's decision can reverse the harm, and often it takes years of stress and misery to attempt to win that decision. This is obviously worthwhile in cases of physical injury or ongoing harm that requires some sort of intervention. For money-related concerns, however, what do we really gain by pursuing "justice" (i.e., a court's acknowledgment that we were right) or "fairness" (i.e., balancing the scales by insisting on some kind of retribution)? The realization that both sides of a conflict have their own perception of what is fair, combined with my journey toward an abundance mindset, sparked a rise in my consciousness. I didn't need the money, and I certainly didn't need to lose more energy to being angry. Focusing on my parents had taken the sting out of my initial reaction. Rather than reigniting that anger, I held onto my sense of gratitude for their full recovery and added to it a sense of gratitude that I didn't need the money and didn't have to stay involved in the drama of it all. My co-founder evidently needed something that I didn't, and I had no reason to fight him on the basis of principle. So I signed away my right of first refusal to maintain my shareholding and moved on.

I'm not saying that this is what you should do or that letting someone exploit you is a good idea. I'm not saying that my co-founder was right or justified in his actions. My point is that the gift abundance has given me is the ability to let go of my attachment to the circumstance long enough to realize it didn't matter to me who was right in that situation. It was more important for me to be free to enjoy my life with my family than it was to become mired in animosity and distress. The money and holdings that were at stake could be replaced, but the relationships I have with my family and even my co-founder are irreplaceable. Choosing to veto my co-founder's investment might have given me some level of satisfaction in the past, but it never would have made things fair and couldn't have improved anything that mattered. In that sense, I couldn't have even gained any satisfaction from it.

Our level of consciousness determines what we focus on and what matters to us. Without gaining awareness of all of our blind spots—including and especially a sense of scarcity that makes us think everything is a one-to-one exchange of finite materials that must be balanced fairly or meted out from a just authority—even good models can devolve over time. Cooperatives can get caught up in profits—not unlike the one formed to avoid death taxes that we saw in the previous chapter. Nonprofits morph into for-profits or collapse. Individuals get caught up with what's happening around them. And without including care for the global community, we're susceptible to becoming the new 150—those who control everything, concentrate resources, and leave others to hopefully survive on their own.

To repeat the recurring theme we're uncovering: there is no silver bullet to get around those in power, but we have to start somewhere. And that "somewhere" may just be right where we are, learning to thrive in community.

Don't forget, however, that "community" includes us all. No one belongs at the bottom of the pyramid. In fact, the very concept that society must be shaped like a pyramid is a lie. Here is how we're going to lift everyone up.

Chapter 11
Thrivir

at All Levels

The change in thinking I'm asking for in this book is not necessarily easy. We see the flaws, but we struggle to imagine alternatives. While the global political system is clearly geared toward rewarding the wealthy, it's hard not to believe that at least some politicians have our respective country's interest at heart. Or we might find ourselves in agreement over the flaws of our current system as we know it, but still sometimes wonder how society might have been limited without it. We are all susceptible to Stockholm syndrome thinking when it comes to the various forms of our current system.

But rather than validating past growth based on the structures that surrounded it, why not reevaluate our potential future based on inclusive growth and the community that can support it? Instead of asking what our world would be like now if we hadn't been driven by competition, what if we were to ask a new question altogether: What might we become if we began to change now?

Given the progress humanity has made, there really is no reason for a percentage of the global population to still live in poverty—except for the problem of economic growth. We seem to be unable to reach the last two billion people while still prioritizing making superprofits, and it is no longer sustainable to grow at any cost. Case in point: the US accounts for less than 5 percent of the world's population, yet it accounts for consumption of 25 percent of the world's resources. Clearly, the American dream is not a model that can be scaled to reach the rest of the world.

At the 2005 Make Poverty History rally in London, Nelson Mandela said, "Like slavery and apartheid, poverty is not natural. It is man-made, and it can be overcome and eradicated by the action of human beings."

In the way that we should have zero tolerance for racism, as our consciousness rises, we will find we have zero tolerance for extreme poverty. The United Nations' Sustainable Development Goals outline a vision for a better world—for all countries—by 2030. Goal one is to end poverty in all its forms everywhere.

While few of you have experienced—or could even imagine—living on less than two dollars a day, what feels impossible for some is reality for many. In 2015 the World Bank estimated that 10 percent of the world's population lives in extreme poverty, commonly defined as surviving on $1.90 a day or less.

Now, that is down from nearly 36 percent in 1990; 200 years ago, it was at 90 percent. Serious progress has been made—but the trend has dropped in the last decade. Instead of keeping pace, global progress in reducing extreme poverty has ground to a halt. In fact, the pandemic pushed 70 million more people into extreme poverty in 2020, the largest one-year increase since global poverty monitoring began in 1990. As a result, an estimated 719 million people subsisted on less than $2.15 a day (adjusted for inflation) by the end of 2020.[1]

We know that inequality isn't going away, but that doesn't excuse the extreme inequality that we're seeing now. The real questions aren't whether we can all have the same things, but whether everyone can have enough to live a decent and dignified life. Can we end poverty?

What are the actual chances of eliminating it, given the size and scope of the causes that remain? Is there such a thing as zero poverty? I believe that together we can answer these questions—and that we have an obligation to try. But the effort is largely left to governments, philanthropists, and economics. With economics clearly moving in the wrong direction and governments under pressure to cut expenditures, that leaves philanthropic organizations to do the work—and there is only so much they can do. As a percentage of global economic activity, philanthropy accounts for less than 1 percent of money movement. No wonder progress has slowed.

With half the world's population struggling to make ends meet, it's worth remembering that there was a time and economic system in which people didn't have to worry about meeting their basic needs. And it may surprise you which time and system that was.

Until the end of the 16th century, it was a given throughout medieval Europe that when food prices rose, there would be a consequent surge in mortality rates as people starved to death and diseases spread among the malnourished. Vagrancy came to be seen as a serious crime during the Tudor period. Many people felt threatened by the presence of the poor, believing they were spreading the plague or likely to rise up in rebellion, especially as some were ex-soldiers. In response, the Elizabethan Poor Laws of 1598 and 1601 turned the situation in England on its head. These laws made each parish responsible for looking after its poor (those who were settled in its constituency) and punished only the vagabonds (wandering poor).

As Hilary Cooper and Simon Szreter explain in their book *After the Virus: Lessons from the Past for a Better Future*, for the first time in history, it became illegal to let anybody starve:

> *The laws were clear and simple, and required each of over 10,000 English parishes to set up a continuous relief fund to support the*

vulnerable. This included the lame, the ill and the old, as well as orphans, widows, single mothers and their children, and those unable to find work. Occupiers of land (landowners or their tenants) had to pay a tax towards the fund in proportion to the value of their holding.

Overseen by local magistrates, the system's transparency provided no loopholes for avoiding the tax. In fact, it encouraged a flourishing culture of charitable giving which provided almshouses, apprenticeships and hospitals for the parish poor to alleviate destitution.[2]

Several economic pressures of the time explain both the rise of poverty and the crime of vagrancy. The population of England and Wales was increasing rapidly, which meant more people were competing for jobs and land. At the same time, England was becoming a wealthier country through increased trade and commerce. Naturally, some merchants and landowners benefited from that growth more than others. Most people were still very poor, and many were unemployed.

The cost of living was also on the rise. Tenant farmers rented or leased land from wealthy nobles or merchants, but when richer farmers and merchants began to enclose land for sheep farming, the cost of renting land rose rapidly. This was known as rack-renting, and it deprived many tenants of their land.

Tenant farmers who were able to work were reliant on the harvest for their survival. Though there were many bad harvests in the 16th century, the four years from 1594 to 1597 stood out as particularly bad, amounting at times to famine, perhaps in the worst sequence of events in the entire century.[3]

Poverty was also made worse by inflation. The prices of essential goods, including food, rose as the population grew, forcing some people to leave their homes in search of help and food. Taxes also increased at this time to pay for foreign wars against France, Scotland, and Spain, which exacerbated inflation that hit the poor hardest. Yet here's what happened when community support became the rule rather than the exception:

> With this proliferation of localized mini-welfare states, England became the first country in Europe by more than 150 years to effectively put an end to widespread famine. And it also enabled England subsequently to enjoy by far the fastest rate of urbanization in Europe.
>
> Between 1600 and 1800, huge numbers of young people left rural parishes to find work in cities, safe in the knowledge that their parents would be supported by the parish in times of need—and that they themselves would receive help if things didn't work out. Long before the first steam engines arrived, the Poor Laws had created an urban workforce which enabled the industrial revolution to take off.[4]

Now, more than 400 years later, we face a similar crisis—rising unemployment, runaway inflation, and huge inequality between the techno-elite and the masses. And 400 years ago, we learned that when people didn't have to worry about meeting their basic needs, prosperity soared for all.

£ € $

In *The Psychology of Money: Timeless Lessons on Wealth, Greed, and Happiness*, Morgan Housel describes an era before the pursuit of superprofits:

> Real income for the bottom 20 percent of wage-earners grew by a nearly identical amount as the top 5 percent from 1950 to 1980. In the '50s and '60s, there wasn't much available to differentiate between rich and poor people.

Harper's Magazine *noted in 1957: The rich man smokes the same sort of cigarettes as the poor man, shaves with the same sort of razor, uses the same sort of telephone, vacuum cleaner, radio, and TV set, has the same sort of lighting and heating equipment in his house, and so on indefinitely. The differences between his automobile and the poor man's are minor. Essentially they have similar engines, similar fittings.*[5]

Humans measure their standing in society against their peers, and for 35 years of the post-war period, there was not much comparison to be had. In general, people's lifestyles looked relatively similar. All that changed from the '80s onwards.

Two major contributing factors were at play in that era. The first was Reaganomics—when policies like privatization shifted wealth from the state to individuals—and the second was the sudden, vast increase in consumer choice. In 1909, Henry Ford famously said, "Any customer can have a car painted any color that he wants, so long as it is black." But when product proliferation set in, consumerism followed. This resulted in more wealth flowing from the masses (consumers) to fewer individuals (manufacturers).

Even though it is fair to say that selfishness, materialism, and greed were unexpected and unwelcome by-products of this era and not inherent to the policies themselves, governments set the trend in motion and mass media did the rest. Suddenly, we were all keeping up with the Joneses. Competition moved us away from community and toward individualism—where we still measure our standing in society against our peers, but now it's a race to an ever-expanding top.

In September 1982, the first Forbes 400 list hit newsstands. Five years later, they found 140 billionaires, including 96 outside of the US, for the World's Billionaires List. Thirty-five years after that, the number had grown to 2,668 (with 735 from the US), representing $12.7 trillion in net worth. Similarly, the first Sunday Times Rich List, a list of the 1,000 wealthiest people or families residing in the UK, was published in 1989. Today, countless lists have emerged all over the world. There are now "40 Under 40" and "30 Under 30" lists for metropolitan areas and small towns alike. Everyone wants to stand out. Everyone wants to win. Once we started trying to out-do the other, the spiral was set in motion, and we're still spinning around it today.

This brand of megaprofit capitalism stretched across borders as well, creating competition between countries.

Instead of Western countries building empires whose extraction was limited by geography, Western corporations have now built global empires with the ability to extract from virtually the whole world. Global corporations and financiers convinced government officials to give them favorable tax and regulatory treatment in the form of deregulation and privatization. They pressured countries to compete against each other for the opportunity to host their businesses. They then cherry-picked what worked best for them by locating their production facilities in one country, their tax affairs and banking in a second—typically a tax haven—their call centers and back office in a third, and their swanky headquarters in a fourth.

This gave them the leverage they needed to stay ahead of governments and resulted in countries vying with each other to offer the most lenient environmental and social regulations and the lowest wage and tax rates. Often governments took on substantial debt to subsidize corporations with tax breaks and other financial incentives. For example, due to favorably low corporation tax and other generous government incentives, a wide range of tech giants have their European headquarters in Dublin, with many based in the "Silicon Docks" alongside many growing startups—even though the majority of their workforce is based in other European countries including the UK. No doubt this has benefited Ireland—to the tune of $16 billion a year in software exports—but it has come at a cost to other European countries where the software is being consumed, and the difference between the low rate corporations pay in Ireland and what they should have paid in tax is pocketed by shareholders.

But it is a lot worse in developing countries. Take Nigeria for example—the second largest economy in Africa. Nigeria has four mobile service operators, including Nigerian-owned Globacom, which has been active in the country since 2003. Yet with only 21 percent market share, the majority of their mobile industry remains foreign-owned. MTN, a South African company, holds the largest share of the mobile market, accounting for 44 percent of total mobile subscribers, followed by Globacom with 21 percent, Airtel (an Indian company) with 20 percent, and Etisalat (a United Arab Emirates company) with 15 percent, according to the National Communications Commission of Nigeria. As a result, almost 80 percent of mobile profits end up leaving the country.

Sector after sector repeat this pattern, from fast-moving consumer goods produced by the likes of Unilever, P&G, etc. to everything that comes from China. In the startup world, competition at this level is celebrated. The entry of American and Chinese venture capitalists as well as Japanese mega investor, SoftBank, into Africa is meant to be an accomplishment. What's more, the major startups in Africa are run by foreigners, and most are registered in the US even if they have local founders. Mobile operator profits are not the exception—almost all profits made on the African continent will leave it.

When profits are exported instead of goods and services, it takes value away from that country—putting even more pressure on their currency. If a country imports more than it exports, there is less need for its currency outside of its borders, which decreases its value. The one exception is the US, only because the US dollar is the de facto global reserve currency.

Yet the goal for any VC-funded startup is to destroy competition and own the market—and in that regard, Africa is touted as the land of opportunity. Recently, an American financial services startup gained traction in West Africa by charging only 1 percent for domestic transfers, dropping under the market price by 70 percent. As you can imagine, customers flocked to the service and embraced it with open arms. The startup raised $200 million series A funding at a valuation of $1.7 billion. This is capitalism at its best—competition benefited the consumer and brought in funding for the startup. There's one catch: in the developed world (including the BRICS countries of Brazil, Russia, India, China, and South Africa) domestic transfers are free. For the most part, regulators have stepped in and mandated zero pricing models. So let's not be fooled by this startup's intentions—they are benefiting from the lack of consumer regulation on domestic transfers. Nothing more.

As soon as a startup controls the market, the extraction can begin. Prices increase and additional services are offered at higher prices—all to a captive audience, enhanced by the network effects we discussed in chapter 3. In other words, even in the 21st century, as it is embedded into the very fabric of our current economic system, we continue to plunder in the name of progress. The rich get richer and the poor stay poor. The only difference between what's playing out now in Africa's major economies is that this time it is *techno*-colonialism plundering the continent. Similarly, *techno*-feudalism has run rampant across the globe, with austerity policies from many governments making the general public poorer and the post-pandemic cost-of-living crisis adding fuel to the fire, with no Elizabethan Poor Laws in sight.

When citizens in a country increase their consciousness, countries can collaborate with each other like members in a community, creating a system of reciprocity in which the economic benefits are shared more inclusively. The economies of countries are not equal and never will be, but there is no reason why we can't move toward creating value *for* them without extracting value *from* them.

The world has, for the most part, accepted that feudalism and colonialism belong in the past. But here they are perpetuating those systems, in a sneaky sort of way, driven by technology and hidden mindsets that we have to root out.

£ € $

If we truly do want everyone to thrive, we need an economic model that will perpetuate that. Let's quickly revisit the five principles of inclusive economics, with a global goal of thriving—not just surviving—in mind:

1. **Growth:** Enough goods and services will be produced to enable broad gains in well-being and greater opportunity for all. Good job and work opportunities should grow and incomes increase, especially for the poorest. Economic systems should transform for the betterment of all, including poor and excluded communities.

2. **Participation:** People need to be able to participate fully in economic life and have greater say over their future in it. Everyone should be rewarded for their efforts, not just those who control the capital.

3. **Opportunity:** Upward mobility should be accessible to more people. This includes equitable access to adequate public goods; services (e.g., UBS); physical infrastructure such as public transport, education, clean air, and water; and digital infrastructure such as the internet, identification, bank accounts, payment, and open data exchange.

4. **Stability:** Economic systems should be increasingly resilient to shocks and stresses, especially to disruptions with a disproportionate impact on poor or vulnerable communities. Ultimately, human well-being should be the central goal of economic performance and social progress, not how someone is faring economically.

5. Sustainability: We must preserve or restore nature's ability to maintain its ecology while producing the ecosystem of goods and services that contribute to human well-being.

Each of these tenets relies on assumptions of abundance: that growth is always possible, there is room for everyone, and that both our planet and our humanity can be preserved along the way.

Extraction and the extreme accumulation of wealth, on the other hand, are based on scarcity—unsurprisingly, because capital itself was once scarce. The mindset itself runs deep: pre-1980s, software was open sourced and shared, which allowed for improvements. Many of the modifications developed by universities were openly shared, in keeping with the academic principles of sharing knowledge. All that changed as software became a lucrative business and IBM, AT&T (Unix), and Bill Gates pushed for the licensing of software—creating the scarcity-based closed-source business model (with some help from the government).* Thankfully, the academic and hobbyist communities fought back in the '80s and '90s, and the abundance mindset gave birth to the current open source movement.†

Profit-driven motives are thought of as incentives that are important to increasing productivity, but taking as much as you can is an extractive, scarcity-based way of thinking. The mindset of scarcity has outgrown its usefulness, if it ever had any, and so has its justification. Money is now available in literal abundance, and has been since 1971 when it was detached from gold bullion. Governments can increase money supply at will, as they did for years after the global financial crisis and

---

* Software was not considered copyrightable before the 1974 US Commission on New Technological Uses of Copyrighted Works decided that "computer programs, to the extent that they embody an author's original creation, are proper subject matter of copyright."

† In 1998, after Netscape released the source code for Mozilla, the term "open source" was coined and led to the creation of the Open Source Institute.

during the pandemic. While economists used to think that printing money causes inflation, it's not necessarily the risk they believed it to be. For sure, hyperinflation can happen when this gets out of hand, like it did in Zimbabwe and Venezuela in recent years. But the current levels of inflation we are seeing around the world, especially in the US and Europe, are not a result of the $12 trillion that was created during the pandemic. After the global financial crisis, similar sums were created but didn't lead to inflation. In fact, the only real difference between the two events is that one was about Wall Street and the other Main Street. Finance was affected during the financial crisis as it was in the pandemic, but supply was not.

By contrast, the various lockdowns around the world due to COVID decreased the supply of virtually everything as the global economy shrank by 25 percent—an amount that can't be recreated out of thin air. We would have faced this level of inflation without printing a single dollar, simply because demand outstripped supply as soon as economies started reopening and growing again. One could say that if none of that money had been printed, we would not have the funds to drive that demand,* but even countries that didn't print any money are experiencing similar inflation—and it's far worse for those countries, as they were already poorer to begin with.

Recall the progression of neoliberalism we discussed in chapter 3—when neoliberalism went global, the big financial capital cities around the world connected in order to ensure that a common set of neoliberal policies could be pursued across the globe. Now, let's look at how that played out: in April 2020, when the price of oil dropped to zero and even went negative (because the demand for oil had dropped off a cliff and all oil reserve tanks were full), hedge funds (surprise, surprise) bought a lot of very cheap oil. What did they do with all of it, you ask?

---

* The data shows that there has not been an increase in pre-pandemic aggregate demand.

They hired oil tanker ships to store the oil, waiting for their opportunity to sell it. However, in mid-2021, as the economy started opening up again and the demand for oil increased, tankers were available in short supply and moving newly extracted oil got expensive, when it was possible at all. The cycle spiraled until the Russia-Ukraine war began, exacerbating the situation, while oil companies made billions more.

Hint: the amount of oil available in the earth is about the same if not more since new oil fields are constantly being discovered, and the cost of extracting oil has only marginally increased. The scarcity was only perceived, but it was enough to substantially increase oil prices. Similarly with gas, as storage across reserves decreased during the pandemic, the price of wholesale gas skyrocketed, but as it turned out, consumption was lower than expected. The increase in the price of oil and gas was a major driver of inflation across the global economy.

Now, there are limits to what's available in a moment in time—there's a difference between scarcity thinking and things that are actually scarce. Yes, there was a finite amount of toilet paper in the world at the beginning of the pandemic, but there was enough for everybody until people went out and bought as much toilet paper as they could (scarcity thinking), creating a self-fulfilling prophecy of the toilet paper becoming scarce. Until we decided to hoard toilet paper, supply wasn't a problem—and we wouldn't have hoarded anything if we were thinking about our community. It was a mini crisis driven purely by individualism. Similarly, in September 2021, there was a rumor in the UK that petrol and diesel at gas stations were running low. Guess what happened? Everyone went to fill their tanks up, resulting in the rumored shortage (Reuters reported that 50 to 90 percent of fuel stations in some regions of England had run dry),[6] creating long queues and full tanks of fuel in cars that were going nowhere! Oil is finite, but even when supply is constrained, we're not actually going to run out. Global prices aren't set by true supply and demand—they're rigged to respond to (or to manipulate) our perception of it all. It's not a lack of supply but a perception of lack that drives the machine.

Conscious millennials are some of the first to think oil companies are categorically bad, but for the most part these companies are a mirror of society. Our constant quest to compete influences our behavior, which creates a herd mentality that capitalism, left unchecked, is primed to respond to in the most extractive way possible. From mining our planet, to mining human labor, to mining people for their time, we're now mining computers for cryptocurrency in another move patterned off these outdated mindsets.

Bitcoin was created in January 2009 in response to the global financial crisis. The point was to create limits on currency, in contrast to governments that can print as much money as they want. So a new, scarce resource was created—there will never be more than 21 million bitcoins. In theory, it's supposed to mimic gold. In reality, it was not a great distribution model. About 500 people own the majority of bitcoins and because there isn't any more of it, the power is concentrated in those hands alone. Some of them were already rich, while some got there with Bitcoin. All were rewarded just for being at the right place at the right time.

Over the last 10 years, Bitcoin was embraced by some as a hedge against our current economic system—Wall Street and regulators, who were seen as unfair or corrupt. This was even more pronounced in countries where the sovereign currency was crashing (Venezuela, Argentina, Zimbabwe, etc.). As an anonymous currency, it attracted illicit use as well. But most of all, its increasing value created hype that led to even more value, climbing from 2014 onward until a combination of pandemic boredom, government stimulus checks, and zero interest rates kicked off an orgy of speculative betting that sent its value into the stratosphere—the value of a single bitcoin reached a high of $68,990.90 in November 2021.

Spare a thought for James Howells, who had 7,500 bitcoins on a hard drive that he mistakenly threw away in 2013, like a winning lottery ticket that blew away in the wind. Poor chap has been desperately trying his best to get permission to dig up the landfill to recover the hundreds of millions it represents.

Like anything driven by scarcity, the Bitcoin madness was all mostly due to FOMO. Even companies got involved in the rush, with Tesla and others buying billions of dollars' worth of bitcoin as it was on its way up. No one wanted to be left behind. But as the recession started to hit, all the spare liquidity that was parked in bitcoin was needed. The currency that was meant to hold value against inflation and government intervention was hit by interest rate hikes and ultra-high inflation, and thus the exodus began. In 2022, investors ditched Bitcoin in droves, and its value came crashing down as everyone scrambled to get out. Not everyone did. Michael Saylor of MicroStrategy infamously lost $970 million. Life savings were obliterated. Chat rooms that once served as forums for crypto enthusiasts became littered with suicide hotline numbers. All in all, cryptocurrencies that collectively topped $3 trillion in value in November 2021 plunged below $1 trillion six months later.

The Bitcoin dream was that software-based money would rebalance the scales against currency controlled by governments. As the dream turned to nightmare, critics have been quick to say "I told you so." Others claim that this is simply another tech boom-and-bust cycle and are urging others to hang on through the so-called crypto winter or even ice age. Maybe they're right and it is just a cycle. Or maybe it is the biggest Ponzi scheme yet, just like Sam Bankman-Fraud's—sorry, *Bankman-Fried's*—FTX. Time will tell.

One thing is certain: those with an abundance mindset are free—from the rat race, from the never-ending effort to increase their net worth, and from the FOMO driving it all.

£ € $

A commonly voiced misconception is that people who build not-for-profit companies do so because they simply cannot build for-profit companies—that they are some sort of a failure, or they haven't tried hard enough. The truth is, you can only think of building a not-for-profit company if you escape scarcity. Acumen founder Jacqueline Novogratz has been a huge inspiration and continues to inspire me on my journey. Her investment fund is, in my view, one of only a few true impact investors—a global nonprofit changing the way the world tackles poverty by investing in sustainable businesses, leaders, and ideas. People who start nonprofits, social enterprises, co-ops, and B Corps are the ones who have the greatest impact on increasing general welfare, and founders like Jacqueline demonstrate the fact that even highly skilled people like her who could have amassed billions can live in abundance and are motivated to work hard to achieve their missions.

We're sold the narrative that hard work pays off, and that some are successful while others aren't because the former were driven and hard-working. But can we honestly say that a farmer who works 10 hours a day while living hand to mouth is seeing his hard work paying off? Plenty of people put in the hours yet never reap the benefits because hard work is only one of many factors that determine "success." The best illustration of this I've seen of this is the work of Adam Donyes, the founder and president of Link Year, a Christian program designed for students who have completed high school but haven't yet started college.

In a video published on YouTube in November 2017, a group of American college students are lined up in an open field and the organizer announces a race where the winner gets $100. Before he says "go," he lists off some statements. If the statements are true for the competitors, they can take two steps forward. If not, they stay put. Below are some of those statements:

Take two steps forward if both of your parents are still married.

...if you grew up with a father figure in the home.

...if you had access to private education.

...if you never wondered where your next meal would come from.

As some students take great strides forward with smiling faces, others are still on the start line in sober isolation. At the end, it is mostly white students who are near the finish line while others, largely people of color, are still at or near the original starting line. Donyes tells the students:

Every statement I've made has nothing to do with anything any of you have done. It has nothing to do with decisions you've made.

I guarantee that some of these Black dudes could smoke all of you, and it's only because you have this big of a head start that you're possibly going to win this race called life. Nothing you have done has put you in the lead you're in right now.

He ends on this note, as the students can be seen in a prayer circle: "If you didn't learn anything from this activity, you're a fool."[7]

To be clear, the lesson is not to teach white people sympathy or pity or shame, but to challenge the institutions that require a person to be privileged in order to guarantee food, housing, education, and access to basic infrastructure. The video isn't perfect because it doesn't show the whole picture and it's tough to shove all aspects of it into a short exercise, but it does draw attention to issues that many people choose to ignore.

Harald Schmidt, assistant professor in the Department of Medical Ethics and Health Policy at the University of Pennsylvania's Perelman School of Medicine, says this:

Inequality isn't just between races—it's between income and wealth, too. In this society, unfortunately, it's a fact that black communities have historically and structurally been disadvantaged. But there's nothing inherent about being black that says you have less stable families.

Ownership is an important element that's not fully addressed here. It's important for people to understand that. It's naive to think you got to where you are completely on your own esteem. You might as well claim you have taught yourself to walk and read on your own.[8]

Unfortunately, the way our current economic system works, it is very much in the interest of the few to gain from the many—and far easier to do so when power and resources are limited. As a result, people are not paid what they deserve for their work, but rather paid as little as possible, creating outsized benefit for the person with more economic power. A farmer who is desperate to sell their produce has to do so immediately, and this allows the buyer to offer a lower price, knowing that the farmer has to sell now or the produce will rot. The buyer holds more power at that moment. In developing countries, a solar fridge might allow the farmer to keep their produce fresh, which would help them get a better price thanks to the ability to wait. But this is only possible if the farmer has the purchasing power to buy the solar refrigerator in the first place. Small-scale farmers aren't always so fortunate.

It's safe to say that everyone reading this book won the postal code lottery by the simple virtue of the families we were born into. Perhaps we each experienced that "win" differently, but access to this book, to literacy itself, and to the ability to take time to read is undoubtedly a win—by most measures, we are all privileged. Can we become aware of, and grateful for, everything we've received by no merit of our own? That's the first step: to recognize that our achievements are not entirely down to our efforts—and not only because of the socioeconomic factors Donyes's video highlights. Parents, teachers, classmates, friends, colleagues, etc. all played their part in our success. If we can recognize that we have benefited from a community around us, we are much more likely to participate in that community in a way that allows everyone to thrive.

£ € $

Another narrative we're sold is that people living on the streets are lazy, don't work hard, or that there is something wrong with them— mentally or physically. But in reality, many people who need help are traumatized in some way and find themselves without housing after experiencing a shock: domestic violence, abuse, a sudden job loss, or addiction and mental health challenges. And many people living unhoused find themselves estranged from family and friends. But every one of us yearns for family and connection, and for them, it can be especially hard to find a welcoming community. For those who rely on food banks, it's not just for food but also for a connection to others. Everyone deserves a nonjudgmental space where they can feel welcome.

The idea that we're all in this society together and we have an obligation to take care of each other seems so basic. Yet it is antithetical to most of the rhetoric of individual achievement.

In 2021, I came across an amazing charity called Recycling Lives. Founded in 2008 in the UK, their mission is to reduce homelessness and reoffending by supporting men and women with stable housing and employment and redistributing food to reduce food waste and tackle food poverty. Listening to their stories gave me goosebumps—as I believe it would to anybody with a heart. Despite their amazing work, they are only able to reach a small fraction of those who need help.

But what if governments played a bigger role in scaling these kinds of services to everyone in society?

A world in which we all have access to UBS might seem like a utopian fantasy, but it really isn't that far-fetched. The big fear is that if people don't have to work, they won't—especially the younger generations who are often called "entitled."* But these complaints are always from boomers and older Gen X, who benefited from free or subsidized college education, comparatively cheaper access to house ownership, and a boatload of other handouts. Not to mention that it's the younger generations who are footing the boomers' retirement bill. Young millennials and Gen Z are hungry for reform, and they want to see change.

The problem as I see it is that boomers and older Gen X worked hard during their working lives regardless of privileges and handouts. They did the 9-to-5 grind. They worked for 40 years without mini-retirements or career breaks. They didn't have the flexibility to choose their hours and not much choice around their line of work either. They were grateful they had a job, and they did their bit. In comparison, millennials and Gen Z are questioning everything, and even though we are working hard and sometimes harder as boundaries have blurred, we come across as entitled or not hardworking. Of course, some people feel entitled, but it is unfair to paint the whole generation as entitled.

As a result, boomers and older Gen X, who are also our current lawmakers, are resisting change in a desperate attempt to cling on to their perceptions. Brexit in the UK is a perfect example: older generations overwhelmingly wanted to go back to the isolationism of the past,

---

* People who feel "entitled" often display one or more of the following behaviors: they take more than they give, they feel they deserve the benefits of something without paying the cost of something, they feel like they should have the results without having to sacrifice, and they want success without putting the work in. Entitled people exist across all generations.

while the younger generation embraced globalism and change.*⁹ And, like with the failure of Brexit, the older generations' resistance to change has proven wrong time and time again.†¹⁰

With the traditional 9-to-5 no more, we actually have it worse. It's much harder to stop working at a fixed time, which has led to longer hours in general. Even for Gen Zs who have their dream job—social media influencer—it's not a bed of roses. Their audiences have expectations and endless options to look elsewhere for content, and influencers have to deal with being trolled, and even when they are on holiday they are constantly on the lookout for new content to post. It's a new type of rat race, and while you may not have sympathy for them, the point I want to make is that even those who are living their "dream" are not really. UBS means people won't have to work just for the sake of having to pay their bills (as the basics are taken care of), but as I've realized, we will always be driven to create. Empirical studies and pilot programs exploring UBI's impact on work behavior have shown mixed results. Our natural inclination to create, innovate, and express ourselves is driven by various intrinsic motivations such as personal fulfilment, passion, curiosity, and the desire to make a positive impact on the world. While money can serve as a motivator for some, many individuals find satisfaction and joy in the act of creation itself, regardless of financial rewards.

But UBS alone is not enough, as it is an inefficient method to cover personal and individual living costs associated with needs such as

---

* One survey by Lord Ashcroft Polls conducted on the day of the referendum indicated that approximately 64% of those aged 65 and older voted to leave the EU. Another survey by YouGov suggested that around 58% of those aged 50 to 64 voted to leave. In contrast, various surveys suggested that around 70–75% of voters aged 18 to 24 voted to remain in the EU.

† Brexit regret has reached record levels, according to a new poll that shows just 9% of Brits consider it to be more of a success than a failure. According to a YouGov survey, 62% of people describe it as more of a flop—including 37% of Leave voters.

personal hygiene—people need some agency to select what works best for them, thus requiring any UBS to be supplemented by some form of cash transfers that can be used by citizens to satisfy personally specific living costs.

UBI and UBS put together still cannot remove all privileges, but they would go a long way in giving everyone the ability to cover their basic needs and a platform from which everyone can thrive. UBI trials were underway* before the pandemic, and during the pandemic many countries conducted de facto UBI experiments—stimulus checks, furlough, etc. Neither UBI nor UBS will occur overnight. But due to the advances in technology I discuss in the next chapter, it's clear that we are entering an age of abundance—energy, food, and everything we *need* will soon be extremely cheap to produce. As a result, I believe we are moving toward increased universal access to cash and services.

Still wondering how we can afford to provide all of this and who is going to pay for it? In the UK, a 2017 study by former senior government official Jonathan Portes and Professor Henrietta Moore, director of University College London's Institute for Global Prosperity, put

---

* Some examples of UBI trials and experiments that were initiated before the pandemic include:

Finland: In 2017, Finland launched a two-year UBI experiment that provided a monthly payment to a randomly selected group of unemployed individuals. The experiment aimed to study the effects of UBI on employment, well-being, and other social and economic factors.

Ontario, Canada: The province of Ontario began a three-year UBI pilot project in 2017. The project provided a basic income to a group of low-income individuals and families to assess its impact on poverty reduction and other outcomes.

Stockton, California, USA: In 2019, the city of Stockton, California, launched a UBI pilot program known as the Stockton Economic Empowerment Demonstration (SEED). The program provided a monthly cash payment to a group of low-income residents.

Kenya: The GiveDirectly organization conducted a large-scale UBI experiment in rural Kenya, known as the "Basic Income Guarantee" program. The program provided direct cash transfers to eligible participants to study the impact on poverty, employment, and other factors.

forward a comprehensive proposal, estimating an annual cost of about £42 billion and earmarking a massive reduction in the personal tax allowance to pay for it. The value for an individual using all services would represent £126 of net weekly earnings, which would also stand to benefit the poorest in society the most.

This is why we are Generation Hope. Those of us who are increasing our consciousness will recognize that taking a community approach to caring for all versus an individualistic approach of fending for yourself is a better way forward for humanity. As Martin Luther King, Jr. said: "An individual has not started living until he [or she] can rise above the narrow confines of his [or her] individualistic concerns to the broader concerns of all humanity."

£ € $

Thanks to the progress in the 20th century, made possible by both technology and capitalism, we entered the 21st century with the ability to meet our biggest challenges and the possibility of abundance—creating unprecedented levels of prosperity for all. The UN's Millennium development goals (2000–2015) highlighted the general trend in saving lives and decreasing poverty. According to research by the Brookings Institution, at least 21 million extra lives were saved due to accelerated progress and as many as 471 million people have been lifted out of extreme poverty.[11] But as long as an extractive scarcity mindset dominates our economic system, no one can really thrive. Even the few at the top are stuck in the system, feeling inadequate in at least some ways. That's what scarcity does. If you're worth $5 million, you may be living someone's dream, but you're made to feel like a poor millionaire.

It's not going to be easy. Scarcity thinking is part of our DNA—a built-in way to make sure we survive at all costs—and the message is constantly

"An individual has not started living until he [or she] can rise above the narrow confines of his [or her] individualistic concerns to the broader concerns of all humanity."
—*Martin Luther King, Jr.*

reinforced by the way society values status and success, all in order to increase consumerism and keep the machine running.

My father has an abundance mindset, but growing up, I tuned into what society was telling me. Being super rich was the only metric to measure success, and that's what I wanted. Ironically, I see the cycle repeating itself with my son. At six years old, he already wants to become super rich because of all the stuff he sees around him. My father's influence eventually rubbed off on me, and I hope my son will be as fortunate.

As evidence that the conscious millennial movement is growing, how we view success is shifting. An illustration by Liz Fosslien (@lizand-mollie), bestselling author and expert on emotions at work, recently went viral, denoting all the ways success should be measured. On the top it showed a circle divided in half—salary and job title—under a banner that says "how we are taught to measure." At the bottom, under a banner that says "a better measure," a circle is divided into six parts, with mental health and physical health covering 50 percent, followed by liking what you do, free time, salary, and job title comprising the rest. It struck a nerve with people, many of whom are no doubt considering leaving their jobs or on the other side of doing so because they want something more than just a paycheck.

That said, it is a bit too simplistic to cut success into a pie chart—perhaps a Venn diagram might be better. I see the slice for "liking what you do" as a centerpiece that almost everything else flows from—but not in the sense that you have to do a job that you like. Rather, if we find contentment in what we are doing in life, a way to *like* our lives, then the rest can fall into place. I also believe this measure should be applied at a family level for those who have families because give and take is necessary in order to create some balance for everyone in the household. The first step is to redefine how we measure success, which will change as we grow and ultimately move away from the need to measure it at all.

Like success, shifting from a scarcity to an abundance mindset is more than financial. Take something as simple and obviously abundant as praise and compliments—yet they are treated as scarce and therefore become something we crave, overvaluing external validation as the source for our feelings of self-worth. It's much more common to be at the receiving end of criticism, especially given we have a tendency to pay more attention to, remember, and be affected by negative information or experiences compared to positive ones.* However, maxims like "it might get to their head" and others reinforce the scarcity that keeps us from openly encouraging each other.

The most helpful thing I did was to untether my self-worth and happiness from old measurements. I value the opinions of people I respect, but I can't dwell on it for too long if their opinions of something I say or do are negative. I have a good income and do have an iPhone and other amenities. But neither stuff (latest iPhone, Tesla, etc.) nor what people say about us can ever bring fulfillment—thinking that they can pulls us into a never-ending process of acquiring stuff and seeking praise, while frequently getting hurt or being disappointed.

In the end, we suffer whenever we're not living our own life to its fullest. Scarcity limits us to a life full of fear and self-doubt, holding us to our comfort zones, which we think makes life more comfortable. But we're never really comfortable when we're trapped in our own protective castles. The only way to be free is to let go.

It takes work to develop self-worth independent of others' measurements. That's why self-actualization needs are toward the top of Maslow's hierarchy. Self-actualizing people are self-aware, concerned with personal growth, less concerned with the opinions of others, and interested in fulfilling their potential. Their consciousness is growing

---

* In psychological terms, this tendency is called negativity bias.

enough that they know that everyone belongs at the top, and competition isn't required to get there.

Along the way—and I still have so far to go—I have found that we attract people with similar mindsets. When I was living in a scarcity mindset, so were the people around me. Over the years, I continue to meet more and more people with an abundance mindset, and it becomes easier to stay separate from the stories society tells us about worth, value, and success. This is my community, no matter where we might be found.

Later in life, Maslow added Transcendence to his theory, referring to "the very highest and most inclusive or holistic levels of human consciousness, behaving and relating, as ends rather than means, to oneself, to significant others, to human beings in general, to other species, to nature, and to the cosmos."[12] As more and more of us come together, our movement grows stronger and stronger, giving us the ability to actually make the changes we want to see in our world—to transcend the limits we currently feel.

The choice, in that case, is ours. We can continue to live from an extractive model or move to a more equitable one. We can see the world through a lens of scarcity or become grateful for its abundance. The change isn't going to happen by magic. Can we do the personal work it takes to shape an abundant future—full of shared resources, connectivity, and community—or do we live for the moment, in spite of its trajectory toward ultimate destruction?

When individuals raise their consciousness together in community with others who are doing the same, we automatically rise up in Maslow's pyramid—past survival, through belonging, into self-actualization and transcendence. And together, I believe we have the ability to go beyond anything Maslow might've imagined—perhaps finally being able to emulate the Blackfoot communities he admired.

Chapter 12
Tipp

ng the Scales

We've been on quite a journey in this book—across history, around the world, delving into systems and stories. Thank you for reading this far. Now it's time to take a look inside.

In the preface, I mentioned a life coach who I serendipitously met in 2020. Her name is Nicole Dubois, and this is what she told me:

Most of us live from the outside in. Our thinking, emotions, and actions are influenced by the world through our upbringing, culture, education, religion, etc. In business, it comes from the actions of competitors, the newest marketing trends, the stock market, etc. As a result, many of us are filled with anxiety and overwhelm—a sense of dread that we're falling behind. Instead of thriving, our decisions are made ad hoc based on what will allow us to survive.

To live from the inside out, we have to overcome the fears and uncertainties the world hands to us. We can no longer adapt to what other people think of us. We can no longer people-please or be a victim or make ourselves small. We have to take full responsibility for our thoughts, emotions, and actions.

This is the growth conscious millennials and others have been seeing over the past 10 years as our collective consciousness increases. We're much more aware of our carbon footprint, the impact our consumption has on our environment, and the ways we use our time. If we weren't, then climate change could simply be ignored by politicians and corporations—but we won't let them ignore it.

Formerly taboo topics such as mental health are now openly discussed—burnout even became an official medical diagnosis in 2019 when The World Health Organization recognized workplace burnout as an occupational phenomenon.

We have become more accepting of diversity in all forms, reducing judgment of others while increasing our willingness to live and let live.

These changes have not all been well received, which can at times feel like we'll never see the light at the end of the tunnel. But change *is* happening. It only feels slow because we're taught to believe it will happen exponentially, or "zero to one"* as Peter Thiel famously said. To be fair, technology *has* increased exponentially—hardware in particular. Moore's law is the observation that the number of transistors in an integrated circuit (IC) of a fixed size doubles about every two years. His prediction has held since 1975, and while it can't go on at this pace forever, the direction will remain.

But in all other contexts, zero moves to 0.1, to 0.2, then 0.3, eventually to 0.9 and then to 1. It's the last incremental step that makes the transformation look exponential. For example, ChatGPT-3, launched in November 2022, looks exponentially improved compared to previously available AI language models and so will each future iteration (getting there faster and much more powerfully than the previous

---

* Zero to one is a phrase coined by entrepreneur and investor Peter Thiel in his book titled *Zero to One: Notes on Startups, or How to Build the Future*. The central idea behind the phrase is to emphasize the creation of something entirely new and groundbreaking, rather than simply improving or iterating on existing ideas.

version), but it's taken decades of incremental steps to get there—the field of artificial intelligence was officially born and christened at a workshop organized by John McCarthy in 1956 at the Dartmouth Summer Research Project on Artificial Intelligence.

When I first read Peter Thiel's book, *Zero to One: Notes on Startups, or How to Build the Future,* I thought it was brilliant. There is a lot to learn about and a lot I agree with (e.g., Facebook's network effects). However, as I've dug deeper, I've come to appreciate that even for those who are aiming for moonshots, change is an incremental process. And while the last decade has been full of tragedy and upheaval, it has also led to a positive increase in consciousness. Our shared wisdom and knowledge, from documentaries to books to more direct ways of communication, is moving us through incremental growth much faster, adding to the illusion of exponentiality. No change happens instantaneously or in isolation. Like individual success, the tipping point of a movement comes from many factors coming together over time.

Here are just some of the many ways we can see our consciousness rising:

1. Conscious Consumerism

Conscious consumerism is here to stay. It may always be nice to buy new things, but one of the major ways society has changed in recent years has been through our desire to shop more sustainably or to upcycle and borrow/rent rather than buy new stuff to meet temporary needs. The market for secondhand clothing is exploding, and sales are expected to grow 127 percent by 2026, three times faster than the apparel market overall.[1] I constantly come across new services targeting conscious consumers, for example, SuperLooper, which provides a pre-loved baby clothes rental service for UK parents. The Buy Nothing Project, a global conglomeration of community-based groups, now has over 7 million community members who give (or recycle) consumer goods and services (called "gifts of self") in preference to conventional commerce.

By contrast, the wedding industry in the US alone totaled more than $70 billion in 2022. To put this into context, if the "United States of Matrimony" were a country, it would rank number 88 out of 217 nations of the world in terms of GDP. The social expectations that come with such normalized extravagance are real, and resisting them requires a steely resolve. Take Natalie and George, for example, who found that resolve quite easily because they had much bigger things to worry about: a daughter diagnosed with a life-threatening form of blood cancer takes precedence over the social expectations of the wedding-industrial complex.

Natalie worked through her local BuyNothing chapter to find a wedding dress that fit with just a few alterations performed by her mother. The fresh flowers at the wedding came from George's parents' garden. George borrowed his father's best suit. The photographer swapped his services for George's help on his motorcycle. The wedding was for family and very close friends only; the reception was a backyard barbecue with friends supplying the food and drinks. The total cost? Zero. All the couple's funds were free to be directed toward care for their daughter who, as of summer 2023, is now in remission.

Not all spending shifts tip toward zero, however: research from Unilever reveals that a third of consumers now choose to buy from brands they believe are doing social or environmental good.[2] This is a stark contrast from how consumers used to behave a decade ago, representing a sizable shift in how we have consciously decided to respond to the threat of climate change.

Just 10 years ago, the concept of veganism was alien to most of us, but there is a growing movement toward eating sustainably—from small dietary and lifestyle changes like reducing red meat intake or buying local and ethically/sustainably sourced meat, to deciding to become a vegan or vegetarian. The dairy and meat industries account for a huge percentage of the world's total gas emissions, with the beef industry alone emitting 150 billion gallons of methane every day. What's more, the amount of land and water required for livestock is incredibly uneconomical: globally, 85 percent of agricultural land is used for animal agriculture, and 441 gallons of water (that's not a typo) are needed to produce just one pound of boneless beef.[3] In response, one in five of us claim that we have modified our meat consumption—physical health is still the primary reason, at 56 percent, but 39 percent of people claim to reduce how much meat they eat for the greater good alone. A staggering 20 percent of people also claimed to reduce meat intake due to feelings of guilt.

For those who find it difficult to make a permanent switch, flexitarianism or casual vegetarianism are increasingly popular options—plant-based diets that reduce your carbon footprint and improve your health can still allow for the occasional meat dish to ease a craving or a social interaction. As our consciousness grows, we realize that all-or-nothing thinking is also an illusion, as is the need to name or label our choices in a performative way that signals that we're doing more than others.

And let's not leave out the wealthy: Sir Lewis Hamilton, the seven-time Formula 1 World Champion, became a vegan in 2017, saying the transition was sparked by a vegan friend he met in New York who "opened his eyes to the realities of food production."[4] He sold his private jet in 2019 because he wanted "to live a healthier and greener lifestyle," and naturally, the carbon emission of the private jet was not in line with those goals.[5] His Instagram posts went from photos of him and his mates jetting to exotic holidays to captions that encouraged his huge fanbase to care about our planet.

2. Conscious Humanitarianism

While conscious consumerism is about saving the planet, conscious humanitarianism is more about the harm that has been inflicted on humans. It shows up in two forms: one is commercially driven and the other is politically driven.

Commercial cruelty includes child labor and poor ethics, when people are being treated like cattle in order to reduce end costs. These practices have been brought to light more in recent years as both consumers and those who work in commercial organizations have begun to object.

Political cruelty covers a huge spectrum, from armed conflicts and civil war to dictators and governments that are democratic in name only. From the Arab Spring to Ukrainian resistance, people are standing up for their freedom, often at the cost of their lives.

It's worth noting that both forms of cruelty are driven by our current economic system, which values money and power over anything else. The consciousness we're reaching in these areas is bringing awareness to the change needed in our economic system, and hopefully similar action will soon follow.

3. Conscious Community

Liberals and conservatives alike can embrace the idea of conscious community, defined by Dennis Pitocco, the inspiring founder of 360° Nation, as a place where:

> *People are bound together by choice, founded upon a universal good-faith commitment to listen, understand, respect, empathize with, and support one another. A place for giving and receiving without judgment. An authentic, fresh, uplifting exercise in relational diplomacy—recognizing that the relationship between people of diverse backgrounds and expertise is the foundational building block for uniting the world. Rich, adult conversations. Thoughtful engagement. Real relationships. Humanity at its very best.*[6]

As we saw at the end of chapter 8 with the Blackfoot people, many First Nations cultures see the work of meeting basic needs, ensuring safety, and creating the conditions for the expression of purpose as a community responsibility, not an individual one.

In believing that we need to make it on our own, we lost our way.

Community without consciousness will remain transactional. Consciousness is the next step in the growing community movement, bringing strong teams, relationships, families, and communities together in the pursuit of something greater than the systems we've been given. I hope that during my lifetime we can add conscious governments to this list as well. But if that doesn't happen, I won't lose hope.

Your purpose of life doesn't have to be grand or Mother Teresa-esque to count or make a difference. You already count. We need fewer people trying to change the world and more people trying to change their *own* worlds. Because change starts within us. If we can't change ourselves, it's unlikely we can change anything.

As entrepreneur and philosopher Derek Sivers says:

> We're told we all need to be leaders, but that would be really ineffective. The best way to make a movement, if you really care, is to courageously follow and show others how to follow. When you find a lone nut doing something great, have the guts to be the first person to stand up and join in.[7]

£ € $

I discovered Derek Sivers in early 2020 when I watched his TED Talk "How to Start a Movement," a fascinating three-minute talk that I highly recommend. He explained that being a first follower is an

In believing that we need to make it on our own, we lost our way.

under-appreciated form of leadership because the first follower trans-forms a lone nut into a leader.[8] I immediately started looking for my first follower.

To me, Sivers came across as someone who is more interested in giving to society than taking from it, which led me down the Derek Sivers rabbit hole. I read all about him, bought his books, and listened to his podcast.

I learned that he is an American writer, musician, programmer, and entrepreneur. He is best known for being the founder and former president of CD Baby, an online CD store for independent musicians. And after he sold CD Baby for $22 million in 2008, he gave away the proceeds from the sale of his company to charity.

When asked why, he said this:

> Two friends were at a party at a billionaire's extravagant estate. One said, "Wow! Look at this place! This guy has everything!" The other said, "Yes, but I have something he'll never have: enough." And he continued, "I live simply. I don't own a house, a car, or even a TV. The less I own, the happier I am. The lack of stuff gives me the priceless freedom to live anywhere anytime."
>
> So I didn't need or even want the money from the sale of the compa-ny. I just wanted to make sure I had enough for a simple comfortable life. The rest should go to music education, since that's what made such a difference in my life.[9]

Inspired by what Sivers had done, I wondered how I could follow in his steps. I didn't have a company to sell, but I still owned shares in my first startup, which I had exited in 2019. Looking at them through the filter of Sivers's story, I could see that those shares were caus-ing me mental stress, especially each time there were shareholder communications or meetings. I didn't agree with the direction the company was going in. My mindset was on its way to being one of abundance, and I realized there was something I could do: I gave away all my shares.

I made a list of everyone who helped me on my journey with that startup—65 people—and I gave 80 percent to them and 20 percent to charity. None of them know yet and will only find out when there is a liquidation event (when someone buys the company). I'm grateful to my co-founder who agreed to be the custodian in the meantime.

I discovered Sivers at exactly the right time—a full 10 years after he gave that talk. After I signed the paperwork, I wrote to Derek to thank him for inspiring me. He replied: "WOW! It's so cool that you did that. And I love the fact that you didn't even tell them. Admire you for setting that up."

Now, I'm not a millionaire, and it's not that I have pots of money that made me able to give that away. My shares were worth multiple times my current savings or net worth. But for most people, the more money they have, the harder it is to give a similar percentage away. Waiting until you're wealthy to be generous is just as unrealistic as my childhood dream of making millions so I could help people.

I also didn't do it because I'm altruistic. I did it because I was able to change my mindset away from scarcity. I stopped trying to grab everything I could. I stopped believing it rightly belonged to me or was owed to me.

Wanting to be super rich meant I was part of the problem. The problem wasn't what I had or didn't have, but the mindset I nurtured. Actions reflect desire, and focusing on wealth kept my consciousness low even as I tried to do the right thing.

This change in mindset also means that I no longer plan to build for-profit startups. Instead, I am using my time to build nonprofit startups and public utilities with multilateral development agencies. But the thing is, the scarcity that drove me to want to be super rich and the abundance that freed me from chasing millions are on two sides of a spectrum. It takes intentional work to move incrementally from one side toward the other. The shift is not binary, and even when you get to an abundance mindset, it isn't static. You continue to move forward and backward though smaller bands of the same spectrum, probably throughout your entire life.

Of course, it is easier to maintain an abundance mindset when you're not under financial pressure, but as I found out in November 2022, even if you're not chasing money, you can get burned out.

After the hellish experiences during the various lockdowns many of us have already conveniently forgotten, I felt like I had created a nice work-life balance, working four days a week and taking Wednesdays off to ensure time to recharge mid-week (when you have young kids, the weekend isn't time off). I was living in abundance, not trying to extract the last bits of efficiency. Everything was fine, until it wasn't. There wasn't a specific reason or cause for my sudden burnout; it was very much cumulative.

Coming off a relaxed summer, work travel returned with a bang. In the past, I could travel at the drop of a hat. It was normal for me to have a bag almost always half packed so I could hop on a plane or train, often for just the day. Post-pandemic, it almost feels like I forgot what it was like to travel. I've had many misadventures during my travels, but that fall of 2022, I boarded the wrong *plane* for the first time. I got on the plane, pizza in hand, to find someone in my seat. Not wanting to make a fuss, I sat in an empty seat nearby. As luck would have it, another passenger came along and said I was sitting in their seat. After I confronted the guy in my seat, he asked me if I was going to

Syracuse—a far cry from the trip to New Orleans, where I was expected to speak at a conference. Just before it was too late, and with my pizza still in hand, I got off the plane and onto the right one on the other side of the double-aerobridge. Phew!

Ten days later, I was off on another work trip. I got to the airport early (unusual for me pre-pandemic), went through security with my boarding pass on my phone, and had a leisurely dinner. Only at the time of boarding, I realized that I didn't have my passport. I can tell you that it was an interesting experience clearing immigration to get back into the country without a passport. Here I was thinking that I had things figured out, but trying to step back into pre-pandemic life with a post-pandemic mindset brought me back to reality.

The hardest part of it all was that I had no reason to get so burned out. I wasn't required or even told to travel in order to preserve my job (survive), and I no longer believed I needed to work crazy long hours to thrive. But I was enjoying my work and I had stopped taking Wednesdays off. I started working too many hours again, including working on weekends, and managed to burn out even without consciously chasing wealth or status. When I realized what was happening, and at the encouragement to be present from a yoga instructor, I stopped everything that I could—and a lot of things that I didn't realize I could stop. I released tasks, archived my entire inbox, and took Wednesdays off again. Slowly but surely, I shifted back across the scale toward abundance.

A month later, I was expecting to receive a payment that was promised to me for work done over the previous six months, but my paycheck didn't materialize. It was a further two months before I received payment. During that time, my mindset temporarily slid back toward scarcity—partly due to the overtones of the cost-of-living crisis, but mainly due to a considerable period of negative cash flow (eight months). But this time it didn't take intentional work to slide back toward abundance.

After some dark moments, as soon as I realized what happened, I automatically shifted back, even before I received the payment—accepting that I would be fine even if I didn't receive the payment and knowing that this was only a temporary setback. After all, an abundance mindset is living with a belief that there are enough resources in the world for everyone. In practical terms, it shifts our perspective and results in us being grateful for whatever the universe provides. I just needed a reminder. I was truly grateful for all that I have, and with that, I let go once again.

Looking back, I realized that even after I slid backward, I was still very much ahead of my previous scarcity mindset. Yet at times I still question myself: What if I'm wrong about my choices and they leave me poorer or destitute in the future? Poorer, possibly. Destitute, unlikely.

I've come to realize that the intangible assets we create over decades in our professional lives can always be leveraged to create value. These assets—our knowledge, experience, and perspective—are what uniquely makes each of us who we are. This is why rich networks and diverse and inclusive workplaces are so important. Each perspective is its own unique, if intangible, value. Intangible assets are also how millionaires who go broke are able to return to making millions again. Their past experience carries its own leverageable value.

I reinforce my abundance mindset through a faith in the universe and belief that it will provide for me, but I also ground that faith and belief in reality. These intangible assets present one caveat that I protect against with a disability insurance policy and not just a belief in cosmic provision. Not only does this protect my family and me in case of physical disability, it also acknowledges the importance of my mental health. An illness or injury that affects my brain affects my ability to create more of that intangible value, and since no one else can do that for me, I mitigate that risk with a disability insurance policy.

With that said, my conviction around abundance is reinforced in two ways. On a micro level, it feels so good to live with an abundance mindset. I am so much happier and I fight with people a whole lot less (both in reality and in my head—just imagine the hours we spend rolling in our misery). Not because my circumstances have changed, but because I've changed my perspective of my circumstances.

In this way, the angst and frustration that we feel as individuals is the hope that we're looking for. It is a sign that we no longer feel limited by models of scarcity and loss. The steps you take from here will be your own, since going "off the beaten path," by definition, is to forge your own unique way. Take heart that simply questioning whether the worn, default pathways are the only option you have, even just considering that there must be another way, means you are shifting toward the perspective of abundance.

And on a macro level, I believe we have been moving toward abundance for some time. The transition to green energy represents a shift from scarcity to abundance, fundamentally changing the dynamics of energy production and consumption. This shift has empowered nations to move toward energy independence. Unlike our previous dependence on fossil-rich countries, the distribution of solar and wind energy resources across the globe is thankfully much more equitable, offering the potential for a more balanced and decentralized energy landscape. While fossil fuels are finite and scarce resources, solar and wind energy sources are abundantly available and have the potential to be harnessed everywhere.

It's not just clean energy, either. Technology in all spheres of life continues to develop rapidly. Human genome sequencing, wearable devices, and other biotech advances may allow doctors to detect many conditions before they become serious. Nanosatellites might help us keep track of our natural resources in order to manage our carbon budget. Vertical farms in cities could provide healthier, more nutritious food and reduce the resources we consume with our current ways of farming and the need to transport our food across continents.

Because technologies deliver more computational power and cheaper energy every year, a decade from this publication, computational power will likely be over a hundred times cheaper than it is now. And that tremendous computing power, increasing at least a hundred-fold in any given decade, is what we have at our disposal as either utopian or dystopian future pathways emerge. AI could destroy countless jobs or incite nuclear war and destroy our civilization. Equally, it could fight the climate crisis, fuel a renewable energy revolution, make us more efficient, and accelerate a shift to UBI/UBS.

Historian Yuval Noah Harari, author of *Sapiens: A Brief History of Humankind,* says:

> *Since 1945 we have known that nuclear technology could generate cheap energy for the benefit of humans—but could also physically destroy human civilisation. We therefore reshaped the entire international order to protect humanity, and to make sure nuclear technology was used primarily for good. We now have to grapple with a new weapon of mass destruction that can annihilate our mental and social world.*

He goes on to say:

> *We should regulate AI before it regulates us. Whereas nukes cannot invent more powerful nukes, AI can make exponentially more powerful AI.*[10]

This is why I believe it comes down to every one of us: if we don't raise our consciousness and shift our mindset—currently set in scarcity and accumulation—we're heading down a dangerous path.

Our current mindset has led many of us to believe that we're doomed—especially young millennials and Gen Z. A friend recently said of the climate crisis: "We're all fucked." She explained that all of our individual efforts to recycle and reduce consumption are a drop in the ocean compared to the harm that industry and governments are causing. That is statistically true, but as consumers of industry and citizens of governments, we actually get to decide whether it continues being true. At the time of this writing, things might look bleak, but I believe that quietly the ground is swelling, the movement is growing, and slowly, one action at a time, there is an incremental move toward consuming less, recycling more, supporting businesses with our shared values, and holding our governments accountable (albeit the last one is even slower—but it is happening too).

We only tell ourselves that we need to get somewhere *else* first before we can do any "real" good—but more and more people are realizing that we can't afford to defer helping others until some point in the future that may or may not come, especially as we look toward a future that may or may not come. That is why millennials are engaging in philanthropy at an early age, long before the age older business owners began forming charitable funds as tax havens—because we're learning that we can do good *now*, parallel to making a living. We're realizing that there is joy in generosity and reciprocity as we move away from trying to monetize everything—from small acts like giving away things we don't need on free-sharing platforms like Olio (versus selling them on eBay or Craigslist) to larger givebacks like Sivers has done.

Traditional Corporate Social Responsibility (CSR) programs[*] tend to reinforce feelings of positive association after a purchase—that little bit extra that makes you feel you made the right decision. For example,

---

[*] Corporate Social Responsibility (CSR) refers to a business approach that involves companies taking responsibility for the impact of their activities on society, the environment, and various stakeholders beyond their immediate shareholders.

reading the Starbucks Foundation leaflet while you sit drinking your cappuccino adds a bit of inspiration to complement the caffeine. But in a globally connected age, our generation wants to take a more active role in philanthropy than just signing checks. It is rather like signing up for a charitable donation because you were stopped in the street. You may feel happy to give some money, but you can't help wondering if that should be all there is to it. We seek influence, agency, learning, and self-development. We want to be active in our contributions.

Mother Teresa once said: "The more you have, the more you are occupied, the less you give. But the less you have the more free you are. Poverty for us is a freedom. It is not mortification, a penance. It is joyful freedom. There is no television here, no this, no that. But we are perfectly happy."[11]

Even Zig Ziglar, the late and great salesman and motivational speaker—who was all about getting more—summed it up nicely as well: "You can have everything in life you want, if you will just help enough other people get what they want."[12]

Often, we do things for friends, family, and even total strangers without expecting anything in return. For example, giving directions to a stranger. At that moment when we're stopped in the street, our first instinct is to help. We're not thinking "What's in it for me?" Not every action we take is remunerated; we also derive experiential value—the joy of helping others without expecting anything in return. Yet the world tries to get people to think they should be compensated somehow, or else why should they bother? The antidote to this selfishness is an abundance mindset, where there is literally no limit to how much you can help others.

A decade ago, I used to give my time freely to people who needed help. But with the rise of social media came the rise of FOMO. For many people, FOMO takes the form of wondering things like: Are they having fun without me? Are they going to bond over conversations I'm not able to join? For me, FOMO wasn't about social interactions, but financial gains or profitable investments. For many years, I had a great amount of FOMO that I wasn't maximizing my returns or making the right investment decisions. So I learned to guard my time. I put a value on it and focused on my objectives. I thought I was doing the right thing, but in every interaction I was thinking about "what's in it for me." I had gone the wrong way—using people to further my goal of wealth was creating more scarcity, and I was not being authentic. Since that realization, I have gotten off the FOMO train and gone back to the way I offered my time to others in the past, without expecting anything in return. It's exhilarating, rewarding, and frees me to be my authentic self with no hidden agenda.

I recently came across the alternative acronym JOMO—the joy of missing out: "a feeling of contentment with one's own pursuits and activities, without worrying over the possibility of missing out on what others may be doing or achieving."[13]

In his book *The Joy of Missing Out: The Art of Self-Restraint in an Age of Excess*, Danish psychology professor Svend Brinkmann urges us to go back to the old-fashioned ideas of restraint and moderation. He says: "Opting out and saying no are skills we lack both as individuals and as a society."[14]

As I mentioned in chapter 6, in the search for financial freedom, we can be lured into buying course after course and book after book, each of them promising we can make six figures a month in passive income. Sure, 1 percent succeed, but these people would probably have succeeded even without a course. The course authors use these extraordinary examples to sell their courses and also to shame those who don't make it—look at all these people who followed the course material and succeeded; there must be something wrong with you if you didn't.

I've watched a number of people get frustrated over having really good content that they can't turn into millions like the courses all promise. They beat themselves up because they think they're doing something wrong. It's a terrible cycle for those caught up in it—and I know, because I've been there.

But if we hold an abundance mindset for our content, magical things can happen—I say this from experience as well. From that perspective, I didn't write this book to build or monetize an audience. It's quite the opposite. I'm sharing what I've learned and paying it forward, showing you that the ripples start from us rather than living from old patterns and waiting for change to trickle down. If this book helps even one person change their mindset, I trust that the ripples will contribute to a wave.

The scales tip toward JOMO when you become the change you want to see, not only for you individually, but in the business model you adopt and the way that you do your work.

JOMO is a way to live an intentional life from the inside out, rather than from the outside in. But to get here, you have got to be comfortable in your own skin. In our conditioning to be competitive, it will be tempting to compare your growth in consciousness to others' seemingly exponential changes around you. Remember: each of us is on our own individual journey. Increasing our consciousness can begin by simply experiencing the present moment and by slowing down to connect deeply to our core values, mission, and vision. JOMO represents a more fulfilling way of life that's enriching for ourselves as well as our fellow humans, with the added bonus of protecting the planet we all share.

£ € $

In 2010, 40 signatories joined the newly founded Giving Pledge, a promise by the world's wealthiest individuals and families to dedicate the majority of their wealth to charitable causes. As of 2023, there are 241 signatories. I've personally pledged to give away half my wealth, whatever that becomes—though I couldn't officially do this as the Giving Pledge is focused on billionaires (those with a net worth of $1 billion or more) or those who would be billionaires if not for their giving. This kind of commitment should be for everyone—from millionaires and billionaires to ordinary people like you and me.

There's no real reason to hold onto wealth beyond our means, not even for the sake of generational wealth. If I do a good job parenting, I trust that my kids won't need an inheritance—creating value for society will come naturally to them and will help them find their place in the world. This belief is well-founded: it is the drive to create that separates us from every other species. As Anne Folan, my dear friend you met in chapter 5, told me:

> *Everyone talks about the purpose of life as if it was some unfathomable mystery, but nothing could be simpler. We are here on this earth to create. Some people create written works, some music, some painting, some sculpture, some lines of code, some small businesses, some large businesses, some casseroles or furniture or a beautiful party that the guests remember for the rest of their lives.*

Similarly, Kurt Vonnegut, the late American writer known for his satirical and darkly humorous novels, said: "Nobody will stop you from creating. Do it tonight. Do it tomorrow. That is the way to make your soul grow—whether there is a market for it or not! The kick of creation is the act of creating, not anything that happens afterward."[15]

Even a proverbial child on the beach will grab a piece of driftwood and draw a stick figure of his mom or dad or a fish. People talk about robots taking over the world and displacing humans, but a robot does not share the instinct, the drive, the fundamental need to create that we all have. In fact, no other creature except us creates in this way. This is why I also believe that, regardless of how many jobs robots take, we humans will always have something to do.

When we think of creating, we often think of creating physical things. But for millennia before consumerism, we have created the intangible—poetry, stories, dancing, music, religion, and spirituality.

The question that leaves us with is this: What world do we want to create?

One that allows only some of us to thrive, or one that allows all of us to thrive?

I know what you're thinking. Creating a world that includes everyone is going to take a long time, and it's going to be really hard. But every time I have that thought, something tells me that it's going to happen, that it's not going to take long at all, and it's not going to be hard. That voice has only gotten louder in our post-COVID shift amidst the acceleration of our mindfulness and our ability to challenge the status quo.

I'm inspired by the words of John McAvoy, who is today an Ironman Triathlete—however, he was previously a high-profile armed robber. After he found redemption through the power of sport and was eventually given parole after a total of 10 years behind bars, he said:

> *I alone cannot change society for the better, but I can radically transform my consciousness, overturning the conditioning that limits my potential. We can all do this one by one. Over time we can change ourselves to the degree that society changes from the inside-out, giving birth to a new way of being. Manifesting our birthright of living*

in a peaceful and abundant world. Have no fear, trust yourself, live
your full potential.

You may not have a jet or a business or shares to sell, but if you hold
yourself to a sort of all-or-nothing mentality, you'll keep doing nothing indefinitely. This movement is about consciousness and growth,
not performance, and it's a personal, incremental journey that will
take the rest of our lives, within the context of a strong connection
to community.

In the years to come, I believe our social norms will continue to change,
particularly the deeply ingrained guilt society has conditioned us to
have. From social and cultural norms to expectations of compliance,
misfits are frequently shunned. I often see this conditioning starting
in the stories I'm meant to read to my kids. But it's not going to stay this
way. While things like body shaming, mental health, and other taboo
topics are being addressed at the surface level now, over time we will
go deeper. It will become clear that our conditioning and norms are
connected to our economic system, and we will find ways to let them
go. Self-compassion and speaking to ourselves with kindness will make
us more resilient when we mess up along the way, as we all do. It will
help us take responsibility for those actions without taking on all the
toxic guilt we have been meant to absorb.

As consciousness rises, gratitude rises with it. We perform the greatest
mental gymnastics when we try to convince ourselves that we are the
sole reason for our success, that we did it all on our own, and that our
success was only because of our own efforts. We posture and signal
to the world that we are somehow better than we were, or better than
someone else. Gratitude melts all that competition away and makes
us less self-centered. When feelings of hopelessness do threaten to
strike, I recommend finding a blank piece of paper and writing down
all that you are grateful for—the people in your life and all the big and
small things that bring you joy.

The truth we often choose to ignore, as Folan so eloquently explained to me, is that:

> *Nothing on this earth belongs to us, not even our body. Neither do we determine how much time we have left—all of it is a gift. If you believe your time is truly yours, then you should know how much you have left. None of us do. We're only responsible for the use of our time, and how we choose to use it is up to each one of us.*

> *...You're writing about economics, which is determined by politics, which is cultural, which is spiritual—ultimately leading to, "What do you believe?" And everybody believes in something.*

To paraphrase Albert Einstein, we cannot change the world without changing our thinking. Attitude changes everything. By not putting money at the center of your universe, as our current economic system wants you to do, you begin to think differently—and thought has a much bigger impact than you can imagine.

The more I let go of my desire to be super rich, the more I am able to align with the person I want to be. Like so many of us, money had been my primary value, no matter what I told myself. With the wholesale collapse of faith in the 21st century, money became our God. To change our economic system, we need to change our beliefs, our spirituality, our culture, and our politics too. Not just from one thing to another, but to something better and new—a third way*—based on inclusive economics. Something that we can co-create together.

---

* As mentioned before (but it's worth repeating), the term "third way" refers to a political, social, or economic philosophy that seeks to find a middle ground or alternative approach between traditional ideologies. It often emerges as a response to perceived shortcomings or limitations of existing systems. The concept of a third way suggests that there is an alternative path that combines elements from different ideologies to create a more balanced, practical, and inclusive solution.

Change is happening. It has happened to me. It is happening to you now. And that's how meaningful change often happens: incrementally, 0.1 by 0.1, those small steps eventually adding up to a change so profound it will appear to have happened exponentially.

Increment by increment, we are getting closer and closer to tipping the scales.

Conclusion

The global financial crisis in 2008 exposed that our current economic system is broken and that growth at all costs is unsustainable, not just from an economic standpoint with crash after crash, but more importantly, with the impact it is having on our planet. Much of how the world works today is based on unconscious, legacy economic thinking that never worked for all and still doesn't work for most. Very few of us question whether our economic system and its patterns serve humanity. For most, it is routine, and it is accepted at a subconscious level without awareness of the harm it is causing. Unless we raise our consciousness, these problems will remain far away from us—existing in some distant place, leaving us with a feeling that none of them will affect us.

As we come to the end of our journey together, I want to tell you a story about someone who smoked cigarettes for years. She is a well-educated, sophisticated person, but that doesn't really matter; at this point, everyone knows that smoking kills. It says so, in so many words, on every package, with skull and crossbones helpfully added to drive the point home for those who cannot read (at least throughout Europe and Canada). But it seems those warnings don't matter either. Especially for younger people, death and heart disease and emphysema are abstract, hypothetical future risks, far less powerful than the impulses of the present moment. This particular person started smoking in her early twenties when she was fronting bands in local pubs. The force of habit was powerful—until the day her voice would not reach a high B-flat, a note that was well within her range. She quit smoking that night and never picked up again.

This example shows us that awareness and education are not enough to create change. Being aware of consequences but unable (or unwilling) to act on that awareness keeps us making decisions from an unconscious state. Sometimes you're aware, but you dismiss it because the impulses of old patterns are too great. You almost can't help yourself. This choice isn't from an unconscious state, but from a place of low consciousness—because your awareness and consciousness aren't congruent.

Only when you become truly conscious about something—with a deeper understanding that connects that awareness to something you directly value, something that aligns with the meaning you perceive your life to have—does the way you behave toward that thing begin to change. For her, the health warnings and statistics, real as they were, ultimately mattered less than the individual meaning she saw for her own life as a musician. It took that B-flat for the penny to drop and for her consciousness to finally align with her awareness about smoking.

Incidentally, while her career as a musician was threatened by smoking, it also contributed to her starting the habit in the first place. Have you ever watched the movie *Grease*? A millennial favorite, the closing scene shows Sandy's transformation into someone who is cool. The signifier? Both what she was wearing *and* that she was smoking. This film is still beloved, even though the "smoking is cool" imagery doesn't hold as much weight today.*

---

* It is worth noting that more than a billion people still smoke and that number increased to 1.1 billion in 2019.

Similarly, while being and wanting to be filthy rich is still "cool" in many ways—just look at your Instagram feed—the perception has already started to change. Those of us who set out to make our millions by any means necessary are beginning to rethink the impact of our choices. In the years to come, I believe megaprofit capitalism will be as outdated as smoking is now—some will always choose their addiction to profit over their own personal growth, but it will no longer be a quality most people aspire to.

Of course, at the turn of the millennium, Gen X, who believed they had succeeded through drive, hard work, and intelligence, had to find ways of spending their newfound wealth while showing they were not being materialistic. So, according to journalist David Brooks, they "developed an elaborate code of financial correctness to display their superior sensibility." He explains:

> *Spending lots of money on any room formerly used by the servants was socially defensible: A $7,000 crystal chandelier in the living room was vulgar, but a $10,000, 59-inch AGA stove in the kitchen was acceptable, a sign of your foodie expertise.*[1]

The extremes will always exist, but the extremes don't have to shape a new economic system—we get to do that, choice by everyday choice.

Fortunately, choices like the ones mentioned above are only about status, not survival. And what elevates status has been and will be constantly redefined. A fascinating example: between 1813 and 1815, the Prussian royal family urged all citizens to contribute their gold and silver jewelry toward funding the uprising against Napoleon during the War of Liberation. In return, the people were given iron jewelry such as brooches and finger rings, which became a symbol of patriotism and loyalty. Those who continued wearing gold and silver jewelry were seen as selfish and suffered a loss of status. As a result, the people who sacrificed their wealth instead of displaying it enjoyed a higher social status. In today's digital age, status in some circles might be equated with the blue Twitter check mark that indicated a certain number of social media followers and general recognition (before Musk took over Twitter, renamed it as X, and the check mark suddenly indicated something else entirely). Not so long ago it used to be gold and platinum credit cards or your airline status, which became passé when the internet made us lose interest in social signifiers that only a finite number of people could see.

A more personal example: being an author is supposed to be a status thing all on its own. But writing a book is not just one thing anymore, and different options for publishing and promoting a book have become connected to different measurements of status—having that little penguin on the corner of your cover or one of the big five publishers behind you is a strong signal. Over the past two decades, publishing has democratized, at least to some extent. As a result, there are people who swear by self-publishing only, and there are people who think that self-publishing is trash.

While writing this book, I struggled with how I would go about publishing and promoting it. The whole point of writing it was to share a message that could make a difference to a few people's lives, the same way books I read or listen to change my life. For that to happen, I needed the ability to distribute and promote it so that people could find it.

But it has become clear to me that I don't want to join yet another rat race—number of social media followers, newsletter subscribers, preorders, etc. I trust that this book will find the people looking for it, the same way most books have found me: word of mouth recommendations. For a time, I even wanted to become an antihero in this regard, until startup founder coach Evgeny Shadchnev put it to me like this:

> *Trying to be a hero and trying to be an anti-hero have the same dynamic: trying to be someone. Whether we put ourselves on a pedestal*

as the greatest person of all times or as the most unremarkable ever,
we still care about how we come across.

So I'm no longer worried about being a hero *or* an antihero. How I come across doesn't matter—whether or not my message comes across does.

£ € $

Some predict the next billion-dollar startup will only have three employees—a CEO and Product and Operations Leads. Whether it's actually three people or a small handful of employees leveraging outsourced services and AI, the prediction is very plausible—powered by a huge team of AI agents who collaborate with customers to construct a roadmap, drive development, and handle most of the digital marketing and sales functions. Yet, unless such startups are run by people who have raised their consciousness, these advancements will only serve to further concentrate wealth.

We have to think about money in different terms—a means to an end, and not an end in itself. Otherwise, we're just going to prop up our economic system as it continues to produce inequality.

I cannot stress this enough: change on this scale is always incremental before it is seen as exponential, and it cannot be achieved alone.

The design of a new world during and after the Second World War was very much a community-led effort executed on a global scale. Rebuilding the international economic system while World War II was still being fought took 730 delegates from all 44 Allied nations. The result was the Bretton Woods Agreement that established the United Nations. While that was 80 years ago, this shows us that global cooperation can create new systems and models—and from this clarity, it's obvious that the old model isn't the way forward *or* something to feel stuck with.

We need to experiment with new business and funding models. We need innovative ways to engage young people. Waiting for the world to change is futile. We can talk about dangers and we can change what's socially acceptable, but at the end of the day, we are only responsible for ourselves. Similarly, I cannot make you join the growing movement of people who are increasing their consciousness. That is up to you.

The problems in front of us are global, but the choice—whether to divest from the current system and begin participating in and ideating something new—is personal.

Perhaps we can stop worshipping people like Bezos, Buffett, and Branson. We need to be more like Vanguard, not just in helping others create wealth but in the promise of their name: a vanguard is a group of people leading the way in new developments or ideas, just as Bogle, Lewis, Scott, and Arizmendriarrieta did. We need to start and support conscious businesses like We Give a Crap, Toast, and one more you've yet to meet: Happy Maki.

Anna, the founder of Happy Maki, has always loved sushi. While on an atoll in the middle of the Pacific Ocean—6,000 kilometers from the closest continent—she fell in love with the ocean. These two loves felt incompatible to her. She watched the documentary *End of the Line* and realized that "you cannot claim to be an ocean lover and still eat fish," and changed her ordering habits. When the documentary *Cowspiracy* got to her and she realized that "you cannot be an environmentalist and still eat meat," Anna gave up her favorites—rare steak and BBQ ribs—and turned vegan. By 2014, Happy Maki was born, serving vegan sushi, burritos, and bento bowls.

The story doesn't end there: Anna continued to increase her conscious-ness, and in 2020, she realized that our economy needed systemic change. She switched Happy Maki to a gift economy* model, giving patrons the food as a gift while letting them know how much it costs to make. This empowers people to choose how to value the gift and how much they might want to donate in return. By promoting transparency, responsibility, learning, and growth, Anna hopes to address society's issues with money at an emotional level and encourage community support and action to solve problems and build a better world. On her website, she says, "We're experimenting with doing business in a truly kind and transparent way," and the journey hasn't been easy.

In the first year, 37 percent of people who visited Happy Maki chose to donate less than the actual cost of food, 19 percent chose to donate more than the actual cost, and the remaining 44 percent donated the cost alone, resulting in a loss of $24,000. For each meal Happy Maki makes, they feed a child and plant a tree. In four years that's 453,759 meals and 442,510 trees. Just as this book was going to print, Anna has gone back to a conventional model to focus on growing her busi-ness—still a not-for-profit organization, but now in search of other ways to make an impact.

Even the biggest companies in the world are made up of people, and ultimately it is down to either one person or a small group of people to decide how each company operates, just like Anna has done. She notes that thirty-somethings frequently comment that the gift econ-omy model must be a brilliant way to make a lot of money—but that's not her goal at all. If we all keep trying to maximize our own wealth, treating everything like an optimizable transaction, we'll continue to drive inequality. Or we can change our perspective so that "winning"

---

* A gift economy or gift culture is a system of exchange in which valuables are not sold but given without an expectation of remuneration, reciprocity, or future rewards (quid pro quo).

isn't what we've been told it is, so that we see each other as people and money as abundant, and so that even "leaving money on the table" is a good thing, creating a win for our fellow humans rather than a FOMO moment for us.

Your brain is constantly trying to compare in order to find a place to belong, but that doesn't mean you have to play along with society's games and their winners and losers. Remember the show *Whose Line is it Anyway?*, where the rules are all made up and the points don't matter? Our society is a bit like that, at least from an economic standpoint. We get to choose what marks of status we want to pursue—or we can choose to pursue none at all. We can decide to stop asking "Who's better or worse?" and instead lean into belonging by asking "Where do I fit into the puzzle?"

It took me 30 years to realize I was part of the problem. I was trying my hardest to attain success in order to affect change—and it just wasn't happening. I learned about abundance in 2017 and I made a concerted, incremental effort from then on, but it wasn't until 2021 that I finally fully shifted my perspective. Time itself, the people I engaged with, and the books I read along my journey all played a critical role in my transformation. The last year of that time period was filled with intentional work to finally let go of the mindset pieces that were holding me back, and there will undoubtedly be more to go. This is an ongoing journey. The more my consciousness grows and my community alongside it, the more layers of ideology and programming I will uncover and have to decide to face. But we've all got to start somewhere—the stakes have never been higher.

I'll let you in on a little secret—in 2006, I heard a Chinese proverb by Confucius that baffled me: "To know and not to do, is not yet to know."

Initially it went over my head. It didn't land at all. Over time, it made me think—does everything require action? Couldn't we know something

"To know and not to do, is not yet to know."
—*Confucius*

and let that knowledge be enough? I knew some things and I did some things, but it hadn't yet clicked that making conscious choices based on my awareness is really the point of learning in the first place.

Raising your consciousness requires more than hot air. There is no point talking about it unless you are doing it. My grandmother told me something like this when I was 15, playing cricket outside of our house. She came to visit and as she walked past me, she said, "Study, putha," using an endearing term to encourage me to study instead of playing cricket. My backchat to her was full of teenage bravado. I cringe at the memory and how she put me in my place. She replied, "There are many a slip between the cup and the lip. Instead of telling everyone what you're going to do, don't say anything and do it and show us." That moment stuck with me, just like the quote from Confucius, until finally the penny dropped and I realized what it meant to act from a place of consciousness.

The truth is, unless knowledge informs action, it is useless. You can watch all the documentaries and read stacks of books, but if you don't make an effort to put any of that awareness into action, it's just entertainment. We all suffer from the adage that people know what to do, but don't do what they know. Like me several years earlier, you may know something, and you may have made some incremental changes—it wasn't that I was ignoring everything I heard and not taking any action; I was putting a few things into practice where I believed I could. But for a long time, I hadn't *consciously* changed my behavior based on what I had learned.

We're at a historic crossroads, where we can choose to increase our consciousness or remain set in our dangerous ways. Cultivating a deeper consciousness and living with intentionality are the only ways to live a life of abundance to any meaningful extent—which also means that a truly abundant mindset is accessible just by focusing on our consciousness.

I'm not saying it's easy, or that what you've done to this point doesn't count. We're all trying really hard in our own ways. We're all on different journeys, and some things come more naturally to others along the way. Even if we are pessimistic in our analysis of the future, we can still remain optimistic in our actions. Individually, we all have the ability to thrive now. What I've learned is that it's always easier together. And the more of us who choose to thrive, the stronger the movement—and our society—will become.

Your practice of inclusive economics—whether with small steps or big—is the most active way you can affect change in our globally connected world and be a part of solving all the challenges it's facing.

We're living through incredibly transformative times, and you have the ability to shape that transformation. If you weren't up to the task, chances are you wouldn't have read this book, far less gotten to the end of it. That is a signal that you have hope.

I am hopeful because of *you*. You're not participating in the old race anymore. As our time in this book comes to an end, I'm happy to hand you the baton and cheer you on as you sprint to the next marker. We're running together—not in competition but in community.

Jacqueline Novogratz, who you met in chapter 11, put it beautifully in her book, *Manifesto for a Moral Revolution: Practices to Build a Better World*:

> *As we go through life on this tiny, blue planet, the only home we know, imagine the changes that might arise if we each took a step toward making it a home in which all of us could participate, where each person could flourish with peace and justice and a sense of wholeness for many, many generations to come.*[2]

It'll take time for change to happen, but when your level of consciousness taps into a place of abundance—when nothing has to be commodity, and everything can be community—then not even time has to be scarce. The change we create together, choice by choice, gives us more time on this planet and makes more space for each other.

Join me. Join others. Together, we are Generation Hope.

Join
#GenHope

Humanity finds itself at a crossroad, caught in a race between catastrophe and consciousness. At this pivotal moment in time, I firmly hold onto the belief that consciousness will triumph. This conviction isn't a distant hope; it's a choice to embrace change in the here and now.

Ask yourself: What changes will you embrace from this point onward? What changes will you ignite? Are you ready to be part of the resounding chorus of conscious millennials, determined to shape a brighter future?

Consider the ideas that have resonated with you thus far. Are there concepts that have sparked a fire within your mind, illuminating paths you hadn't yet considered? Is there a seed of inspiration beginning to take root? Allow it to unfurl its potential within you.

Yet, seeds and sparks alone are mere potential. The true measure of a change in consciousness lies in action. What will you embark upon? Inscribe your intentions, not just while reading these pages, but deep within yourself. Commit to them as a promise you hold for yourself and for the world.

As you seek to join this movement of change, I extend an invitation: share your journey with me and with the world. Don't let these actions be solitary endeavors—let them reverberate beyond the confines of your own heart and into the community we're all responsible for building. Use the hashtag #GenHope to unite your aspirations with those of countless others who are steering their lives toward consciousness, or email me directly at hi@arunjay.com (I reply to every email).

This book has been created as a public service and I am not earning any money from its publication. If you have benefited from this book, please consider sharing it with your friends and support Acumen with a generous donation at www.acumen.org/donate.

The choice is yours, the path is open, and the time is now. Let's inscribe a legacy of hope, transformation, and conscious action for the generations yet to come.

Appreciation

There is an abundance of reasons to feel gratitude and a multitude of individuals to extend that gratitude toward. My heart swells with joy as I reflect on all the wonderful people who dedicated parts of themselves to bring this book to life. A deep, expanding sense of appreciation fills me, and I am truly thankful to each and every one of you.

This book owes much of its current form to the invaluable assistance of my exceptionally brilliant developmental editor, Brannan Sirratt, whose magic is intricately woven into every page. (And thanks to Rebecca Monterusso for introducing us.)

My dear friend Anne Folan played a pivotal role in crafting key sections of this book and was a constant source of inspiration during our countless conversations over the past two years.

Bec Evans, my book coach, provided me with invaluable writing guidance and I am grateful for her hands-on involvement in the project.

I am incredibly fortunate to have worked with my publisher, Saeah Wood, Amy Reed, and the team at Otterpine. Their attention to detail has been amazing and collaborating with them has been an absolute pleasure.

I am grateful to Thomas Philips for his many contributions. Thomas, you were an early believer, an early reader, and a huge help when this project was young and fragile. I appreciate you and thank you for challenging me every step of the way, and I appreciate your willingness to hurt my feelings in pursuit of a better product.

My gratitude goes out to my posse of early readers who generously devoted their time, provided invaluable edits, and offered sage advice. Each and every one of you played a crucial role in shaping this book. My deepest appreciation for each of you: Janet Shulist, Catherine Lunardon, Tarini Uppal, Evgeny Shadchnev, Katharina Ritter, Aman Mawar, Richard Austin and Ramu Katakam.

I extend my heartfelt thanks to the authors and creators who were the inspiration for this book. My motivation to create and share this work stems directly from my profound appreciation for the transformative influence of similar books. I'd like to specifically mention a few that have had a significant impact:

- *Winners Take All: The Elite Charade of Changing the World* by Anand Giridharadas
- *Manifesto for a Moral Revolution: Practices to Build a Better World* by Jacqueline Novogratz
- *People, Power, and Profits: Progressive Capitalism for an Age of Discontent* by Joseph E. Stiglitz
- *The Psychology of Money: Timeless Lessons on Wealth, Greed, and Happiness* by Morgan Housel

I am deeply grateful for the unwavering help, support, and encouragement I received from numerous friends and family throughout this mammoth project. I genuinely appreciate every gesture of kindness and positivity. Your collective energy was a driving force that carried me through the countless hours it took to create this book for you.

Resources

ThriveNow

ThriveNow brings together and supports a community of purpose-driven leaders to accelerate their impact so humanity and our planet can Thrive. Now.

Accelerating impact as leaders starts with who we are, who we choose to become, and how we connect with the world around us. If we want to see real change, it begins within each of us.

Packed with resources and tools, all available for free, ThriveNow is a platform you can use as you continue on your journey toward increasing your consciousness and moving from a scarcity mindset to one of abundance.

Are you ready to change your thinking, understand your personal definition of thriving, and realize your own power and use it for the good of humanity and our planet?

Visit www.thrive-now.org

Inclusive Action Lab

A better life for every human on earth.

We envision a world where no one has to worry about where their next meal is coming from.

We live in a world of abundance, yet some have such excess while others fight for their survival. This needs to change.

We aim to make digital, financial, and economic inclusion a global reality in the next seven years, and we need your help.

We are deeply researching problems low-income individuals and families have and are developing solutions that will help service providers solve identified needs.

The Inclusive Action Lab is focused on three types of solutions:

1. On a more cooperative basis, allow digital platforms to accumulate less, broker more, and share the rewards more equitably. We need to envision successful digital platforms that are based on profitability, sustainability, and good remuneration to build strong teams and hold them together, while focusing on distributing wealth more equally across the people who genuinely create the value.
2. Create add-on solutions, which extend current solutions to those in what is known as the "hardest to reach" segment of our global population (e.g., offline digital payments that extend mobile money networks to areas without access to network coverage and/or that lack energy access).
3. Provide cost-neutral financial and digital access (e.g., solar kit repayments are cheaper than buying kerosene to burn a lamp and have proven to be a great way to drive penetration because the only barrier is awareness, not cost).

If you could build a brighter future, what would it look like?

Become part of a collective community contributing to a brighter world in innovative and transformative ways.

Visit www.inclusiveactionlab.org

Acumen Academy

The world's school for social change.

Acumen Academy's mission is to unleash a new generation of social innovators and leaders with the determination and grit to build a more just, inclusive, and sustainable world, where success is defined not by how the privileged fare but by how the earth and its poor and vulnerable populations are treated.

Acumen Academy is unique. It's a place where new role models and business models are created and celebrated, where competence meets character, practical skills meet moral imagination, and urgency meets action. Acumen Academy serves a community of social innovators and builders who are willing to embrace the challenge of solving the world's toughest problems while providing the practical tools, practices, and resources needed to create new solutions for an interdependent world. Ultimately, our shared ethos, our commitment to life-long accompaniment, and the unleashing of human energy within our communities will serve a future for all of us.

FREE COURSES: Challenge-based courses and master classes are designed to help you build practical skills to drive change in your community and your business.

FELLOWSHIPS: Join hundreds of fellows and a committed local cohort of leaders intent on building an inclusive, just, and sustainable world.

ACCELERATORS: Join intensive cohort-based sprints that delve deep into practices for scaling your business and taking your leadership to the next level.

Visit www.acumenacademy.org.

Notes

Introduction

1. Institute for Economics and Peace, "Ecological Threat Register" (Press Release), September 9, 2020, https://www.economicsandpeace.org/wp-content/uploads/2020/09/Ecological-Threat-Register-Press-Release-27.08-FINAL.pdf.

2. R. Buckminster Fuller, *Grunch of Giants* (United States: St. Martin's Press, 1983).

3. National Centre for Atmospheric Science, "Air pollution falling across UK cities, latest data shows" (Press Release), March 31, 2020, https://ncas.ac.uk/air-pollution-falling-across-uk-cities-latest-data-shows/.

4. "Coronavirus: Nasa images show China pollution clear amid slowdown," BBC News, February 29, 2020, https://www.bbc.com/news/world-asia-51691967.

5. Ted Millar, "World Leaders' Backs Up Against the Wall at COP 26 as the World Burns," Liberal America, October 26, 2021, https://liberalamerica.org/2021/10/26/tm-world-leaders-backs-up-against-the-wall-at-cop-26-as-the-world-burns/.

6. Andrew Anthony, "Yuval Noah Harari: 'Homo sapiens as we know them will disappear in a century or so,'" *The Guardian*, March 19, 2017, https://www.theguardian.com/culture/2017/mar/19/yuval-harari-sapiens-readers-questions-lucy-prebble-arianna-huffington-future-of-humanity.

7. Fiona Harvey and Damian Carrington, "World is on 'highway to climate hell', UN chief warns at Cop27 summit," *The Guardian,* November 7, 2022, https://www.theguardian.com/environment/2022/nov/07/cop27-climate-summit-un-secretary-general-antonio-guterres.

8. Charlie Mackesy, *The Boy, the Mole, the Fox and the Horse* (New York: HarperOne, 2019).

9. Fuller, *Grunch of Giants.*

Chapter 1

1. "Coronavirus: Worst economic crisis since 1930s depression, IMF says," BBC, April 9, 2020, https://www.bbc.com/news/business-52236936.

2. Thomas K. Grose, "The Worker Retraining Challenge," *U.S. News & World Report*, February 6, 2018, https://www.usnews.com/news/best-countries/articles/2018-02-06/what-sweden-can-teach-the-world-about-worker-retraining.

3. Panhambam S, "Sal Khan: Let's Teach for Mastery—Not Test Scores (Transcript)," The Singju Post, January 12, 2018, https://singjupost.com/sal-khan-lets-teach-for-mastery-not-test-scores-transcript/.

4. Joshua Wöhle, "The Future of Skills Has Arrived: Are You Ready?" LinkedIn post, January 30, 2023, https://www.linkedin.com/pulse/future-skills-has-arrived-you-ready-joshua-w%C3%B6hle/.

5. Access to Medicine Foundation, (website) accessed July 2023, https://accesstomedicinefoundation.org/.

6. World Health Organization, "World Bank and WHO: Half the world lacks access to essential health services, 100 million still pushed into extreme poverty because of health expenses" (News Release), December 13, 2017, https://www.who.int/news/item/13-12-2017-world-bank-and-who-half-the-world-lacks-access-to-essential-health-services-100-million-still-pushed-into-extreme-poverty-because-of-health-expenses.

7. "Mera Doctor," Tracxn, updated July 5, 2023, https://tracxn.com/d/companies/meradoctor/__6kKb4xW5djJYEWiLrDsfg_5TTGE2q8Zo8_F-l-xhx7U.

8. Andrew Gregory, "Police examine 600 cases after damning NHS baby deaths report," *The Guardian*, March 30, 2022, https://www.theguardian.com/society/2022/mar/30/baby-deaths-inquiry-shrewsbury-nhs-trust-condemned-for-repeated-failures.

9. Justinas Baltrusaitis, "70% of the Top 10 Billionaires Generated Wealth from the Tech Industry," *Focus on Business*, March 3, 2021, https://focusonbusiness.eu/en/news/70-of-the-top-10-billionaires-generated-wealth-from-the-tech-industry/4086.

10. Brian Dean, "Amazon Prime User and Revenue Statistics (2023)," Backlinko, updated March 27, 2023, https://backlinko.com/amazon-prime-users.

11. Jeffrey Grabow, "Venture capital continues to exhibit immunity to the COVID-19 pandemic," EY, February 9, 2022, https://www.ey.com/en_us/growth/venture-capital-continues-to-exhibit-immunity-to-the-covid-19-pandemic.

12. Milan Thomas and Yangchen C. Rinzin, "Your Questions Answered: What Is Bhutan's Gross Happiness Index?" Asian Development Blog, March 20, 2023, https://blogs.adb.org/blog/your-questions-answered-what-bhutan-s-gross-national-happiness-index.

13. Margaret Thatcher, interview by Douglas Keay for *Woman's Own* ("no such thing as society"), September 23, 1987, London, Margaret Thatcher Foundation: Speeches, Interviews and Other Statements, https://www.margaretthatcher.org/document/106689.

Chapter 2

1. Douglas Coupland, *Generation X: Tales for an Accelerated Culture* (London, England: Abacus, 2017).

2. Rebecca Leung, "The Echo Boomers," CBS News, October 1, 2004, https://www.cbsnews.com/news/the-echo-boomers-01-10-2004/.

3. Kathryn Tuggle, "3 Reasons Baby Boomers and Millennials Are More Alike Than Anyone Wants to Admit," *The Street,* June 11, 2015, https://www.thestreet.com/personal-finance/3-reasons-baby-boomers-and-millennials-are-more-alike-than-anyone-wants-to-admit-13181859.

4. Emily A. Vogels, "Millennials stand out for their technology use, but older generations also embrace digital life," Pew Research Center, Washington, D.C., September 9, 2019, https://www.pewresearch.org/fact-tank/2019/09/09/us-generations-technology-use/.

5. "Current Population Survey (CPS)," Pew Research Center, accessed July 2023, https://www.census.gov/programs-surveys/cps.html.

6. "Who Are Millennials," Millennial Marketing website, accessed July 2023, https://www.millennialmarketing.com/who-are-millennials/.

7. Christopher Ingraham, "The staggering millennial wealth deficit, in one chart," *The Washington Post,* December 3, 2019, https://www.washingtonpost.com/business/2019/12/03/precariousness-modern-young-adulthood-one-chart/.

8. William Strauss and Neil Howe, *Millennials Rising: The Next Great Generation* (New York: Vintage, 2000).

9. Millennial Marketing, "Who Are Millennials."

10. Matt McGrath, "Climate change: Five things we have learned from the IPCC report," BBC, August 9, 2021, https://www.bbc.com/news/science-environment-58138714.

11. Rebecca Henderson, *Reimagining Capitalism in a World on Fire* (New York: PublicAffairs, 2021).

12. Richard Baldwin, *The Globotics Upheaval: Globalization, Robotics and the Future of Work* (United States: Oxford University Press, 2019).

13. Bureau of Labor Statistics, "Employer Costs for Employee Compensation—March 2023" (News Release), USDL-23-1305 June 16, 2023, https://www.bls.gov/news.release/pdf/ecec.pdf.

14. Daisuke Wakabayashi, "Google's Shadow Work Force: Temps Who Outnumber Full-Time Employees," *The New York Times,* May 28, 2019, https://www.nytimes.com/2019/05/28/technology/google-temp-workers.html.

15. World Economic Forum, "The Future of Jobs Report 2020," October 2020, http://www3.weforum.org/docs/WEF_Future_of_Jobs_2020.pdf.

16. Aaron Smith, "Public Predictions for the Future of Workforce Automation," Pew Research Center, Washington, D.C., March 10, 2016, https://www.pewresearch.org/internet/2016/03/10/public-predictions-for-the-future-of-workforce-automation/.

17. Lee Simmons, "Should We Stop Licensing Doctors and Lawyers?" Stanford Business, March 2, 2018, https://www.gsb.stanford.edu/insights/should-we-stop-licensing-doctors-lawyers.

18. David Brooks, "How the Bobos Broke America," *The Atlantic*, September, 2021, https://www.theatlantic.com/magazine/archive/2021/09/blame-the-bobos-creative-class/619492/.

19. "The end of UK austerity means a tilt towards taxes," Financial Times, June 30, 2017, https://www.ft.com/content/8d6a89e4-5d85-11e7-b553-e2df1b0c3220.

20. Paul Johnson (@PJTheEconomist), "This is actually awful..." Twitter post, October 27, 2021, https://twitter.com/PJTheEconomist/status/1453350780124160007?s=20.

21. Jon Stone, "UK economy damaged by 'own goals' like Brexit and Liz Truss's Budget, economists say" *Independent*, November 19, 2022, https://www.independent.co.uk/news/uk/politics/ifs-budget-own-goals-brexit-liz-truss-jeremy-hunt-b2228051.html.

22. "Global Wealth Inequality," Facts: Global Inequality, Inequality.org, accessed July 2023, https://inequality.org/facts/global-inequality/#global-wealth-inequality.

23. Thomas Shapiro, Tatjana Meschede, and Sam Osoro, "The Roots of the Widening Racial Wealth Gap: Explaining the Black-White Economic Divide" (Research and Policy Brief), Brandeis University, Institute on Assets and Social Policy, February 2013, https://heller.brandeis.edu/iere/pdfs/racial-wealth-equity/racial-wealth-gap/roots-widening-racial-wealth-gap.pdf.

24. "Home Ownership," Ethnicity Facts and Figures: Housing: Owning and Renting (English Housing Survey 2017 to 2018), gov.uk, updated September 15, 2020, https://www.ethnicity-facts-figures.service.gov.uk/housing/owning-and-renting/home-ownership/latest#by-ethnicity.

25. Tiffany N. Ford, Sarah Reber, and Richard V. Reeves, "Race gaps in COVID-19 deaths are even bigger than they appear," Brookings, June 16, 2020, https://www.brookings.edu/articles/race-gaps-in-covid-19-deaths-are-even-bigger-than-they-appear/.

26. Nina Martin and Renee Montagne, "Black Mothers Keep Dying After Giving Birth. Shalon Irving's Story Explains Why." *NPR*, December 7, 2017, https://www.npr.org/2017/12/07/568948782/black-mothers-keep-dying-after-giving-birth-shalon-irvings-story-explains-why.

27. Jeanna Smialek, "Poor Americans Hit Hardest by Job Losses Amid Lockdowns, Fed Says," *The New York Times*, May 14, 2020, https://www.nytimes.com/2020/05/14/business/economy/coronavirus-jobless-unemployment.html.

28. Nick Hanauer, "The Pitchforks Are Coming...For Us Plutocrats," *Politico*, July/August 2014, https://www.politico.com/magazine/story/2014/06/the-pitchforks-are-coming-for-us-plutocrats-108014/.

29. Blake Morgan, "NOwnership, No Problem: Why Millennials Value Experiences Over Owning Things," *Forbes*, June 1, 2015, https://www.forbes.com/sites/blakemorgan/2015/06/01/nownershipnoproblem-nowners-millennials-value-experiences-over-ownership/?sh=57f830b55406.

30. "More than Half of Consumers Would Pay More for Sustainable Products Designed to Be Reused or Recycled, Accenture Survey Finds," Accenture Newsroom, June 4, 2019, https://newsroom.accenture.com/news/more-than-half-of-consumers-would-pay-more-for-sustainable-products-designed-to-be-reused-or-recycled-accenture-survey-finds.htm.

31. Jeff Cox, "A record 4.5 million workers quit their jobs in November," CNBC, January 4, 2022, https://www.cnbc.com/2022/01/04/jolts-november-2021-record-4point5-million-workers-quit-their-jobs.html.

32. Kim Parker and Juliana Menasce Horowitz, "Majority of workers who quit a job in 2021 cite low pay, no opportunities for advancement, feeling disrespected," Pew Research Center, March 9, 2022, https://www.pewresearch.org/fact-tank/2022/03/09/majority-of-workers-who-quit-a-job-in-2021-cite-low-pay-no-opportunities-for-advancement-feeling-disrespected/.

33. thefrontpageofreddit (@thefrontpageofreddit), "Is there anyone at McMurdo..." Reddit: r/antarctica, Reddit post, November 17, 2020, https://www.reddit.com/r/antarctica/comments/jvu1ap/is_there_anyone_at_mcmurdo_that_can_confirm_this/.

Chapter 3

1. Alex Hern, "WhatsApp loses millions of users after terms update," *The Guardian*, January 24, 2021, https://www.theguardian.com/technology/2021/jan/24/whatsapp-loses-millions-of-users-after-terms-update.

2. Zoe Kleinman, "Cambridge Analytica: The story so far," BBC, March 21, 2018, https://www.bbc.com/news/technology-43465968.

3. George Monbiot, "Neoliberalism – the ideology at the root of all our problems," *The Guardian*, April 15, 2016, https://www.theguardian.com/books/2016/apr/15/neoliberalism-ideology-problem-george-monbiot.

4. Robert Reich, "Republicans aren't going to tell Americans the real cause of our $31.4tn debt," *The Guardian*, sec. Opinion, February 1, 2023, https://www.theguardian.com/commentisfree/2023/feb/01/republicans-arent-going-to-tell-americans-the-real-cause-of-our-314tn-debt.

5. Monbiot, "Neoliberalism."

6. David Leonhardt, "The Rich Really Do Pay Lower Taxes Than You," *The New York Times*, October 6, 2019, https://www.nytimes.com/interactive/2019/10/06/opinion/income-tax-rate-wealthy.html.

7. Katelyn Peters, "Is Economics a Science?," *Investopedia*, August 14, 2021, https://www.investopedia.com/ask/answers/030315/economics-science.asp.

8. Andrew Sayer, *Why We Can't Afford the Rich* (United Kingdom: Policy Press, 2015).

9. "Inside Job (2010 film)," Wikipedia, accessed July 2023, https://en.wikipedia.org/wiki/Inside_Job_(2010_film).

10. Sheena McKenzie, Nicole Gaoette, and Donna Borak, "The full 'Putin list' of Russian oligarchs and political figures released by the US Treasury," CNN, January 30, 2018, https://edition.cnn.com/2018/01/30/politics/full-us-list-of-russian-oligarchs-with-putin-ties-intl/index.html.

11. "Carlos Slim Helu & family," *Forbes*, accessed July 2023, https://www.forbes.com/profile/carlos-slim-helu/?sh=6af25231646b.

12. "Mukesh Ambani," *Forbes*, accessed July 2023, https://www.forbes.com/profile/mukesh ambani/?sh=4156606c214c.

13. "Gautam Adani," *Forbes*, accessed July 2023, https://www.forbes.com/profile/gautam-adani-1/?sh=11a705465b0e.

14. Mohammed Haddad and Marium Ali, "How India will overtake China to become the most populous country," Al Jazeera, April 14, 2023, https://www.aljazeera.com/news/longform/2023/4/14/how-india-will-overtake-china-to-become-the-most-populous-country.

15. Arundhati Roy, *Capitalism: A Ghost Story* (Chicago, IL: Haymarket Books, 2014).

16. Sophia Yan, "China's parliament has about 100 billionaires, according to data from the Hurun Report," CNBC, March 3, 2017, https://www.cnbc.com/2017/03/02/chinas-parliament-has-about-100-billionaires-according-to-data-from-the-hurun-report.html.

17. Andrea Shalal, "IMF tells G20 countries to 'keep spending' on COVID-19 crisis," *Reuters*, November 2, 2020, https://www.reuters.com/article/us-imf-economy/imf-tells-g20-countries-to-keep-spending-on-covid-19-crisis-idUSKBN27I1X7.

18. P. Berthon, M. Ewing, and L. L. Hah, "Captivating company: Dimensions of attractiveness in employer branding," *International Journal of Advertising* 24, no. 2 (January 2005) 151–172, https://www.researchgate.net/publication/285707472_Captivating_company_Dimensions_of_attractiveness_in_employer_branding.

19. "Monetary Policy Hub," Atlantic Council website, accessed July 2023, https://www.atlanticcouncil.org/blogs/econographics/global-qe-tracker/.

20. William D. Cohan, "How We Got the Crash Wrong," *The Atlantic,* May 21, 2012, https://www.theatlantic.com/magazine/archive/2012/06/how-we-got-the-crash-wrong/308984/.

21. Gary Leff, "Congress Agrees To Second Airline Bailout. United's CEO Prepares To Ask For A Third.," *View from the Wing,* December 22, 2020, https://viewfromthewing.com/congress-agrees-to-second-airline-bailout-uniteds-ceo-prepares-to-ask-for-a-third/.

22. Gary Leff, "How American Airlines Is Keeping Government Payroll Support For Itself, Not Giving It To Employees," *View from the Wing,* January 13, 2021, https://viewfromthewing.com/how-american-airlines-is-keeping-government-payroll-support-for-itself-not-giving-it-to-employees/.

23. Tim Wu, "Don't Feel Sorry for the Airlines," *The New York Times,* March 16, 2020, https://www.nytimes.com/2020/03/16/opinion/airlines-bailout.html.

24. Brandon Kochkodin, "U.S. Airlines Spent 96% of Free Cash Flow on Buybacks," *Bloomberg,* March 16, 2020, https://www.bloomberg.com/news/articles/2020-03-16/u-s-airlines-spent-96-of-free-cash-flow-on-buybacks-chart#xj4y7vzkg.

25. William Turvill, "US airlines pushing for massive bailout gave $45bn to shareholders in five years," *The Guardian*, March 18, 2020, https://www.theguardian.com/business/2020/mar/18/america-airlines-bailout-shareholders-coronavirus.

26. Matt Levine, "Money Stuff: The Good Times for Airlines Are Over," *Bloomberg*, March 17, 2020, https://www.bloomberg.com/news/newsletters/2020-03-17/money-stuff-the-good-times-for-airlines-are-over.

27. Ciara Linnane, "Stock buybacks have totaled $5.3 trillion over the past decade — has that contributed to U.S. pandemic failures?," *MarketWatch*, July 30, 2020, https://www.marketwatch.com/story/stock-buybacks-have-totaled-53-trillion-over-the-past-decade-has-that-contributed-to-us-pandemic-failures-2020-07-29.

28. Richard Lardner, "Trump outpaces Obama, Bush in naming ex-lobbyists to Cabinet," Associated Press, September 17, 2019, https://apnews.com/article/08dce0f5f9c24a6aa355cd0aab3747d9.

29. Marik Von Rennenkampff, "Trump is flooding the swamp that Obama drained," *The Hill*, February 4, 2020, https://thehill.com/opinion/white-house/481407-trump-is-flooding-the-swamp-that-obama-drained/.

Chapter 4

1. Lawrence Lessig, "The Left and Right Share a Common Enemy: Capitalists Who Corrupt Capitalism," *Evonomics*, January 13, 2016, https://evonomics.com/how-capitalists-corrupt-capitalism/.

2. "'Boss'" Tweed delivered to authorities," History.com, accessed July 2023, https://www.history.com/this-day-in-history/boss-tweed-delivered-to-authorities.

3. Pangambam S, "Larry Lessig: Our Democracy No Longer Represents the People. Here's How We Fix It at TEDxMidAtlantic (Transcript)," *The Singju Post*, January 12, 2017, https://singjupost.com/larry-lessig-our-democracy-no-longer-represents-the-people-heres-how-we-fix-it-at-tedxmidatlantic-transcript/.

4. Thomas B. Edsall, "Putting Political Reform Right into the Pockets of the Nation's Voters," *The New York Times*, December 14, 2011, https://www.nytimes.com/2011/12/15/books/republic-lost-campaign-finance-reform-book-review.html.

5. David Brooks, *Bobos in Paradise: The New Upper Class and How They Got There* (United Kingdom: Simon & Schuster, 2010).

6. David Books, "How the Bobos Broke America," *The Atlantic*, August 2, 2021, https://www.theatlantic.com/magazine/archive/2021/09/blame-the-bobos-creative-class/619492/.

7. *Oxford English Dictionary*, s.v. "post-truth, adj.", last modifed July 2023, https://doi.org/10.1093/OED/3755961867.

8. Peter Dizikes, "Study: On Twitter, false news travels faster than true stories," *MIT News*, March 8, 2018, https://news.mit.edu/2018/study-twitter-false-news-travels-faster-true-stories-0308.

9. Aaron Souppouris, "Clickbait, Fake News and the Power of Feeling," Yahoo.com, July 17, 2019, https://www.yahoo.com/now/2016-11-21-clickbait-fake-news-and-the-power-of-feeling.html.

10. Eillie Anzilotti, "The Case for Paying to Use Google and Facebook," Fast Company, April 11, 2018, https://www.fastcompany.com/40557452/the-case-for-paying-to-use-google-and-facebook.

11. Emily A. Vogels, Lee Rainie, and Janna Anderson, "5. Tech causes more problems than it solves," Pew Research Center: Internet, Science & Tech, June 30, 2020, https://www.pewresearch.org/internet/2020/06/30/tech-causes-more-problems-than-it-solves/.

12. Alice Miranda Ollstein, "FDA Commissioner Califf sounds the alarm on health misinformation," Association of Health Care Journalists, April 30, 2022, https://healthjournalism.org/blog/2022/04/fda-commissioner-califf-sounds-the-alarm-on-health-misinformation-at-ahcj/.

13. Gordon Pennycook and David G. Rand, "Lazy, not biased: Susceptibility to partisan fake news is better explained by lack of reasoning than by motivated reasoning," *Cognition* 188 (July 2019): 39–50 https://doi.org/10.1016/j.cognition.2018.06.011.

14. Brian Chappatta, "Elon Musk Becomes First Person Ever to Lose $200 Billion," *Bloomberg,* December 30, 2022, https://www.bloomberg.com/news/articles/2022-12-30/elon-musk-becomes-first-person-ever-to-lose-200-billion#xj4y7vzkg.

Chapter 5

1. "The Influencer Report," Morning Consult, October 2019, https://pro.morningconsult.com/analyst-reports/influencer-report.

2. "Greensill: David Cameron 'made $10m' before company's collapse," BBC, August 9, 2021, https://www.bbc.co.uk/news/uk-58149765.

3. Greg Heffer, "Greensill collapse: £335m of taxpayers' cast at 'increased risk' due to 'woefully inadequate' checks on firm David Cameron lobbied for," Sky News, November 20, 2021, https://news.sky.com/story/greensill-collapse-335m-of-taxpayers-cash-at-increased-risk-due-to-woefully-inadequate-checks-on-firm-david-cameron-lobbied-for-12472928.

4. "David Cameron: I was paid far more at Greensill than as PM," BBC, May 13, 2021, https://www.bbc.co.uk/news/uk-politics-57104234.

5. Brian Lowry, "Alex Gibney's 'Dirty Money' exposes capitalism run amok," CNN, January 25, 2018, https://edition.cnn.com/2018/01/25/entertainment/dirty-money-review/index.html.

6. Shawn Achor, Andrew Reece, Gabriella Rosen Kellerman, and Alexi Robichaux, "9 Out of 10 People Are Willing to Earn Less Money to Do More-Meaningful Work," *Harvard Business Review*, November 6, 2018, https://hbr.org/2018/11/9-out-of-10-people-are-willing-to-earn-less-money-to-do-more-meaningful-work.

7. Phil Stutz and Barry Michels, *The Tools: 5 Tools to Help You Find Courage, Creativity, and Willpower--and Inspire You to Live Life in Forward Motion* (United States: Random House Publishing Group, 2013).

8. Phil Stutz and Barry Michels, *Coming Alive: 4 Tools to Defeat Your Inner Enemy, Ignite Creative Expression and Unleash Your Soul's Potential* (United Kingdom: Ebury Publishing, 2017).

9. Paul Skinner, *The Purpose Upgrade: Change Your Business to Save the World. Change the World to Save Your Business* (United Kingdom: Little, Brown Book Group, 2022).

10. Vishen (@Vishen), "You don't have to change the world..." Twitter post, April 29, 2019, https://twitter.com/vishen/status/1122892554083680257.

11. Christopher Kelly, "Joshua Fields Millburn Transcript," Nourish Balance Thrive blog, September 22, 2016, https://nourishbalancethrive.com/blog/2016/09/22/joshua-fields-millburn-transcript/.

12. Barry Nielsen, "The Lost Decade: Lessons From Japan's Real Estate Crisis," Investopedia, January 14, 2022, https://www.investopedia.com/articles/economics/08/japan-1990s-credit-crunch-liquidity-trap.asp.

13. Daniel Kahneman and Angus Deaton, "High income improves evaluation of life but not emotional well-being," *PNAS* 107, no. 38 (September 7, 2010): 16489–16493, https://www.pnas.org/doi/full/10.1073/pnas.1011492107.

14. Matthew A. Killingsworth, "Experienced well-being rises with income, even above $75,000 per year," *PNAS* 118 no. 4 (January 18, 2021): e2016976118, https://www.pnas.org/doi/full/10.1073/pnas.2016976118.

15. Joe Pinsker, "The Reason Many Ultrarich People Aren't Satisfied With Their Wealth," *The Atlantic,* December 4, 2018, https://www.theatlantic.com/family/archive/2018/12/rich-people-happy-money/577231/.

16. Kahneman and Deaton, "High income improves evaluation of life."

17. Tom Popomaronis, "Warren Buffett says this is 'the ultimate test of how you have lived your life'—and Bill Gates agrees," CNBC, September 1, 2019, https://www.cnbc.com/2019/09/01/billionaires-warren-buffett-bill-gates-agree-this-is-the-ultimate-test-of-how-you-have-lived-your-life.html.

Chapter 6

1. Dianeharris, "POLL: How Husbands and Wives Really Feel About Their Finances," *Money,* June 1, 2014, https://money.com/love-money-by-the-numbers/.

2. "Survey: Certified Divorce Financial Analyst® (CDFA®) Professionals Reveal the Leading Causes of Divorce," Institute for Divorce Financial Analysts, accessed July 2023, https://institutedfa.com/Leading-Causes-Divorce/.

3. "Planning & Progress Study 2018," Northwestern Mutual, accessed July 2023, https://news.northwesternmutual.com/planning-and-progress-2018.

4. Caroline Castrillon, "5 Ways to Go from a Scarcity to Abundance Mindset," *Forbes,* July 12, 2020, https://www.forbes.com/sites/carolinecastrillon/2020/07/12/5-ways-to-go-from-a-scarcity-to-abundance-mindset/.

5. Patrick Gonzales and Anindita Sen, "Financial Literacy of 15-Year-Olds: Results From PISA 2015," NCES, *Data Point,* NCES 201786 May 24, 2017, https://nces.ed.gov/pubs2017/2017086.pdf.

6. William Samuelson and Richard Zeckhauser, "Status quo bias in decision making," *J Risk Uncertainty* 1 (March 1988): 7–59, https://doi.org/10.1007/BF00055564.

7. Daniel Kahneman and Amos Tversky, "Prospect Theory: An Analysis of Decision under Risk," *Econometrica* 47, no. 2(March 1979): 263–292 https://doi.org/10.2307/1914185.

8. Laurie Santos, "A Monkey Economy as Irrational as Ours," TED Talks, filmed TEDGlobal 2010, July 2010 in Oxford, UK, 19:46, https://www.ted.com/talks/laurie_santos_a_monkey_economy_as_irrational_as_ours?language=en.

9. Jacob M. Nebel, "Status Quo Bias, Rationality, and Conservatism about Value," *Ethics* 125, no. 2 (January 2015): 449–76, https://doi.org/10.1086/678482.

10. "Research Statistic on Financial Windfalls and Bankruptcy," National Endowment for Financial Education, January 12, 2018, https://www.nefe.org/news/2018/01/research-statistic-on-financial-windfalls-and-bankruptcy.aspx.

11. "Why Most of Spread Betting Traders Lose Money?" Independent Investor, accessed July 2023, https://www.independentinvestor.com/spread-betting/why-spread-bettors-lose/.

12. Kelly McLaughlin, "The parents of a 20-year-old who died by suicide after thinking he lost $730,000 on Robinhood are suing the stock-trading app," Business Insider India, February 9, 2021, https://www.businessinsider.in/international/news/the-parents-of-a-20-year-old-who-died-by-suicide-after-thinking-he-lost-730000-on-robinhood-are-suing-the-stock-trading-app/articleshow/80755728.cms.

13. Alex Veiga, "Family of novice investor who killed himself sue Robinhood," Yahoo!life, February 8, 2021, https://uk.style.yahoo.com/family-novice-investor-killed-himself-013932329.html.

Chapter 7

1. Emily Garr Pacetti, "The Five Characteristics of an Inclusive Economy: Getting Beyond the Equity-Growth Dichotomy," The Rockefeller Foundation, December 13, 2016, https://www.rockefellerfoundation.org/blog/five-characteristics-inclusive-economy-getting-beyond-equity-growth-dichotomy/.

2. Ianchovichina, Elena and Susanna Lundstrom. 2009. *Inclusive Growth Analytics: Framework and Application*. Policy Research Working Papers, March 2009. © World Bank. https://doi.org/10.1596/1813-9450-4851. License: Creative Commons Attribution CC BY 3.0 IGO.

3. Alan Berube and John Irons, "Measuring 'inclusive economies' in metropolitan America," Brookings, May 12, 2016, https://www.brookings.edu/articles/measuring-inclusive-economies-in-metropolitan-america/.

4. Joseph Parilla and Glencora Haskins, "Metro Monitor 2023: Examining pandemic-era patterns of inclusive growth across the U.S.," Brookings, February 28, 2023, https://www.brookings.edu/articles/metro-monitor-2023-examining-pandemic-era-patterns-of-inclusive-growth-across-the-u-s/.

5. Jon Alexander and Ariane Conrad, *Citizens: Why the Key to Fixing Everything Is All of Us* (United Kingdom: Canbury Press, 2023).

6. "The Panama Papers: Exposing the Rogue Offshore Finance Industry," International Consortium of Investigative Journalists, April 3, 2016, https://www.icij.org/investigations/panama-papers/.

7. "Paradise Papers: Secrets of the Global Elite," International Consortium of Investigative Journalists, November 5, 2017, https://www.icij.org/investigations/paradise-papers/.

8. "Pandora Papers," International Consortium of Investigative Journalists, October 3, 2021, https://www.icij.org/investigations/pandora-papers/.

9. "Offshore havens and hidden riches of world leaders and billionaires exposed in unprecedented leak," International Consortium of Investigative Journalists, October 3, 2021, https://www.icij.org/investigations/pandora-papers/global-investigation-tax-havens-offshore/.

10. Azeem Azhar, "The Time for 'Catalytic Government' Is Now," Wired UK, December 17, 2022, https://www.wired.co.uk/article/government-economy-innovation.

11. "9 Million Jobs from Climate Action: The Inflation Reduction Act," BlueGreen Alliance, accessed July 2023, https://www.bluegreenalliance.org/site/9-million-good-jobs-from-climate-action-the-inflation-reduction-act/.

12. "UK government launches taskforce to support drive for 2 million green jobs by 2030" (Press Release), GOV.UK, November 12, 2020, https://www.gov.uk/government/news/uk-government-launches-taskforce-to-support-drive-for-2-million-green-jobs-by-2030.

13. Cedefop, "The green employment and skills transformation: insights from a European Green Deal skills forecast scenario," Publications Office of the European Union, 2021, https://data.europa.eu/doi/10.2801/112540.

14. "Green & Just Transition," C40 Cities, accessed July 2023, https://www.c40.org/what-we-do/green-just-transition/.

15. John Appleby and Sally Gainsbury, "The past, present and future of government spending on the NHS," Nuffield Trust, October 17, 2022, https://www.nuffieldtrust.org.uk/news-item/the-past-present-and-future-of-government-spending-on-the-nhs.

16. Appleby and Gainsbury, "Government spending NHS."

17. Appleby and Gainsbury, "Government spending NHS."

18. Nick Hardinges, "PM claims £350m figure on side of Brexit bus was actually 'a slight underestimate,'" LBC, July 7, 2021, https://www.lbc.co.uk/news/brexit-boris-johnson-350-million-figure-side-vote-leave-bus-underestimate/.

19. Appleby and Gainsbury, "Government spending NHS."

20. "Leading 500 Fortune companies based on number of employees in 2022," Statista, accessed July 2023, https://www.statista.com/statistics/264671/top-50-companies-based-on-number-of-employees/.

21. U.S. Government Accountability Office, "Federal Social Safety Net Programs: Millions of Full-Time Workers Rely on Federal Health Care and

Food Assistance Programs," October 19, 2020, https://www.gao.gov/assets/gao-21-45.pdf.

22. Marc Benioff, "We Need a New Capitalism," *The New York Times*, October 14, 2019, https://www.nytimes.com/2019/10/14/opinion/benioff-salesforce-capitalism.html.

Chapter 8

1. E. F. Schumacher, *Small Is Beautiful: A Study of Economics as if People Mattered* (United Kingdom: Abacus, 1975).

2. "Taylor Swift on why she quit 'grand experiment' Spotify," BBC News, November 7, 2014, https://www.bbc.co.uk/news/newsbeat-29949644.

3. "Love Your Job? Someone May Be Taking Advantage of You," Duke University's Fuqua School of Business, April 24, 2019, https://www.fuqua.duke.edu/duke-fuqua-insights/kay-passion-exploitation.

4. Rebecca Giblin and Cory Doctorow, *Chokepoint Capitalism: How Big Tech and Big Content Captured Creative Labor Markets and How We'll Win Them Back* (United States: Beacon Press, 2022).

5. Giblin and Doctorow, *Chokepoint Capitalism*.

6. Yanis Varoufakis, *Another Now* (United States: Melville House, 2021).

7. Josie Cox, "Businesses perform better when they have greater ethnic and gender diversity, study reveals," *The Independent*, January 19, 2018, https://www.independent.co.uk/news/business/news/business-ethnic-gender-diversity-performance-levels-better-study-workplace-office-mckinsey-a8166601.html.

8. Louisa Heinrich, "Sharing, shmaring [part1/2]," January 5, 2016, https://www.louisaheinrich.com/2016/01/05/sharing-shmaring-part-12/.

9. Fernando Duarte, "It takes a CEO just days to earn your annual wage," BBC, January 9, 2019, https://www.bbc.com/worklife/article/20190108-how-long-it-takes-a-ceo-to-earn-more-than-you-do-in-a-year.

10. Maha El Dahan and Ahmed Rasheed, "OPEC+ announces surprise oil output cuts," Reuters, April 2, 2023, https://www.reuters.com/business/energy/sarabia-other-opec-producers-announce-voluntary-oil-output-cuts-2023-04-02/.

11. Molly Kinder, Katie Bach, and Laura Stateler, "Profits and the pandemic: As shareholder wealth soared, workers were left behind," Brookings, April 21, 2022, https://www.brookings.edu/wp-content/uploads/2022/04/Pandemic_Profits_report.pdf.

12. "Markets: Natural Gas: Summary," Trading Economics, accessed July 2023, https://tradingeconomics.com/commodity/natural-gas.

13. Connor Gillies, "Cost of living: Rent hike forces parents-to-be out of home," BBC News, June 17, 2022, https://www.bbc.co.uk/news/uk-scotland-glasgow-west-61846989.

14. Teju Ravilochan, "Could the Blackfoot Wisdom That Inspired Maslow Guide Us Now?" Medium, April 4, 2021, https://gatherfor.medium.com/maslow-got-it-wrong-ae45d6217a8c.

Chapter 9

1. Yanis Varoufakis, *Another Now* (United States: Melville House, 2021).

2. Matt Taibbi, "The Great American Bubble Machine," *Rolling Stone,* April 5, 2010, https://www.rollingstone.com/politics/politics-news/the-great-american-bubble-machine-195229/.

3. Molly Kinder, Katie Bach, and Laura Stateler, "Profits and the pandemic: As shareholder wealth soared, workers were left behind," Brookings, April 21, 2022, https://www.brookings.edu/wp-content/uploads/2022/04/Pandemic_Profits_report.pdf.

4. Kinder, Bach, and Stateler, "Profits and the Pandemic."

5. Yuki Noguchi, "Why Chobani Gave Employees A Financial Stake In Company's Future," NPR, April 28, 2016, https://www.npr.org/sections/thesalt/2016/04/28/476021520/why-chobani-gave-employees-a-financial-stake-in-companys-future.

6. "Semco – Insanity That Works: A Philosophy of Participation and Involvement," Epic Work Epic Life, accessed July 2023, https://epicworkepiclife.com/semco-insanity-that-works/.

7. "Blake Mycoskie, TOMS Founder," TOMS, accessed July 2023, https://www.toms.com/us/corporate/blakes-bio.html.

8. "Impact," TOMS, accessed July 2023, https://www.toms.com/us/impact.html.

9. Ruth Umoh, "Billionaire Warren Buffett won $2.2 million on a bet and gave it to this charity," CNBC, Feburary 16, 2018, https://www.cnbc.com/2018/02/16/warren-buffett-won-2-point-2-million-on-a-bet-and-gave-it-to-girls-inc.html.

10. "The Scott Trust, History, Formation of the Trust," Guardian Media Group, accessed July 2023, http://backup.gmgplc.co.uk.s3-website-eu-west-1.amazonaws.com/the-scott-trust/history/formation-of-the-trust/.

Chapter 10

1. Esteban Ortiz-Ospina, Diana Beltekian, and Max Roser, 2018 "Trade and Globalization," Our World in Data.org, revised October 2018 https://ourworldindata.org/trade-and-globalization.

2. "Janet Yellen calls for a global minimum tax on companies. Could it happen?" *The Economist,* April 8, 2021, https://www.economist.com/finance-and-economics/2021/04/08/janet-yellen-calls-for-a-global-minimum-tax-on-companies-could-it-happen.

3. President Joe Biden (@POTUS), "Here at the G20..." Twitter post, October 30, 2021, https://twitter.com/POTUS/status/1454454364081430530.

4. Mark Bou Mansour, "Tax haven ranking shows countries setting global tax rules do most to help firms bend them," Tax Justice Network, March 9, 2021, https://taxjustice.net/press/tax-haven-ranking-shows-countries-setting-global-tax-rules-do-most-to-help-firms-bend-them/.

5. Sam Meadows, "362 perfectly acceptable ways to avoid tax," *The Telegraph*, October 19, 2019, https://www.telegraph.co.uk/tax/news/362-perfectly-acceptable-ways-avoid-tax/.

6. Deborah Orr, "Neoliberalism has spawned a financial elite who hold governments to ransom," *The Guardian*, June 8, 2023, https://www.theguardian.com/commentisfree/2013/jun/08/neoliberalism-financial-elite-governments-ransom.

7. Larry Elliott, "$427bn a year lost to tax abuse by firms and rich individuals, study finds," *The Guardian,* November 19, 2020, https://www.theguardian.com/business/2020/nov/20/427bn-a-year-lost-to-tax-abuse-by-firms-and-rich-individuals-study-finds.

8. "$427 billion lost to tax havens every year," Global Alliance for Tax Justice, November 20, 2020, https://globaltaxjustice.org/news/427-billion-lost-to-tax-havens-every-year/#:~:text=Alex%20Cobham%2C%20chief%20executive%20of,a%20system%20programmed%20to%20fail.

9. Stuart Jeffries, "Frankie Boyle's Farewell to the Monarchy review—looks like he's blown his chance of an OBE," *The Guardian*, April 30, 2023, https://www.theguardian.com/tv-and-radio/2023/apr/30/frankie-boyles-farewell-to-the-monarchy-review-looks-like-hes-blown-his-chance-of-an-obe.

10. Michael Holder, "Global sustainable investing assets surged to $30 trillion in 2018," GreenBiz, April 8, 2019, https://www.greenbiz.com/article/global-sustainable-investing-assets-surged-30-trillion-2018.

11. Jessica Aizarani, "Energy imports in the UK – statistics & facts," Statista, January 31, 2023, https://www.statista.com/topics/4938/energy-imports-in-the-united-kingdom-uk/#topicOverview.

12. Damian Carrington, "Revealed: Oil sector's 'staggering' $3bn-a-day profits for last 50 years," *The Guardian,* July 21, 2022, https://www.theguardian.com/environment/2022/jul/21/revealed-oil-sectors-staggering-profits-last-50-years.

13. "ATTN Davos Attendees: In Tax We Trust," In Tax We Trust, accessed July 2023, https://www.intaxwetrust.org/.

14. Michelle Fox, "Why We Need a Global Wealth Tax: Picketty," CNBC, March 10, 2015, https://www.cnbc.com/2015/03/10/why-we-need-a-global-wealth-tax-piketty.html.

15. "Sideways solutions and inverted explanations: A recap of session 10 of TEDGlobal 2014," TEDBlog, October 9, 2014, https://blog.ted.com/a-recap-of-session-10-of-tedglobal-2014/.

Chapter 11

1. The World Bank, "Global Progress in Reducing Extreme Poverty Grinds to a Halt" (Press Release), October 5, 2022, https://www.worldbank.org/en/

news/press-release/2022/10/05/global-progress-in-reducing-extreme-poverty-grinds-to-a-halt.

2. Hilary Cooper and Simon Szreter, *After the Virus: Lessons from the Past for a Better Future* (United States: Cambridge University Press, 2021).

3. W. G. Hoskins, "Harvest Fluctuations and English Economic History, 1480–1619," *The Agricultural History Review*, 1964: 23–46, https://www.bahs.org.uk/AGHR/ARTICLES/12n1a3.pdf.

4. Cooper and Szreter, *After the Virus*.

5. Morgan Housel, *The Psychology of Money: Timeless Lessons on Wealth, Greed, and Happiness*, (United Kingdom: Harriman House Limited, 2020).

6. Guy Faulconbridge and Alistair Smout, "Fuel pumps run dry in British cities, sowing supply chain chaos," Reuters, September 27, 2021, https://www.reuters.com/world/uk/uk-gas-stations-are-running-dry-english-cities-retailers-association-says-2021-09-27/.

7. Dexter Mullan (@TRIGERPULLER), "Privilege activity (Adam Donye) take 2 steps," YouTube video, November 29, 2017, https://youtu.be/a5l9fLkd5g4.

8. Korin Miller, "As a Video about White Privilege Goes Viral Again, Experts Caution It Could Actually Cause More Damage," Yahoo!movies, June 3, 2020, https://uk.movies.yahoo.com/as-a-video-about-white-privilege-goes-viral-again-experts-caution-it-could-actually-cause-more-damage-170528763.html.

9. Peter Raven, "One in Five Who Voted for Brexit Now Think It Was the Wrong Decision," YouGov UK, November 17, 2022, https://yougov.co.uk/topics/politics/articles-reports/2022/11/17/one-five-who-voted-brexit-now-think-it-was-wrong-d.

10. Faye Brown, "Brexit: Poll suggests just 9% of Britons think decision to leave European Union more of a success than failure," *Sky News*, May 22, 2023, https://news.sky.com/story/brexit-poll-suggests-just-9-of-britons-think-decision-to-leave-european-union-more-of-a-success-than-failure-12887197#:~:text=Brexit%20regret%20has%20reached%20record,including%2037%25%20of%20Leave%20voters.

11. John W. McArthur and Krista Rasmussen, "Change of pace: Accelerations and advances during the Millennium Development Goal era," Brookings, January 11, 2017, https://www.brookings.edu/articles/change-of-pace-accelerations-and-advances-during-the-millennium-development-goal-era/.

12. Abraham H. Maslow, *The Farther Reaches of Human Nature* (United Kingdom: Penguin Publishing Group, 1993).

Chapter 12

1. "Resale Report 2023," thredUP, April 2023, https://cf-assets-tup.thredup.com/resale_report/2023/thredUP_2023_Resale_Report_FINAL.pdf.

2. "Research: Unilever Consumer Study Shows a Third of Consumers Prefer Brands Doing Social or Environmental Good," Engage for Good, accessed July 2023, https://engageforgood.com/unilever-consumer-study-shows-third-consumers-prefer-brands-social-environmental-good/#:~:text=or%20Environmental%20 Good-.

3. J. L. Capper, "The environmental impact of beef production in the United States: 1977 compared with 2007," *J Anim Sci* 89, no. 12 (December 2011): 4249–61, https://doi.org/10.2527/jas.2010-3784.

4. Liam Gilliver, "Lewis Hamilton shares 'go-to' vegan snack he eats daily – and how a friend inspired him to go plant-based," Vegan Food & Living, August 11, 2022, https://www.veganfoodandliving.com/news/lewis-hamilton-shares-go-to-vegan-snack-he-eats-daily/.

5. Abhay Tyagi, "Eco-Warrior Lewis Hamilton Reveals the Only Reason He Bought a $29 Million Worth Snazzy Private Jet," Essentially Sports, September 27, 2022, https://www.essentiallysports.com/f1-news-eco-warrior-lewis-hamilton-reveals-the-only-reason-he-bought-a-29-million-worth-snazzy-private-jet/.

6. Melissa Hughes, "What Does a conscious community look like?" Melissa Hughes blog, February 27, 2020, https://info.melissahughes.rocks/neuronugget/what-does-a-conscious-community-look-like.

7. Derek Sivers, "First Follower: Leadership Lessons from a Dancing Guy" (transcript of TED Talk), Derek Sivers website, February 11, 2010, https://sive.rs/ff.

8. Derek Sivers, "First Follower: Leadership Lessons from a Dancing Guy," TED Talks, recorded at TED2010, February 2010 in Long Beach, CA, 3:10, https://www.ted.com/talks/derek_sivers_how_to_start_a_movement.

9. Derek Sivers, "Why I Gave My Company to Charity," December 4, 2009, https://sive.rs/trust.

10. "Yuval Noah Harari argues that AI has hacked the operating system of human civilisation," *The Economist*, April 28, 2023, https://www.economist.com/by-invitation/2023/04/28/yuval-noah-harari-argues-that-ai-has-hacked-the-operating-system-of-human-civilisation.

11. Edward W. Desmond, "Interview with Mother Theresa: A Pencil in the Hand of God," *TIME*, December 4, 1989, https://content.time.com/time/subscriber/article/0,33009,959149-2,00.html.

12. Kevin Kruse, "Zig Ziglar: 10 Quotes That Can Change Your Life," *Forbes*, November 28, 2012, https://www.forbes.com/sites/kevinkruse/2012/11/28/zig-ziglar-10-quotes-that-can-change-your-life/?sh=387eda5d26a0.

13. Svend Brinkmann, *The Joy of Missing Out: The Art of Self-Restraint in an Age of Excess* (United Kingdom: Wiley, 2019).

14. Matthew Rigberg, "JOMO – the Joy of Missing Out: How We Can Liberate Ourselves from Overstimulation Through Restraint and Moderation," Rice Psychology Group, January 10, 2019, https://ricepsychology.com/behavior/jomo-the-joy-of-missing-out-how-we-can-liberate-ourselves-from-overstimulation-through-restraint-and-moderation/.

15. "Kurt Vonnegut Jr. Quotes," Goodreads, accessed July 2023, https://www.goodreads.com/quotes/420191-nobody-will-stop-you-from-creating-do-it-tonight-do.

Conclusion

1. David Brooks, "How the Bobos Broke America," *The Atlantic*, September, 2021, https://www.theatlantic.com/magazine/archive/2021/09/blame-the-bobos-creative-class/619492/.

2. Jacqueline Novogratz, *Manifesto for a Moral Revolution: Practices to Build a Better World* (United States: Henry Holt and Company, 2020).

About the Author

 Arunjay is a former serial entrepreneur and recovering wealth-chaser, having realized in May 2020 that by wanting to be super rich, he was part of the problem.

Arunjay left a career in investment banking and has spent over a decade in international development, working with the GSMA and the Bill & Melinda Gates Foundation, among other development agencies, to increase financial inclusion through cross-border payments and digital public infrastructure. In a previous life, he mentored over 20 inclusive fintech startups with DFS Lab and was a venture builder with Catalyst Fund. He diligently advocates for a zero-fee customer payment model in his first book, *The Power of Micro Money Transfers*. In 2020, Arunjay created the Inclusive Action Lab, a nonprofit that is incubating moonshot ideas focused on ending poverty for the last billion people by 2030.

Connect with Arunjay:
www.arunjay.com
www.linkedin.com/in/arunjay

Printed and bound by CPI Group (UK) Ltd, Croydon, CR0 4YY

11/12/2023

03620333-0001